Inventing the Enemy

Inventing the Enemy uses stories of personal relationships to explore the behavior of ordinary people in five Moscow factories during Stalin's terror. Communist Party leaders targeted specific groups for arrest and strongly encouraged Soviet citizens and party members to take an active role in the terror by "unmasking the hidden enemy." In response to this call, a flood of accusations poured into the secret police (NKVD) and local party organizations. By 1937, every workplace was convulsed by hypervigilance, intense suspicion, and the hunt for hidden enemies. Forced to lie in order to protect loved ones, people faced terrible choices and dilemmas in their struggles to reconcile political imperatives with personal loyalties. Coworkers, spouses, friends, and relatives disavowed and denounced one another. The strategies that many adopted to protect themselves – including naming names, volunteering preemptive denunciations, and shifting blame – all helped to spread the terror. Drawing on formerly secret archival sources, *Inventing the Enemy* explores personal relationships and individual behaviors within a pervasive political culture based on fear and "enemy-hunting."

Wendy Z. Goldman is a professor of history at Carnegie Mellon University. She is the author of *Terror and Democracy in the Age of Stalin: The Social Dynamics of Repression* (Cambridge, 2007); *Women at the Gates: Gender and Industry in Stalin's Russia* (Cambridge, 2002); and *Women, the State and Revolution: Soviet Family Policy in Social Life, 1917–1936* (Cambridge, 1993); and a coeditor (with Donald Filtzer, Gijs Kessler, and Simon Pirani) of *A Dream Deferred: New Studies in Russian and Soviet Labour History* (2008).

Inventing the Enemy: Denunciation and Terror in Stalin's Russia

Wendy Z. Goldman

Carnegie Mellon University

CAMBRIDGE
UNIVERSITY PRESS

CAMBRIDGE UNIVERSITY PRESS

Cambridge, New York, Melbourne, Madrid, Cape Town,
Singapore, São Paulo, Delhi, Tokyo, Mexico City

Cambridge University Press
32 Avenue of the Americas, New York, NY 10013-2473, USA

www.cambridge.org
Information on this title: www.cambridge.org/9780521145626

First published 2011

Printed in the United States of America

A catalog record for this publication is available from the British Library.

Library of Congress Cataloging in Publication data

Goldman, Wendy Z.
Inventing the enemy : denunciation and terror in Stalin's Russia / Wendy Z. Goldman.
p.   cm.
Includes bibliographical references and index.
ISBN 978-0-521-19196-8 (hardback) – ISBN 978-0-521-14562-6 (pbk.)
1. Soviet Union – Politics and government – 1936–1953.   2. Soviet Union – Social
conditions – 1917–1945.   3. Political purges – Social aspects – Soviet Union – History.
4. Political culture – Soviet Union – History.   5. State-sponsored terrorism – Social
aspects – Soviet Union – History.   6. Kommunisticheskaia partiia Sovetskogo Soiuza –
Purges – History.   7. Working class – Soviet Union – History.   8. Interpersonal relations –
Soviet Union – History.   9. Factories – Russia (Federation) – Moscow – History.
10. Moscow (Russia) – Social conditions.   I. Title.
DK268.4.G65   2011
947.084′2 – dc22   2011002164

ISBN 978-0-521-19196-8 Hardback
ISBN 978-0-521-14562-6 Paperback

This book is dedicated to my husband,
Marcus Rediker,
who seeks and loves the challenge of new realms

CONTENTS

ACKNOWLEDGMENTS

Many people have generously helped to make this book possible. Donald Filtzer read the entire manuscript with meticulous care and discussed interpretative questions about the terror with me at length. His thoughtful comments have been invaluable to my work in recent years. Melanie Ilic kindly shared her knowledge of several Web sites devoted to the victims of repression, preeminently that hosted by Memorial, and thereby helped me to discover the fates of some of those who were arrested or purged from the Party. Igor Kurukin has proved ever helpful and resourceful in locating elusive but crucial information. Lydiia Naumova, head of the reading room in the Central Archive of Social-Political History of Moscow (TsAOPIM), assisted me in navigating the archive's many restrictions. Barry Schles, former head of interlibrary loan at Carnegie Mellon University's Hunt Library, went above and beyond the call of duty in helping me to find rare materials. William Chase, Carmine Storella, and Lynne Viola all offered excellent comments on and suggestions about the manuscript at various stages. J. Arch Getty and Paul Hagenloh shared their statistical knowledge of arrests, executions, and categories of victims. My wonderful colleague Naum Kats has aided my research over the years in countless ways. I am grateful to Dmitri Zhilinskii for permission to use his haunting painting *1937*, which is currently part of the collection in the Tretiakov Gallery, for the cover of this book.

Numerous parts of this book have benefited from stimulating comments made by colleagues in far-flung venues: the Modern European History Research Centre, Oxford University; the Faculty of History in the State University – Higher School of the Economy, Moscow; the Conference on Stalinist Terror, University of Leeds; the Department of History, Brown University; the European History Colloquium, Cornell University; the European Social Science History Conference, Lisbon; the annual meeting of the American Historical Association, Washington, D.C.; the Association for Slavic, East European and Eurasian Studies; the "Fear" seminar, Shelby Cullom Davis Center for Historical Studies, Princeton University; and the Department of History and the School of Law, University of Miami.

The exchange between Carnegie Mellon University (CMU) and the Russian State University for the Humanities (RGGU) facilitated my work in archives and libraries in Moscow, as did the generous support of my home department (History) at CMU. I am indebted to Efim Pivovar, Irina Karapetiants, Svetlana Petukhova, John Lehoczky, and Joe Trotter for their continuing financial and administrative support for the exchange. I am also grateful to my Russian colleagues at RGGU: Galina Babkova, Sergei Karpenko, Aleksei Kilichenkov, Igor Kurukin, and Vladimir Strelkov. Dorothy Straight was a marvelous copy editor, who brought both style and the mastery of language to the manuscript.

Finally, I would like to thank my husband, Marcus Rediker, who has always urged me to write with a larger audience in mind and to bring the great dramas of history to life. His own work sets a high standard for emulation.

Inventing the Enemy: Denunciation and Terror in Stalin's Russia

INTRODUCTION

" ... how thin the line between high principles and blinkered intolerance, how relative all human systems and ideologies, and how absolute the tortures which human beings inflict on one another."

– Eugenia Ginzburg, Communist Party member, arrested 1937[1]

B EGINNING IN THE SUMMER OF 1936, WORKPLACES AND institutions throughout the Soviet Union were gripped by a rising fever of denunciation. From the shop floors of the factories to the private chambers of the highest ruling bodies, Soviet citizens actively hunted for internal enemies among their coworkers, fellow students, comrades, and colleagues. After the murder of S. M. Kirov, head of the Leningrad party organization, in December 1934, the leaders of the Communist Party had accused former oppositionists of engaging in terrorist conspiracies and begun to target them for arrest. Over the next two years, the NKVD (People's Commissariat of Internal Affairs) arrested a wide range of people, including former leftists and rightists, industrial managers, military leaders, cultural figures, party and union officials, and entire social and national

1 Eugenia Semenovna Ginzburg, *Journey into the Whirlwind* (New York: Harcourt Brace Jovanovich, 1967), p. 113.

groups that were deemed to be potentially disloyal. The campaign against terrorists, spies, and industrial saboteurs attracted broad and eager popular participation. The Party, the unions, and other mass organizations urged their members to search out hidden enemies among their social and professional contacts, in their apartment buildings, on collective farms, and even within their own families. The hunt resulted in a flood of denunciations, imprisonments, and executions.

I. V. Stalin and members of the Politburo, convinced that foreign and domestic enemies posed a threat to the Soviet state, initiated, encouraged, and ultimately halted the hunt for enemies. Yet once the hunt began, following several highly publicized propaganda campaigns, it developed a powerful dynamic of its own. Popular belief and fear intermingled to create a toxic atmosphere. As ordinary people answered the call for vigilance, increasing numbers of their fellow citizens fell victim to NKVD arrests. In the factories, the hunt for enemies intensified in tandem with arrests: as more people were denounced by others, arrests multiplied. Family members, coworkers, mentors, and bosses disappeared into prison. Speakers at mass meetings and writers for factory and national newspapers railed against the spies and terrorists who threatened the country.

Factory employees seemed willing enough to accept this message so long as the arrests did not affect anyone they knew personally. When the NKVD arrested their relatives, comrades, or coworkers, they were deeply shocked. Was it possible that these intimates and acquaintances were really hidden enemies? Amid the nationwide fury over terrorists and spies, citizens were isolated and shamed by the arrests of friends and family members. Many who had initially been persuaded by the state's claim that terrorists were operating inside industrial, military, and state institutions began to grasp that *everyone* was subject to arrest. This internal shift, from belief in the state's campaign to fear of becoming its target, became evident in people's outward behavior. The growing dread of personal vulnerability produced a pervasive mistrust of others. People developed twisted, often aggressive strategies for self-protection. The poisonous atmosphere seeped into even the closest and most private of human relationships. No one in the Soviet Union remained unaffected or unmarked by the political culture of these years. What began as a state-sponsored war on terrorism had grown into a full-blown terror.

This book explores the transformation of the political culture based on a unique body of sources in the Central Archive of Social Political History of Moscow: the stenographic reports of Communist Party meetings held in five Moscow factories between 1934 and 1939. Paired with daily factory newspapers, these reports enable us to reconstruct in detail what happened in the factories, to plot the spread of terror through the actions of specific individuals, and to piece together who did what to whom. The factories involved, representing both heavy and light industry, were Dinamo, which made electric locomotives and machines; Serp i Molot, a steel plant; Trekhgornaia Manufaktura, a textile factory; Krasnyi Proletarii, a machine fabricator; and Likerno-Vodochnyi Zavod, a distillery.[2] The stenographic reports, verbatim transcripts of party meetings, permit us to witness how the terror unfolded on the local level – to eavesdrop, so to speak, on closed meetings held more than seventy years ago.[3] They allow us to track party members and other factory employees over time, to learn about their backgrounds and secrets,

2 The state considered Dinamo, Serp i Molot, and Krasnyi Proletarii to be "leading" factories of special importance to the industrialization effort. See *Istoriia rabochikh Moskvy 1917–45 gg.* (Moscow: Izdatel'stvo 'Nauka,' 1983), p. 425.
3 A stenographer, present at the meetings of the party committees and primary party organizations, produced a verbatim transcription. This practice dated back to the 1920s. See Igal Halfin, *Intimate Enemies: Demonizing the Bolshevik Opposition, 1918–1928* (Pittsburgh: University of Pittsburgh Press, 2007), p. 29.

to observe their interactions with their coworkers – in sum, to watch a grand drama unfold in intimate human terms. Unlike memoirs of the terror, which reconstruct the past from the remembered experience of a lone individual, most often a victim, the stenographic reports follow victims, participants, and perpetrators as they act in real or present time. Unlike diaries, they show multiple perspectives uninflected by a single subjectivity. Additional archival and published sources on national, regional, and city events enable us to place the microenvironments of the factories within a larger political context and to trace the dynamic interplay between orders from above and events and responses from below. This book can be read independently or as a companion volume to my *Terror and Democracy in the Age of Stalin: The Social Dynamics of Repression* (Cambridge University Press, 2007). Whereas that work focused on industrial tensions, power struggles in the unions, and workers' responses, this one explores personal relationships and individual behavior within a pervasive political culture of "enemy hunting."

The study of individual behavior within the world of the factories raises intriguing questions about mass participation in the terror. Many historians have argued that the terror was strictly a top-down affair, launched and managed by Stalin with the aim of eliminating any threat, whether potential or real, to his personal power over the Party and the state. This view has proponents on both the right and the left wings of the political spectrum. On the right, it first found expression in the Cold War notion of "totalitarianism," describing the system of total political control that allegedly characterized both Nazi Germany and the Soviet Union.[4] On the left, historians

4 The adjective *totalitarian* made its first appearance in the 1920s in reference to Italian fascism, was next used in the late 1940s to describe German fascism, and then gained broad popularity during the Cold War. Focusing on the political system and eschewing class analysis, adherents of the concept offered little

sympathetic to socialism, including but not limited to Trotskyists, tended to emphasize Stalin's obsession with purging oppositionists who provided an alternative, democratic path to socialism that challenged his power.[5] More recently, scholars focusing on state power within a wider, pan-European perspective have revived the totalitarian framework based on archival materials that revealed Stalin's significant role in the terror and the Politburo's orders for mass arrests of specific social and national groups. According to this view, repression was a form of violent social engineering, aimed at eliminating those individuals and groups that did not fit into an ideologically determined socialist community.[6]

to distinguish fascism from socialism. See Michael Geyer, "Introduction: After Totalitarianism – Stalinism and Nazism Compared," in Geyer and Sheila Fitzpatrick, eds., *Beyond Totalitarianism: Stalinism and Nazism Compared* (New York: Cambridge University Press, 2009), pp. 1–37; Hannah Arendt, *The Origins of Totalitarianism* (New York: Harcourt Brace Jovanovich, 1968); Robert Conquest, *The Great Terror: A Reassessment* (New York: Oxford University Press, 1990); Richard Pipes, *Russia under the Bolshevik Regime* (New York: Alfred A. Knopf, 1994); Martin Malia, *The Soviet Tragedy: A History of Socialism in Russia: 1917–1991* (New York: Free Press, 1994); Stéphane Courtois, Nicolas Werth, Jean-Louis Panné, Andrzej Paczkowski, Karel Bartosek, and Jean-Louis Margolin, *The Black Book of Communism: Crimes, Terror, Repression* (Cambridge, Mass.: Harvard University Press, 1999); Alexandr Solzhenitsyn, *The Gulag Archipelago 1918–1956: An Experiment in Literary Investigation* (New York: Harper & Row, 1973).

5 Roy Medvedev, *Let History Judge: The Origins and Consequences of Stalinism* (New York: Columbia University Press, 1989); Vadim Zakharovich Rogovin, *Stalin's Terror of 1937–1938: Political Genocide in the USSR* (Oak Park, Mich.: Mehring Books, 2009).

6 Amir Weiner, ed., *Landscaping the Human Garden: Twentieth-Century Population Management in a Comparative Framework* (Palo Alto, Calif.: Stanford University Press, 2003); Hiroaki Kuromiya, *Freedom and Terror in the Donbas: A Ukrainian-Russian Borderland, 1870s–1990s* (New York: Cambridge University Press, 1998), and *The Voices of the Dead: Stalin's Great Terror in the 1930s* (New Haven, Conn.: Yale University Press, 2007); Peter Holquist, "'Information Is the Alpha and Omega of Our Work': Bolshevik Surveillance in Its Pan-European Perspective," *Journal of Modern History*, vol. 69, no. 3 (1997), pp. 415–50; David Hoffman, *Stalinist Values: The Cultural Norms of Soviet Modernity, 1917–1941* (Ithaca, N.Y.: Cornell University Press, 2003); Hoffman and Yanni Kotsonis,

Other historians, more concerned with social, institutional, and economic history, reject the primacy of a monolithic ideology and instead depict a dynamic of power marked by vacillation, bureaucratic infighting, differences of opinion, and popular participation. In place of Stalin's personal drive for "totalizing power," they emphasize the influence of uncertainty, confusion, and a welter of social tensions in exacerbating the terror. Centering their research on conflicts within industrial enterprises, scientific institutions, collective farms, military units, and party organizations, these writers suggest that numerous other factors may have contributed to Stalin's excisionary violence.[7] Several historians link the terror to the broader

eds., *Russian Modernity: Politics, Knowledge, Practices* (Basingstoke, Hampshire: Palgrave Macmillan, 2000); Paul Hagenloh, *Stalin's Police: Public Order and Mass Repression in the USSR, 1926–1941* (Baltimore: Johns Hopkins University Press, 2009); Golfo Alexopoulos, *Stalin's Outcasts: Aliens, Citizens, and the Soviet State, 1926–1936* (Ithaca, N.Y.: Cornell University Press, 2003).

7 These include William J. Chase, *Enemies within the Gates?: The Comintern and the Stalinist Repression, 1934–1939* (New Haven, Conn.: Yale University Press, 2001); Sheila Fitzpatrick, "Workers against Bosses: The Impact of the Great Purges on Labor-Management Relations," in Lewis H. Siegelbaum and Ronald Grigor Suny, eds., *Making Workers Soviet: Power, Class and Identity* (Ithaca, N.Y.: Cornell University Press, 1994), pp. 311–40; Fitzpatrick, *Stalin's Peasants: Resistance and Survival in the Russian Village after Collectivization* (New York: Oxford University Press, 1994); J. Arch Getty, *Origins of the Great Purges: The Soviet Communist Party Reconsidered, 1933–1938* (New York: Cambridge University Press, 1985); Getty, "State and Society under Stalin: Constitutions and Elections in the 1930s," *Slavic Review*, vol. 50, no. 1 (1991); Getty and Oleg V. Naumov, *The Road to Terror: Stalin and the Self-Destruction of the Bolsheviks, 1932–1939* (New Haven, Conn.: Yale University Press, 1999); Getty and Roberta T. Manning, eds., *Stalinist Terror: New Perspectives* (New York: Cambridge University Press, 1993); Manning, "Government in the Soviet Countryside in the Stalinist Thirties: The Case of Belyi Raion in 1937," *The Carl Beck Papers in Russian and East European Studies*, no. 301 (1984); E. A. Rees, ed., *Centre-Local Relations in the Stalinist State, 1928–1941* (Basingstoke, Hampshire: Palgrave Macmillan, 2002); Gábor Rittersporn, *Stalinist Simplifications and Soviet Complications: Social Tensions and Political Conflicts in the USSR, 1933–1953* (Reading, U.K.: Harwood, 1991); Asif Siddiqi, "The Rockets' Red Glare: Technology, Conflict, and Terror in the Soviet Union," *Technology and Culture*, vol. 44, no. 3 (July 2003);

social history of the 1930s, and the state's struggle with entrenched social, class, and regional interests.[8] New work has also set the terror in the context of a longer history of Soviet policing of various social groups, beginning with the deportation, arrest, and execution of kulaks and other rural, allegedly antistate groups during the collectivization drive of 1929–30. After the introduction of internal passports in 1932, police conducted mass sweeps of urban areas to round up dispossessed, criminal, and marginal populations that were then sentenced through boards (troiki) established outside the official judicial system. The mass arrests, absence of specific charges, and extrajudicial sentencing provided a template for the subsequent arrests of targeted social and national groups in 1937–38.[9] A very few historians have trained their gaze on the individual. Relying on diaries, interviews, and other sources, they have explored the "Soviet self" and the extent to which Soviet citizens internalized

Peter H. Solomon Jr., Soviet Criminal Justice under Stalin (New York: Cambridge University Press, 1996); Robert W. Thurston, Life and Terror in Stalin's Russia, 1934–1941 (New Haven, Conn.: Yale University Press, 1996); Thurston, "Reassessing the History of Soviet Workers: Opportunities to Criticize and Participate in Decision-Making," in Stephen White, ed., New Directions in Soviet History (New York: Cambridge University Press, 1992).

8 Wendy Z. Goldman, Terror and Democracy in the Age of Stalin: The Social Dynamics of Repression (New York: Cambridge University Press, 2007); James R. Harris, The Great Urals: Regionalism and the Evolution of the Soviet System (Ithaca, N.Y.: Cornell University Press, 1999); David Priestland, Stalinism and the Politics of Mobilization: Ideas, Power and Terror in Inter-War Russia (New York: Oxford University Press, 2007).

9 Lynne Viola, V. P. Danilov, N. A. Ivnitskii, and Denis Kozlov, The War against the Peasantry, 1927–1930: The Tragedy of the Soviet Countryside (New Haven, Conn.: Yale University Press, 2005); Viola, The Unknown Gulag: The Lost World of Stalin's Special Settlements (New York: Oxford University Press, 2007); Viola, "The Role of the OGPU in Dekulakization, Mass Deportations, and Special Resettlement in 1930," The Carl Beck Papers in Russian and East European Studies, no. 1406 (January 2000). On the history of Soviet policing, see Hagenloh, Stalin's Police; David R. Shearer, Policing Stalin's Socialism: Repression and Social Order in the Soviet Union, 1924–1953 (New Haven, Conn.: Yale University Press, 2009).

the views of their leaders and the ideals of the new socialist society.[10]

These innovative studies, looking at a range of contributing factors from Politburo orders to social and institutional tensions to personal subjectivities, have yet to be synthesized into a new paradigm. New findings have provoked fresh debates over the reasons for the terror, the actual decision-making process, and the specific identities of the victims. Some historians now maintain that the threat of war provided the main impetus for the elimination of potentially disloyal groups, seemingly justifying a prophylactic purge of a possible "fifth column."[11] Others counter that the terror in fact predated Hitler's takeover of Eastern Europe, and that no significant international events correlated either with the terror's onset or with its end.[12] Still other historians emphasize domestic factors, most particularly the pressure imposed by regional party leaders to purge their areas in preparation for upcoming multicandidate, secret-ballot elections

10 Anna Krylova, "The Tenacious Liberal Subject in Soviet Studies," *Kritika: Explorations in Russian and Eurasian History*, Winter 2000; Natalia Korenevskaya, Veronique Garros, and Thomas Lahusen, eds., *Intimacy and Terror: Soviet Diaries of the 1930's* (New York: New Press, 1995); Jochen Hellbeck, *Revolution on My Mind: Writing a Diary under Stalin* (Cambridge, Mass.: Harvard University Press, 2006); Halfin, *Intimate Enemies;* Halfin, *Stalinist Confessions: Messianism and Terror at the Leningrad Communist University* (Pittsburgh: University of Pittsburgh Press, 2009); Orlando Figes, *The Whisperers: Private Life in Stalin's Russia* (New York: Metropolitan Books, 2007).

11 This idea was first advanced by V. M. Molotov in *Molotov Remembers: Inside Kremlin Politics, Conversations with Felix Chuev* (Chicago: Ivan R. Dee, 1993). See also Oleg Khlevniuk, "The Objectives of the Great Terror, 1937–38," in Julian Cooper, Maureen Perrie, and E. A. Rees, eds., *Soviet History, 1917–53: Essays in Honour of R. W. Davies* (Basingstoke, Hampshire: St. Martin's Press, 1995), pp. 172–74; Shearer, *Policing Stalin's Socialism*, pp. 314–15.

12 Marc Junge and Bernd Bonwetsch, "'Everywhere, Nothing but Enemies': The 'War Threat' and the Great Murder of the Little People in the Soviet Union 1937 to 1938," unpublished paper presented to the Terror Conference, University of Leeds, Leeds, U.K., August 2010.

to the soviets. Historians also differ over the degree of strategizing involved: some contend that the mass operations were planned in advance, while others hold that they were carried out only in response to petitions from regional party leaders.[13] Finally, historians also disagree about the terror's victims. Some now assert that the majority of them were not the managerial elites, party members, and former oppositionists who figured so prominently in earlier accounts, but rather dispossessed and criminal elements and targeted national groups. They posit that the terror was the culmination of policing campaigns against nonpolitical, marginal populations. Others still insist on the primacy of politics. The debate is further complicated by the fact that individual victims often did not even fit into the category under which they were arrested, and many had multiple identities that could not be represented by a single label. In the national operations, for example, some of the targeted immigrant groups contained a high percentage of Communists and socialists. Although these individuals were arrested as part of national groups, their elimination had an enormous political impact on the international Communist movement. Historians are still striving to understand the connections among the successive waves of violence and the relative importance of policing techniques, politics, social instability, and international events in launching and shaping the terror. And they still differ widely over even the most basic questions regarding the motivations of the leadership, the role of mass participation, and the dynamics of power.

13 Shearer, *Policing Stalin's Socialism*, pp. 322–34; Hagenloh, *Stalin's Police*, pp. 232–51; J. Arch Getty, "State and Society under Stalin: Constitutions and Elections in the 1930s," *Slavic Review*, vol. 50, no. 1 (1991); Getty, "'Excesses Are Not Permitted': Mass Terror and Stalinist Governance in the Late 1930s," *Russian Review*, vol. 61 (January 2002), pp. 113–38.

Inventing the Enemy concentrates less on the high politics of the era than on the behavior of ordinary people in the factories. It attempts to elucidate, through a close examination of speech and behavior, how such people reacted to the terror, treated one another, and tried to protect themselves and their families. It focuses on both individual and group behaviors in the context of the orders and campaigns mandated from above. The factory newspapers and stenographic reports reveal frightened and self-righteous human beings who felt a desperate need to denounce one another, defend themselves, and respond to charges made against them with aggressive counteraccusations. The sources also show the various but ultimately limited ways in which many people tried to help others during a chaotic and dangerous period. The stenographic reports and other archival materials make it possible to piece together a microhistory of the terror, bringing to life the political culture, the actions and reactions of ordinary citizens, and the role those citizens played in creating the terror. Individual perpetrators, participants, and victims emerge vividly in the transcripts and accounts of shop, party, and factory-wide meetings. Over time, we watch party members attack, "unmask," and expel their comrades, only to become victims themselves in turn. The sources expose individual strategies for defense and survival, as well as the impact of those strategies on the larger group. They enable us to unravel a tangled web of mutual denunciations and to see how the terror unfolded on the local level. Under close and patient scrutiny, the sources yield the secrets that party members concealed, the choices and the actions that made up the terror in every workplace.

The people who live in these pages were not well known; they were not celebrated intellectuals, party leaders, writers, or revolutionaries. They were workers, shop heads, party organizers, local officials, engineers, and managers. Most of them were party members, though not all. Their names were unknown at the time to anyone except their fellow workers, family, and friends. They kept no records of their own and wrote nothing about their views or experiences. Much about their inner thoughts and motivations remains unclear. Yet the record of their actions, and of the events that befell them, illuminates a mass political culture that might otherwise appear opaque. Their personal loyalties, interests, and emotional attachments intersected with central orders and campaigns to give form to the repression that we have come to call the Great Terror. Their stories, deeply personal yet broadly shared, reveal the human face of both accusers and accused.

The party organizations in the factories, as in all workplaces and institutions, encompassed a vertical cross section of employees, from the director to the workers. Yet even the factory leadership – the directors, managers, engineers, shop heads, and party activists – though often the object of attack, could hardly be considered an established elite. Catapulted into positions of authority by the rapid upward mobility propelled by Soviet industrialization, most of the factory leaders had themselves been ordinary workers at the start of the decade, and few boasted any education beyond a brief, narrow technical or political training. They came from peasant or working-class families, had relatives in factories and on collective farms, and were still connected to those humble social milieus. The Party actively sought members from modest backgrounds. The majority of its membership in the 1930s, while arguably more politically aware and ambitious than the "average" citizenry, nonetheless remained closely connected through family ties to the mass of workers and peasants, the two largest groups in Soviet society. The experiences of party activists on the local level were thus inextricably tied to those of other common people. When a party member was expelled or arrested, the family that must absorb the blow was composed of ordinary, unexceptional people. And although the Party was undoubtedly an epicenter of repression, the shock waves reverberated outward to encompass all of Soviet society through the dense ties between party members and their classes of origin.

Most historians agree that the political terror began in December 1934 with the Kirov murder, accelerated with the appointment of Nikolai I. Ezhov as head of the NKVD in November 1936, and ended with Ezhov's removal in November 1938. The arrests and executions reached their apogee between 1936 and 1938, during Ezhov's tenure – a period known in Russian as the Ezhovshchina, or "time of Ezhov." In 1937–38, approximately 2.5 million people were arrested for both political and nonpolitical crimes. The NKVD was responsible for the majority of these arrests, seizing 1,605,259 people in total, of whom 1,372,382 were accused of counterrevolutionary offenses. Out of the total number arrested, 1,344,923 were convicted, and between 681,692 and 683,000 executed.[14] Among the more prominent victims were party and military leaders, heads of industry, former oppositionists, and cultural figures. Yet proportionally, the victims included a much larger share of dispossessed and disenfranchised individuals, foreign Communists, and members of various national groups, all arrested under the rubric of

14 Some of the people convicted may have been arrested before 1937. J. Arch Getty, Gábor Rittersporn, and Viktor Zemskov, "Victims of the Soviet Penal System in the Pre-War Years: A First Approach on the Basis of Archival Evidence," *American Historical Review*, vol. 98, no. 4 (October 1993), pp. 1022–24. According to data from the Tsentral'nyi Arkhiv Federal'noi Sluzhby Bezopasnosti Rossiiskoi Federatsii (TsA FSB), f. 8os., o. 1, d. 80, and cited by V. N. Khaustov, V. P. Naumov, and N. S. Plotnikova, eds., *Lubianka. Stalin i glavnoe upravlenie gosbezopasnosti NKVD, 1937–8. Dokumenty* (Moscow: Izdatel'stvo 'Materik,' 2004), pp. 659–60, the NKVD arrested 1,575,259 people in 1937–38.

"mass and national operations." In the summer of 1937, the Polit-buro issued secret orders for regional NKVD units to effect mass arrests of groups considered to be a threat to Soviet security. In July 1937, "Order 00447" set target numbers for the imprisonment and execution of recidivist criminals, village clergy, religious activists, former kulaks, *lishentsy* (nobles, industrialists, and others deprived of voting rights), and other supposed "hostile elements." This was followed by "Order 00485," which led to the mass roundup of Polish nationals, and "Order 00486," which mandated the arrest of the wives of men convicted of counterrevolutionary crimes. Additional orders targeted alleged spies from Germany, Romania, Finland, Latvia, and other countries. Many of these "national" victims were Communist and left-wing refugees from Fascist and other repressive regimes. People swept up in the mass and national operations con-stituted the great majority of arrests and executions in these years.[15]

Yet the orders for these operations, despite their stated aims, net-ted many victims who did not directly belong to the targeted groups and often had no connection at all to the target category under

15 On mass and national operations, see "Zapiska N.I. Frinovskogo v Politburo TsK VKP (b) s Prilozheniem Operativnogo Prikaz NVKD SSSR No. 00447," in Khaustov et al., eds., *Lubianka*, pp. 273–81; Getty, "'Excesses Are Not Permit-ted'"; Paul R. Gregory, *Terror by Quota: State Security from Lenin to Stalin, An Archival Study* (New Haven, Conn.: Yale University Press, 2009); Hagenloh, *Stalin's Police*, pp. 227–87; Oleg Khlevniuk, "The Objectives of the Great Ter-ror, 1937–1938," in Cooper et al., eds., *Soviet History*; Barry McLoughlin and Kevin McDermott, "Rethinking Stalinist Terror," McLoughlin, "Mass Opera-tions of the NKVD, 1937–9: A Survey," Nikita Firsov and Arsenii Roginskii, "The 'Polish Operation' of the NKVD, 1937–8," and David Shearer, "Social Disorder, Mass Repression and the NKVD during the 1930s," in McLoughlin and McDermott, eds., *Stalin's Terror: High Politics and Mass Repression in the Soviet Union* (Basingstoke, Hampshire: Palgrave Macmillan, 2003); Shearer, *Policing Stalin's Socialism*, pp. 320–70; A. Iu. Vatlin, *Terror raionnogo masshtaba: "massovye operatsii" NKVD v Kuntsevskom raione Moskovskoi oblasti, 1937–8* (Moscow: Rosspen, 2004).

which they were rounded up. Workers in and of themselves, for example, were never explicitly targeted by the mass and national operations, yet many were nonetheless taken into custody. In March 1938, the deputy commissar of the NKVD, M. I. Frinovskii, wrote to the head of the Sverdlovsk provincial NKVD, D. M. Dmitriev, about the projected quota of 10,024 arrests set for the national operations in Sverdlovsk province. Frinovskii noted with asperity that according to Dmitriev's own figures, he had arrested 4,142 people during the German operation, of which only 390 were in fact Germans. The vast majority, nearly 96 percent (3,968 people) were instead former kulaks and their children, of which some 92 percent (3,647 people) were now workers. Likewise, in the Polish operation, Dmitriev arrested 4,218 people, of whom just 390, again, were Poles. Here, too, the overwhelming majority of those whom Dmitriev arrested as "Polish spies," 91 percent (3,798 people), were former kulaks and their children, of which group 93 percent (3,552 people) were now workers. The numbers for the other national categories were similar.[16] These figures suggest that the demographic of Soviet factory workers, or at least of those from kulak backgrounds, was hit hard by the national operations. The terror was thus a complex and layered phenomenon: its victims varied widely, encompassing a broad range of political beliefs, social positions, nationalities, and occupations. The Moscow show trials, the Kemerovo trial of industrial saboteurs, and the mass and national operations all targeted different groups, and a shocking number of "ordinary" people – workers and their children – were victimized even though they did not fit into the particular category singled out for arrest. The NKVD

16 Khaustov et al., eds., *Lubianka*, p. 659.

arrested people in mass sweeps and assigned them after the fact to social categories to which they did not belong. Thus operational orders did not necessarily correlate with the actual social, political, or national composition of the victims. Moreover, the orders for the mass and national operations were not revealed to the general population, who therefore experienced these arrests as part of an ongoing public campaign against hidden terrorists, spies, and wreckers.

In the Moscow factories, the trials and the national campaign against wrecking launched a raft of denunciations. The NKVD was not permitted to arrest local party members without prior permission from the first secretary of the city party committee, who based his decision on a variety of determinants, including information provided in denunciations.[17] The editors of factory newspapers also played a key role here, criticizing shop heads and others by name in print and calling for full investigations of sundry accusations. Each day, a front-page article would feature some new suspect, usually a manager, director, shop head, party organizer, or technical expert, who was pilloried for working and living conditions. Party meetings, once devoted to issues of production, political education, and mass organizing, were now given over entirely to the scrutiny of party members. Public exposure, accusation, denunciation, investigation, expulsion, and arrest were linked in a vicious circle. Each new arrest set in motion an investigation of the victim's associates, and each new investigation resulted in more arrests. The hunt for internal enemies, sparked by party directives and mass campaigns, soon found new fuel in the tensions of the workplace, individual

17 I am indebted to Vladimir Khaustov, head of the History Faculty, FSB Academy, for clarifying this procedure.

fears, and associational ties. Millions of people actively participated in creating and sustaining this political culture of terror, just as millions were victimized by it. Often these people were one and the same.

At the factory level, the terror combined political attacks on former oppositionists with arrests of social and national groups and mass participation in the hunt for enemies. One historian suggests that the "Great Terror" was in fact many separate "terrors," each with its own distinct history and logic.[18] Yet as the following pages will show, the Soviet people did not experience these elements of terror as separate and discrete. The orders that launched the mass and national operations, for example, were kept secret. Vague rumors of mass arrests circulated among prisoners in the camps, but beyond the small group of Politburo leaders and NKVD officials who issued and carried out the orders, no one else knew of their existence. A Russian newspaper first published them only in 1992.[19]

By focusing on the microenvironments of the factories, we can see how arrests, operational orders, and public campaigns merged to create the terror on a local level. Soviet citizens experienced its various phases as a series of concussive assaults. Party members in the factories worked side by side with foreigners who had immigrated to the Soviet Union to live in the world's first socialist country. A family might count among its members loyal Communists as well as former oppositionists, ex-priests, relatives who had fought with the White armies, former traders, and peasants exiled during collectivization. Party members and other citizens often withheld details about their social backgrounds on job and school applications

18 Sheila Fitzpatrick, "Varieties of Terror," in Fitzpatrick, ed., *Stalinism: New Directions* (London and New York: Routledge, 2000), p. 258.
19 Hagenloh, *Stalin's Police*, pp. 1, 6.

or during periodic party membership reviews.[20] Every family was the product, in one way or another, of two decades of turbulent Soviet history, and thus vulnerable, often at multiple points, to successive waves of repression against the state's so-called enemies.

This messy period, with its multiple phases, campaigns, and categories of victims, not only defies easy conceptualization but also resists a commonly accepted designation. In short, historians cannot even agree what to name it, employing instead a variety of metonyms, or figures of speech composed of particular attributes associated with the thing itself. Soviet party leaders at the time called the upheaval the "great cleansing work."[21] Later, "1937," for the year that marked the height of the mass campaigns, arrests, and executions, became a popular shorthand term. Russians often refer to the interval as the Ezhovshchina, or "time of Ezhov," defining it by Nikolai Ezhov's tenure as head of the NKVD. With the discovery of the "mass and national operations," many historians began to call it "the mass repressions." One writer, urging that a distinction be drawn between 1937–38 and other, less murderous periods of mass repression, has suggested that these two years be renamed "the mass purges."[22] Western historians frequently employ such designations as "the purges," "the Great Terror," or, more loosely, "Stalinism." In part, the failure to settle on a single term reflects differences over when the period began and ended, who was responsible for it, and which groups should be counted as its victims.

20 Halfin, *Intimate Enemies*, pp. 145–50; Sheila Fitzpatrick, *Tear Off the Masks!: Identity and Imposture in Twentieth-Century Russia* (Princeton, N.J.: Princeton University Press, 2005).
21 "Po Bol'shevistski Ispravit' Dopushennie Oshibki," *Kirovets*, February 5, 1938, p. 1.
22 Shearer, *Policing Stalin's Socialism*, p. 286.

As metonyms, each of these alternatives captures a major feature of the period, but each is also a misnomer for what it glosses over or omits. "The purges" or "mass purges" refers to the "cleansing" or expulsion of potential or perceived enemies from the Communist Party, institutions, and the country as a whole. This term most closely approximates the party leaders' understanding of their own activities at the time. Yet both "purge" and "great cleansing" fall short as accurate descriptors in that they fail to differentiate between a largely benign organizational practice of the 1920s and the murderous variant of it undertaken in the late 1930s. Party and state institutions had a longstanding custom of reviewing their members and employees and periodically purging their ranks of socially suspect groups, criminals, and passive members. In 1937–39, however, this practice turned deadly, and expulsion from the Party in particular commonly prefigured the loss of employment and housing, arrest, a camp sentence, or execution. The "purge," as an organizational tool, thus assumed a more sinister meaning.

For its part, the "Ezhovshchina" narrowly limits the period to Ezhov's tenure, thus ascribing almost all blame and responsibility to him. Ezhov, as head of the NKVD for two years, did actively promulgate the idea that the Soviet Union was beset by a vast, hidden conspiracy of enemies. He presided over the most intense time of arrests and executions, and his dismissal brought to an end the mass and national operations and extrajudicial trials. Yet he was not solely responsible for the executions and arrests, which instead involved a complex interaction among various levels of the Party, the NKVD, the workplace, and ordinary citizens. (Ezhov was himself ultimately arrested and executed on the charge of spying for foreign powers.) Moreover, party leaders relied on extrajudicial bodies before Ezhov was appointed to head the NKVD, and the political culture of fear and denunciation lingered long after he was deposed. The state would continue to manufacture charges against and conspiracies by its citizens until Stalin's death, in 1953.

The historian Robert Conquest first coined the term the "Great Terror," and it still stands as perhaps the most popular conception of the period in the West. This vivid and convenient tag suggests a twofold meaning, referring to Stalin's campaign of terror against the Soviet people even as it points to the experience of the people themselves. Yet "Great Terror" obscures an essential historical fact in a subtle sleight of hand: the arrests actually began as an *anti*terrorist campaign, a response to Kirov's assassination and to fears of terrorists, spies, and internal enemies. The inversion of the term begs a critical question: how does a broadly popular, state-sponsored campaign against "terrorism" turn into a "terror?" How does a war against targeted "terrorists" become a mass terror predicated on the widespread participation and victimization of ordinary citizens?

While granting that no one term can successfully capture all the facets of the period, this book uses the simple word *terror* to describe events in the factories. In a study concerned with political culture, experience, and behavior, it seems to best express the factories' prevailing atmosphere. The first chapter, "The Terror: A Short Political Primer," briefly traces its subject's development, from the state's early fears of terrorists to the flourishing of mass terror. Focusing on the peculiar language of the times, the chapter explains how specific phrases and political concepts influenced popular understanding and behavior. The next three chapters – "Comrades and Coworkers," "Family Secrets," and "Love, Loyalty, and Betrayal" – are built around the strongest and most basic of human connections. They use individual stories to explore how the terror affected intimate relationships among coworkers, family members, friends, and lovers. Each chapter examines the drama of denunciation, investigation, expulsion, and arrest that was played out in response to state orders and mass campaigns. Collectively, the chapters reveal a tragic process in which staunch "true believers," eager at first to aid the Party in its hunt for internal enemies, wrestled with growing doubts as coworkers, bosses, parents, siblings, friends, and neighbors disappeared into prisons. Many of those who initially denounced others were themselves soon swept away. Denouncers became victims as factory employees and party members vigilantly sought to root out the enemies in their midst. The last chapter, "The Final Paroxysm," treats the end of the terror and the purging of the most aggressive "denouncers" for their role in the arrests of others. The removal of this group from party ranks, and these individuals' own disappearance into the camps, signaled the waning of the terror and the beginning of a gradual return to relative normalcy. Finally, a brief conclusion, "A History without Heroes" considers the range of possible behaviors during the terror, the small acts of human decency that occurred, as well as the limits of resistance.

The stenographic reports used here to examine how citizens behaved during the terror do not tell us what individuals thought or felt in their hearts. They do, however, show us how people acted, and these actions, no matter what they believed or how they felt, had powerful consequences. In the factories, the human agents of the terror were not only the NKVD officials who made arrests; they were also the people who penned denunciations, wrote defamatory articles in the factory and wall newspapers, and accused shop heads of causing accidents. They were the party committee members who spearheaded investigations and voted for the expulsion of comrades, the district committee members who pressured party and shop committees to comb their membership lists for enemies, the engineers who recast technical disagreements as wrecking, and hundreds of others. Named and nameless, they were all of those who brought the hunt for enemies into the workplace and created an environment in which no one knew who the next victim might be.

Party, union, workplace, and other institutional meetings were the main collective arenas in which people identified and denounced the alleged enemies among them. These meetings were public performances. The participants, keenly aware of how others viewed and judged them, publicly demonstrated their own loyalty as they questioned, attacked, and investigated others. They followed common scripts and used specific language that structured both the form and substance of the meetings. People understood the limits of public speech and silence. They knew, for example, that they could not openly question the actions of the NKVD without risking serious consequences, or fail to take part in the victimization of others even if they were disgusted by it. They often used aggressive speech as a cover for their own secrets or political weaknesses, aware that silence would be construed as tacit support of the "enemy." Each successive meeting offered a new set of disciplinary lessons, in which the group instructed its members in the evolving limits of speech and behavior. Yet performances were also linked to real risks and results. Speakers and audience alike knew that they were involved in a genuine and deadly engagement. Moreover, common scripts did not necessarily produce predictable outcomes. The accused fought hard to defend themselves, votes were often split, and the actions of individuals could be and were erratic and unpredictable. People quickly learned and adopted the strategies they needed to survive.

In the factories, the terror was the sum of thousands of human actions in an evolving interplay with central party policies. The terror placed human relationships under intense pressure, twisting intimate bonds and fomenting profound mistrust. It forced people to make painful choices, to lie, to keep secrets, to betray friends and family. Rank-and-file party members, workers, managers, engineers, and others participated fully and actively. Their lived experience of terror is the subject of this book.

1: The Terror: A Short Political Primer

COLUMNS FOR THE GREAT MAYDAY PARADE BEGAN FORMING early in the morning in Moscow on May 1, 1937. Tens of thousands of people streamed through the streets, searching for the marching groups from their factories, schools, government institutions, and cultural organizations. Bakhmutskii, a zealous party organizer from Dinamo, Moscow's foremost electric machine plant, was in charge of his factory's contingent. His eyes intently scanned the swelling crowd as he checked to see who was present and, more important, who was still missing. During the anniversary Revolution Day parade the previous November, some party members had arrived later than the workers, and shamefully, many of Dinamo's employees had not shown up at all. This time, Bakhmutskii would note who had stayed home.[1] Along the great snaking throng, workers from Serp i Molot, a steel plant, Trekhgornaia Manufaktura, a textile factory, Krasnyi Proletarii, a machine-building factory, and Likerno-Vodochnyi, a distillery, among hundreds of other enterprises, could be seen forming up in jostling rows behind fluttering

[1] Tsentral'nyi Arkhiv Obshchestvenno-Politicheskoi Istorii Moskvy (TsAOPIM), f. 432, o. 1, d. 179, l. 108.

red banners. The wording on the banners, emblazoned in gold and black, had been composed by party leaders and disseminated first to the Central Committees of the republics, then through regional, city, and district committees to the party committees in the factories and other workplaces. Handmade signs, proudly lettered with heartfelt slogans, were nowhere to be found in this year's parade. The "official" slogans, published in the newspapers for all to read, had an ominous tone that seemed at odds with the celebratory holiday tradition:

"Strengthen Revolutionary Vigilance!"
"End Political Carelessness in Our Midst!"
"Unmask to the End Each and Every Double Dealer!"
"Destroy the Enemies of the People, the Japanese-German-Trotskyist Wreckers and Spies!"
"Death to Traitors to the Motherland!"[2]

The crowd, too, was in an edgy and anxious mood. Beneath the smiles and greetings, the workplace joking and ribbing, people were tacitly aware of the numerous comrades, coworkers, managers, and shop heads who were missing from their ranks. The thousands of Dinamo employees readying themselves to march this day had seen a number of their colleagues arrested over the preceding months. The mostly female workers of Trekhgornaia Manufaktura had lost their director to prison. Many more had meanwhile vanished from Serp i Molot, Likerno-Vodochnyi, and other factories and workplaces. By Mayday 1937, almost every marcher had a relative, friend, neighbor, or coworker who had disappeared, and almost every party member was keeping a secret. Some had failed to report the arrest of a relative or friend to their local party organization; others worried

2 "Lozungi k 1 Maia 1937 goda," *Kirovets*, April 27, 1937, p. 1.

about indiscreet remarks they had made, their ties to bosses or coworkers who had been arrested, or unfortunate details of their family origins or their past. Party members spoke fervently in public about the need to "unmask hidden enemies," but by this time many had realized that they themselves were also at risk of being arrested for one reason or another. Even some of the most ardent party members, who had denounced and accused others, were now sitting in prison. The banners called for vigilance against traitors, spies, and wreckers, but many of those who marched behind them feared that they, too, might one day soon be revealed as enemies.

A GIANT LINGUISTIC MACHINE

By 1937, the Soviet state had reduced a vibrant multiplicity of revolutionary voices and ideas to a single, narrow discourse prescribed by the Party. Like the slogans dictated from above for the Mayday banners, carefully defined words and phrases delimited the channels of discussion and analysis. The Party controlled political speech through its organizational network, which functioned as a vast linguistic machine for the generation and implementation of concepts, phrases, slogans, and catchwords. Political language originated in the speeches and communications of party leaders and filtered down through the Party's organizational pyramid via resolutions adopted by Central Committee plenums and provincial, town, district, and factory meetings. The reigning bodies of mass organizations in turn replicated the process within their own ranks. Newspapers then conveyed this language to the general population, reprinting major speeches and popularizing the Party's "line," or policy positions. The resolutions adopted in March 1937 by the sixth plenum of the All-Union Central Council of Trade Unions (VTsSPS), for example, were drawn directly from the platform passed by the Party's Central Committee plenum two weeks earlier. The VTsSPS plenum laid down the "marching orders" for more than one hundred separate unions, which then copied the Central Committee's resolutions word for word in their own meetings and organizational hierarchies. The language, parroted faithfully by midlevel and local union officials, served as shorthand for mass mobilizations and national campaigns. In this way, hundreds of thousands of local officials, journalists, and educators disseminated a political vocabulary crafted by a handful of leaders.

The Party made every effort to ensure that ordinary people understood its positions and political language. Organizers in the factories were routinely charged with talking over national events with workers in shop, shift, dormitory, and factory-wide meetings. After the first Moscow show trial, in August 1936, for instance, party organizers read aloud and discussed newspaper articles about the trial in meetings held throughout the factories. The local party organizations appointed official "discussants" (*besedchiki*) to emphasize specific political points. District party leaders organized instructional meetings for the heads of factory party committees, shop organizers, and discussants, during which they explained the meanings of the newest slogans, phrases, and concepts and provided the "correct" answers to questions that workers might be expected to pose. The district committees taught both political vocabulary and concepts to party organizers in the factories, who then passed the language on to workers. The Party, from top to bottom, thus went well beyond providing just a basic education for its members. From political instructors in the middle to an army of *besedchiki* at the base, the Party employed a vast staff to engage officials and ordinary people in constant political discussions built on specified concepts, slogans, and catchphrases. This language, though seemingly easy enough to master, was hardly transparent or self-evident at the time to those being inculcated in it. Each phrase was a distillation of political aims emerging from national and international events, and as such represented a whole realm of political knowledge. To many Soviet citizens, especially the illiterate and uneducated, all of this remained a strange and mysterious tongue. Eugenia Ginzburg, a party member arrested in 1937, would later recall an old peasant woman she met in prison who insisted that she was being held as a "tractorist." Initially puzzled, Ginzburg soon realized that her cellmate must in fact have been arrested as a "Trotskyist." The woman, no more familiar with Trotskyism than she was with Euclidean geometry, told Ginzburg in helpless confusion, "But as God's my witness I never went near one of those cursed things. . . . They don't put old women like me on tractors."[3]

Throughout the 1930s, the Party tightened its control over political speech. Language not only expressed the aims of power but attained a fierce power of its own. By 1937, certain words and phrases – including "Trotskyist," "wrecker," "lickspittle," "Fascist hireling," "hidden enemy," "masking" and "unmasking," "enemy of the people," "party and union democracy," and "suppression of criticism" – were constitutive elements of the political discourse even as they also dictated organizational practices and behaviors. Party members and ordinary people spoke publicly and privately in this new language, assimilating its most basic assumptions. In party meetings, it structured a deadly game with strict rules for accusations and responses, aggression and self-protection.

3 Eugenia Semenovna Ginzburg, *Journey into the Whirlwind* (New York: Harcourt Brace Jovanovich, 1967), p. 182.

None of these words and phrases was entirely new, but after the murder of Sergei M. Kirov, head of the Leningrad party committee, in December 1934, they became increasingly characteristic of political speech. Party leaders soon linked Kirov's murderer to prominent former oppositionists such as G. E. Zinoviev, L. B. Kamenev, and L. D. Trotsky and promoted a new political discourse around hidden terrorists and conspiracies. Within a short time, ordinary people began employing this language in their interactions with one another – so much so, in fact, that these phrases became the common currency of exchange, a normal, fully accepted way to describe, interpret, and understand work, social relations, and daily life. Local party organizations and workplaces became the focus of the search for conspirators. In the factories, for example, party members and workers were quick to blame leaky roofs, industrial accidents, and broken machines on "wrecking" perpetrated by "hidden enemies." Coworkers recast strained or conflicted relationships in political terms and wrote denunciations of one another to their local party organizations and the NKVD.

ACCUSATIONS AND *ZAIAVLENIIA*

The Russian people had a long tradition, dating back to the tsarist period, of complaining in writing to authorities. In the 1930s, peasants and workers sent letters not only to newspapers but also to district and regional prosecutors, local and regional party leaders, and the NKVD. The texts of such letters comprised, in the words of one historian, "a grab bag of all the crimes, shortfalls, mistakes, defects, and black marks" that might be attributed to the writers' targets. By denouncing those who misused authority to *other* authorities, the powerless sought a form of justice. Ordinary citizens also denounced one another, submitting accusations of alleged wrongdoing or illegal activities to state officials.[4] This tradition turned deadly after the Kirov murder and then the first Moscow show trial in August 1936. Accusations within the factories led to investigations, which in turn involved the NKVD. Allegations of all types circulated among local party officials, judicial authorities, and the NKVD, fattening dossiers on party members and ordinary citizens alike.

According to longstanding party rules, members were required to present an official declaration, or *zaiavlenie*, whenever they learned of the arrest of a relative, friend, or mentor, overheard a suspicious conversation, suspected "enemy" activity, or received compromising information. A *zaiavlenie* could be either about the writer himself or herself or about another, and it might take the form of a personal confession, a denunciation, a report of a rumor, or even an assertion of a mere suspicion. Workplaces and other institutions also mandated *zaiavleniia* among their operating procedures. A *zaiavlenie* in this sense was simply a declarative written statement, required of party members and regular citizens alike. The Party, however, took things a step further by demanding that its members submit *zaiavleniia* disclosing any information that affected their own standing in, or the political interests of, the Party itself. After the first Moscow trial, flurries of such "informational declarations" blanketed the NKVD and the Party at every level. "To write" became a slang

---

4 Sheila Fitzpatrick, "Signals from Below: Soviet Letters of Denunciation of the 1930s," *Journal of Modern History*, vol. 68, no. 4 (December 1996), pp. 846, 837, 834–35. Among the two hundred denunciation letters that Fitzpatrick viewed, she suggests that "loyalty denunciations," or "Communist against Communist," were the paradigmatic form. Golfo Alexopoulos, "Victim Talk: Defense Testimony and Denunciation Under Stalin," *Law and Social Inquiry*, vol. 24, no. 3 (Summer 1999), pp. 637–54, notes that people who filed petitions for reinstatement of citizenship rights often cast aspersions on others.

synonym for "to denounce." Charges made in *zaiavleniia* did not have to be substantiated by proof or evidence, and their authors were not even held responsible for their contents. Individual *zaiavleniia* might thus contain, along with party members' supposed full revelations about themselves, a generous measure of rumor, gossip, slander, and lies about others. Moreover, whereas there were no penalties for writing a *zaiavlenie* without evidence, not writing one at all could invite serious consequences. Failure to report the arrest of a relative or to go on record with suspicions about a coworker who was subsequently arrested, for example, was grounds for expulsion from the Party. There was therefore a strong impetus to denounce others, if only to protect oneself against the charge of having failed to denounce them. Local party leaders, once able to exercise some discretion in their investigations, were now forced to investigate every *zaiavlenie*, no matter how nonsensical or malicious.

Primary party organizations, shop committees, party committees, and even huge factory-wide party groups discussed *zaiavleniia* in highly ritualized meetings that resembled court trials.[5] Party members in the factories were organized in a pyramidal structure, with the primary party organizations at the base, the shop committees at the middle level, and the party committee, an elected body of ten to fifteen people, at the apex. Directly above the party committees stood the district committee, which in turn answered to the city and regional committees. Party membership cut vertically through the factory and included workers, shop heads, engineers, managers, and the director. Party meetings, from those at the party committee level to the general, factory-wide variety, ranged in size from tens to

5 For a fascinating history of staged mock trials as political education, see Elizabeth Wood, *Performing Justice: Agitational Trials in Early Soviet Russia* (Ithaca, N.Y.: Cornell University Press, 2005).

hundreds of members and encompassed different, often conflicting interests. Some of the larger and more important factories employed hundreds of party members, while many smaller workplaces had none at all. Throughout the 1920s and early 1930s, party committees were occupied primarily with tasks related to production, political campaigns and education, and social welfare. Membership issues comprised only a small part of their work. By the fall of 1936, though, *zaiavleniia* and investigations of cadres had begun to dominate their agendas. When a party member presented a *zaiavlenie*, the members of his or her shop committee were the first to consider the information and decide what action to take. The party committee then met to review this decision, often with the benefit of additional evidence and testimony. At this meeting, the head of the party committee would present the charges, the accused would defend himself or herself, and other members would be encouraged to ask questions. Then the accused would respond, the committee's head would render an opinion, and the members would vote on the outcome. In this venue, unlike a court trial, there were no rules governing the presentation of evidence: hearsay was a mainstay of such proceedings, and members' questions were often openly prejudicial and belligerent. By 1937, party organizations in the factories were focused almost exclusively on the investigation of *zaiavleniia*, as a parade of members came forward to "unmask" comrades, report the arrests of relatives, or confess to minor misdeeds.

UNCOVERING "TERRORISTS" AND "DOUBLE DEALERS"

The state began targeting and rooting out potential political enemies immediately after Kirov's assassination, though its initial response did not have an instantaneous effect on the political culture either of the factories or of local party organizations. On the dark afternoon of December 1, 1934, a former employee of the Institute of Party History, Leonid V. Nikolaev, slipped into an empty corridor in Leningrad party headquarters and shot and killed Kirov. That very night, the government responded by passing an antiterrorist law abrogating civil liberties and judicial rights. Investigations of "terrorism" were to be completed within ten days. The accused were to be informed of the charges against them just twenty-four hours before trial and denied any legal counsel for their defense. Their sentences could not be appealed, and capital punishment, if imposed, was to be carried out at once.[6] The Politburo entrusted Nikolai I. Ezhov, deputy chairman of the Party Control Commission, and Ia. S. Agranov, deputy commissar of the People's Commissariat of Internal Affairs (NKVD), with the murder investigation. Although Ezhov's aggressive investigative techniques and his conspiracy theories would eventually propel him to the top spot at the NKVD, he and Agranov initially limited their search to a small group of suspects.

Stalin and the NKVD first targeted the former supporters of G. E. Zinoviev, a close collaborator of Lenin's who had opposed Stalin and his policies in the late 1920s. Zinoviev had headed Leningrad's party organization until 1926, when he was removed and replaced with Kirov. He still had many supporters within the Party, though the heyday of the "Zinovievite opposition" was long past. Less than a month after Kirov's murder, Nikolaev and thirteen others, including a number of former Zinovievites, were charged with

6 Matthew Lenoe, *The Kirov Murder and Soviet History* (New Haven, Conn.: Yale University Press, 2010), pp. 251–56; Peter Solomon, *Soviet Criminal Justice under Stalin* (New York: Cambridge University Press, 1996), p. 236.

having formed a "Leningrad center" responsible for the assassination. They were arrested, tried, and executed in accordance with the new laws passed in the immediate aftermath of Kirov's murder. A second trial followed soon after, on January 15–16, 1935. Nineteen additional former oppositionists, including Zinoviev himself as well as L. B. Kamenev, a party leader with strong ties to both Lenin and Zinoviev dating back to the prerevolutionary period, were charged with establishing a "Moscow center" that had guided the activities of various counterrevolutionary groups, including the so-called "Leningrad center." Zinoviev and Kamenev both denied that they had played any part in planning Kirov's assassination. Convicted of a lesser charge of "abetting" the murder by encouraging "terrorism," they were sentenced to prison.[7]

Party leaders soon used Kirov's murder as the pretext on which to arrest thousands of former oppositionists who had long since abandoned their oppositional activity. Directly after the trial of the "Moscow center" ended, in January 1935, Stalin reviewed the political situation in a secret letter that was circulated to all party organizations for discussion. Summarizing the leadership's current thinking on the Kirov murder, the letter claimed that Nikolaev, Kirov's assassin, had been a member of a "Zinovievite group," based in Leningrad, that was responsible for the crime. This "Leningrad center" in turn reported to a "Moscow center," which had been unaware of the actual assassination plan but was fully cognizant of the "terrorist moods" of the Leningrad Zinovievites. The two centers were said to share a common "Trotskyist-Zinovievite platform," a phrase that signaled a broader targeting of former left oppositionists

7 Lenoe, *Kirov Murder*, pp. 279–388; J. Arch Getty and Oleg Naumov, *The Road to Terror: Stalin and the Self-Destruction of the Bolsheviks, 1932–1939* (New Haven, Conn.: Yale University Press, 1999), pp. 144–47.

of the 1920s. According to the letter, the defendants, having lost the support of the workers, turned to "individual terror" and external Fascist assistance. While outwardly professing loyalty to the Party's policies and leaders, they were really two-faced "double dealers" (*dvurushniki*), "Judas betrayers with party cards in their pockets," who "masked" their true intentions. Their party cards allowed them to operate freely within Soviet institutions while plotting terrorist acts. The letter noted that while the Party had harbored numerous oppositional groups in the past, it had never before included a group that swore allegiance to party policies while at the same time preparing terrorist attacks against its leaders. It demanded the exclusion, arrest, and exile of all "remnants of antiparty groups within the Party." With the suggestion that "masked" or hidden enemies lurked within the Party's ranks, the letter highlighted a critical concept in the political vocabulary of party members: "masking" and "unmasking" would soon come to occupy a significant place in the new lexicon of repression.[8] Yet how many "masked" enemies were truly lurking in the Party's ranks? The letter referred to only "tens or hundreds of degenerates," a tiny number in view of the arrests that would eventually follow. Shortly after drafting the letter, in January and February 1935, the Politburo, on Stalin's initiative, arrested hundreds of former Zinovievites from Leningrad and sent them into exile.[9]

The campaign against terrorism soon developed a peculiar logic of its own, as interrogations and coerced confessions identified fresh suspects and led to more arrests. In May 1935, Ezhov elaborated

8 On the phenomenon of "masking, " see Sheila Fitzpatrick, *Tear Off the Masks!: Identity and Imposture in Twentieth-Century Russia* (Princeton, N.J.: Princeton University Press, 2005).
9 "Zakrytoe Pis'mo TsK VKP (b): Uroki Sobytii, Sviazannykh s Zlodeiskim Ubiitstvom Tov. Kirova," *Izvestiia TsK KPSS*, no. 8 (1989), pp. 95–100.

a new version of the growing conspiracy in a manuscript enti-
tled "From Fractionalism to Open Counterrevolution and Fascism,"
which he sent to Stalin. In it, Ezhov asserted that former Trotskyists
had also opted for terrorism and abetted the Zinovievites. Tension
increased substantially in the Central Committee early that summer,
when members of the Kremlin service administration were accused
of being involved with another terrorist group intent on assassinat-
ing Stalin and other party leaders. That summer, Ezhov instructed
the NKVD to locate and eliminate a still-hidden "Trotskyist center."
Former members of the left opposition – now in exile, in prison, or
even ensconced in leading posts – were arrested or brought back to
Moscow to be questioned. Their subsequent confessions, extracted
through harsh interrogation techniques, inevitably widened the circle of alleged perpetrators and reinforced the fears of the state.[10]

Gravely worried by Hitler's rise to power, Japanese designs on
Mongolia, hostile border states, and domestic social discontent,
party leaders saw Kirov's murder as part of a larger terrorist threat,
a nascent anti-Stalinist alliance of former oppositionists, disgrun-
tled social groups, and foreign enemies. These fears were not mere
figments of Stalin's imagination. In the words of one historian,
the Soviet Union was indeed "living under siege," ringed by hostile states or, in Soviet parlance, in a position of "capitalist encir-
clement." The embassies were in fact riddled with spies. The head
of the Polish consulate in Kiev gathered intelligence on Soviet railways, industry, and telecommunications and filed regular reports
with Warsaw. Polish intelligence agents organized Polish spies and

10 "O Tak Nazyvaemom 'Antisovetskom Ob"edinennom Trotskistsko-Zinov'-
evskom Tsentr'," *Izvestiia TsK KPSS*, no. 8 (1989), pp. 81–2. On Ezhov's manu-
script, see Wladislaw Hedeler, "Ezhov's Scenario for the Great Terror and the
Falsified Record of the Third Moscow Show Trial," in Barry McLoughlin and
Kevin McDermott, eds., *Stalin's Terror: High Politics and Mass Repression in the
Soviet Union* (Basingstoke, Hampshire: Palgrave Macmillan, 2003), pp. 34–40.

Russian exiles under the aegis of the "Promethean Movement," a shadowy entity aimed at overthrowing the Soviet state. Spies were also active among ethnic Latvians in the northern borderlands and among ethnic Koreans in the Russian Far East. The Japanese would later admit that Stalin's order to arrest and deport this latter group had effectively deprived their Korean spies of cover. Japan additionally collaborated in subversive activities with Poland, Latvia, and Estonia, as well as with émigré Ukrainian nationalists.[11]

In May 1935, the Party initiated a routine screening of its members, comprising a review (*proverka*) followed by a surrender and replacement of party documents (*obmen*). According to its implementation instructions, the screening had a threefold purpose: to weed out members who no longer belonged in the Party, to update membership records, and to ensure that members' documents were in order. No mention was made, in this context, of the Kirov murder. Local party organizations took a nonpolitical approach to the review, expelling those members who were no longer active (and who were now cited for their "passivity"), who were judged to be ill behaved (prone to drunkenness or domestic violence, or possessed of a poor work record), or who had been found guilty of criminal activity (for example, embezzlement, rape, or theft). By contrast, party officials took a more tolerant view of members whose only fault was that they had once sided with oppositional groups, provided that they had abandoned their earlier views. So long as party members were honest about their biographies and past political activities, party organizations by and large did not consider prior oppositionism a cause for expulsion or even censure. The

11 On espionage and counterespionage, see Hiroaki Kuromiya, *The Voices of the Dead: Stalin's Great Terror in the 1930s* (New Haven, Conn.: Yale University Press, 2007), pp. 2, 30, 32, 126, 142, 163.

cumbersome review process would drag on into 1936 as party organizations attempted to put their muddled records in order.[12] Between May and December of 1935, the Party expelled only a tiny fraction of its members for "Trotskyist-Zinovievite" opposition (4,956 people, or just 2.6 percent of its total membership of more than 1.9 million). The NKVD continued to make targeted arrests, but Ezhov's manuscript, which warned of a far wider conspiracy, had evidently been shelved by the leadership, at least for the time being. By the end of the year, 30,174 people had been arrested and sentenced for committing "counterrevolutionary" crimes, a number that would come to seem minuscule in comparison with the mass of arrests and executions that were soon to follow.[13]

In January 1936, the lull was broken. V. P. Ol'berg, a member of the German Communist Party who had fled fascism and acquired Soviet citizenship, confessed that Trotsky had instructed him to assassinate Stalin and create a counterrevolutionary terrorist organization.[14] It is not clear whether interrogators forced Ol'berg to concoct this scenario or whether he unwittingly supplied information that reinforced Ezhov's expanded version of the plot. In any case, as a result, other alleged "Trotskyists" throughout the country were arrested and charged with terrorism.[15] As these investigations

12 On the casual approach to this review, see Wendy Z. Goldman, *Terror and Democracy in the Age of Stalin: The Social Dynamics of Repression* (New York: Cambridge University Press, 2007), pp. 65–67, 86–91.

13 Getty and Naumov, *Road to Terror*, p. 198. J. Arch Getty, Gábor Rittersporn, and Viktor Zemskov, "Victims of the Soviet Penal System in the Prewar Years: A First Approach on the Basis of Archival Evidence," *American Historical Review*, vol. 98, no. 4 (October 1993), p. 1035.

14 William J. Chase, *Enemies within the Gates?: The Comintern and the Stalinist Repression, 1934–1939* (New Haven, Conn.: Yale University Press, 2001), pp. 134–35.

15 "O Tak Nazyvaemom 'Antisovetskom Ob"edinennom Trotskistsko-Zinov'evskom Tsentr'," *Izvestiia TsK KPSS*, no. 8 (1989), p. 82.

in turn "exposed" new terrorist subplots linked directly to Trotsky, the state's narrative of the Kirov assassination began rapidly to evolve. The latest variant now implicated Zinoviev, Kamenev, Trotsky, and additional suspects in an "underground terrorist" conspiracy dating back to 1932. In February 1936, the deputy commissar of the NKVD instructed its local organs to eliminate the "entire Trotskyist-Zinovievite underground" and "uncover terrorist groups." Stalin proposed that Ezhov assume responsibility for the interrogations. During the spring of 1936, NKVD investigators used a variety of illegal methods, including torture, sleep deprivation, psychological abuse, and isolation, to extract and shape confessions from former oppositionists. Stalin entrusted G. G. Iagoda, head of the NKVD, and A. Ia. Vyshinskii, general prosecutor of the USSR, to draw up a list of people who were to be brought to trial. From June 1936 on, Vyshinskii worked to develop the case against the so-called "united center" of prominent former Trotskyists and Zinovievites, the basis for the first of the Moscow show trials.[16]

On July 29, 1936, the Central Committee sent out a second secret letter to the party organizations, this one outlining the case against Zinoviev, Kamenev, and their fellow defendants. Its text showed that the state's view of the Kirov murder had shifted substantially over the previous eighteen months, in tandem with the confessions extracted from various former oppositionists. Zinoviev and Kamenev, initially accused merely of "arousing terrorist moods," were now charged with Kirov's murder and the attempted murders of Stalin and other party leaders. The revised roster of terrorists included Trotskyists as well as Zinovievites, allied in a "united

16 *Ibid.*, pp. 82–84.

Trotskyist-Zinovievite center" dating back to 1932. According to the letter, this center had received instructions from Trotsky to murder Kirov, Stalin, and other party leaders, to organize terror cells within the army, and to seize power in the event of war.[17] A number of German Communists who had escaped Hitler and settled in the Soviet Union were also linked to the center and accused of committing acts of terrorism and espionage on behalf of Russian Fascist émigré organizations and the Gestapo. The letter further claimed that terrorists had infiltrated newspaper staffs, the army, the defense industry, and a variety of other institutions. While focusing its attack on former left oppositionists and foreign Communists, it introduced the possibility that certain former "rightists," including N. I. Bukharin, M. P. Tomskii, and A. I. Rykov, had also participated in the plots against Stalin.[18]

Of greater significance for rank-and-file party members was that the letter reprimanded the local party organizations for failing to uncover hidden terrorists during their general membership review of the previous year. It noted that the NKVD had subsequently arrested party members who had passed muster in the review, an indication of sloppy, careless practices within the local organizations. The letter stressed, "The indelible mark of every Bolshevik under the present conditions should be the ability to recognize an enemy of the Party,

17 One of the defendants was charged with plotting to kill Stalin at a Comintern congress, a charge that set off a chain of arrests in the Comintern. See Chase, *Enemies within the Gates?*, pp. 146–77.

18 "Zakrytoe Pis'mo TsK VKP (b): O Terroristicheskoi Deiatel'nosti Trotskistsko-Zinov' evskogo Kontrrevoliutsionnogo Bloka," *Izvestiia TsK KPSS*, no. 8 (1989), pp. 100–15. Chase, *Enemies within the Gates?*, pp. 162–63, notes that the Party's cadres department notified Georgi Dimitrov, general secretary of the Comintern, that it sent material to the NKVD on three thousand foreign Communists and émigrés living in the USSR who were suspected of being spies, provocateurs, and wreckers.

no matter how well he may be masked." It urged party members to find and expose the enemies hiding in their ranks.[19]

Sixteen defendants alleged to have belonged to the "united Trotskyist-Zinovievite center" were tried in open court in Moscow on August 19–24, 1936.[20] The trial was the first of three Moscow show trials, all of which were to be covered by both Soviet papers and the international press. To the shock of Soviet citizens and others the world over, the defendants, dedicated revolutionaries all, confessed to murdering Kirov, attempting to murder Stalin and other Soviet leaders, and allying with German and Japanese Fascists to overthrow the Soviet government. Vyshinskii, the state prosecutor, charged the defendants with organizing "underground terrorist groups" whose brief was to "seize power at all costs," explaining, "They made use of the most detestable method of fighting, namely, terrorism."[21] The accused all declined the assistance of counsel. Their confessions – which, along with their reciprocal denunciations, constituted the main evidence in the case – were not entirely false; rather, they were a carefully created "amalgam," combining falsified accounts of the defendants' activities (from murder and terrorism to espionage) with an accurate depiction of their deep disapproval of Stalin's policies.[22] Vyshinskii was not wrong in

---

19 "Zakrytoe Pis'mo TsK VKP (b): O Terroristicheskoi Deiatel'nosti Trotskistsko-Zinov'evskogo Kontrrevoliutsionnogo Bloka," *Izvestiia TsK KPSS*, no. 8 (1989), pp. 100–15.

20 *The Case of the Trotskyite-Zinovievite Terrorist Center: Report of the Court Proceedings* (Moscow: People's Commissariat of Justice, 1936). The defendants were G. E. Zinoviev, L. B. Kamenev, G. E. Evdokimov, I. N. Smirnov, I. P Bakayev, V. A. Ter-Vaganian, S. V. Mrachkovsky, E. A. Dreitser, E. S. Holtzman, I. I. Reingold, R. V. Pickel, V. P. Olberg, K. B. Berman-Yurin, Fritz David (I. I. Kruglyansky), M. Lurye, and N. Lurye.

21 *Ibid.*, p. 12.

22 Vadim Zakharovich Rogovin coined the term "amalgam" to describe the confessions in all three Moscow show trials in *Stalin's Terror of 1937–1938: Political Genocide in the USSR* (Oak Park, Mich.: Mehring Books, 2009).

suggesting that many former oppositionists and other party members had strong doubts about Stalin. Repelled by his policies, they nevertheless remained within the Party, outwardly professing loyalty while inwardly harboring reservations.

Stalin and other party leaders were grimly aware of this lurking discontent. Collectivization, famine, and the sharp drop in living standards had embittered many peasants and workers, and party cadres at every level were badly shaken by the painful conditions of life on the collective farms and in the industrial enterprises.[23] With war looming on two fronts, in the east and west, they were afraid that former oppositionists might exploit social dissatisfaction to remove Stalin and alter the Party's political course. This threat provided the logic underlying the state's fantastic charges and spurred its growing obsession with "double dealers" and "masked enemies." Vyshinskii voiced the state's fears forthrightly. He argued that the defendants had never accepted the Party's line under Stalin's leadership: "The united center carefully masked its terrorist activities," he noted. "While preparing the assassination of Comrade Stalin and other leaders of the CPSU, the united center simultaneously strove by all means in its power to give assurances of its loyalty and even devotion to the Party." Yet under the direct influence of Trotsky, its members took "the path of terrorism" and expanded the practice of "double dealing to monstrous dimensions."[24] In the middle of the trial, Vyshinskii announced a new investigation into the "terrorist organization of the former leaders of the right," including Bukharin, Rykov, Tomskii, and others.[25]

23 Wendy Z. Goldman, "Hunger and Politics: Prelude to the Great Terror in the Soviet Union," in Mathias Middell and Felix Wemheuer, eds., *Hunger and Scarcity under Socialist Rule* (Leipzig: Leipzig University Press, 2010).

24 *The Case of the Trotskyite-Zinovievite Terrorist Center*, pp. 19, 21.

25 *Ibid.*, pp. 55–56, 65, 68, 71–72, 115, 117, 126, 133, 178–80. "O Tak Nazyvaemom 'Antisovetskom Ob"edinennom Trotskistsko-Zinov'evskom Tsentr',"

As a stunned public, both inside and outside the Soviet Union, tried to make sense of the trial's startling revelations, the defendants were found guilty of organizing a terrorist center, murdering Kirov, and attempting to murder Stalin and other Soviet leaders. All were shot the day after the trial ended. More than fifty years later, in 1988, the Party and the Supreme Court would officially admit that the confessions, extracted under torture and duress, had been false, and announce the rehabilitation of the victims.[26] At the time, however, the executions were not enough to satisfy the state's obsession with rooting out terrorist conspiracies and hidden enemies. Instead, the NKVD stepped up its investigations of former left oppositionists who had returned to the Party and assumed leading posts in industry.[27] Officials from the Moscow party committee began pressuring local party organizations to use records of the membership screening of the year before to identify and expose the enemies lurking in their ranks. They called on party leaders at the district and factory levels to compel them to check their cadres again. S. Z. Korytnyi, secretary of the Moscow party committee, visited seven districts in September. During one meeting, he brusquely told the district party officials to "stop lying around and doing nothing." He chided, "You have material on forty people that you need to investigate. If one of these people is an enemy, then your dawdling is a crime. You have *zaiavleniia* about forty people. What are you waiting for?"[28] The local organizations, which up to this point had largely ignored instructions about uncovering enemies, at

Izvestiia TsK, no. 8 (1989), pp. 78–81. "Materialy Fevral'sko-Martovskogo Plenuma TsK VKP (b) 1937 goda," *Voprosy Istorii*, nos. 2–3 (1992), pp. 3–4.

26 "O Tak Nazyvaemom 'Antisovetskom Ob"edinennom Trotskistsko-Zinov'evskom Tsentr'," *Izvestiia TsK*, no. 8 (1989), p. 94.

27 Oleg Khlevniuk, *1937-g. Stalin, NKVD i sovetskoe obshchestvo* (Moscow: Izdatel'stvo 'Respublika', 1992), pp. 116–17.

28 TsAOPIM, f. 3, o. 49, d. 119, l. 36.

once began investigating the *zaiavleniia*. They sent letters to party organizations in distant cities to request members' biographical data, their Civil War records, and protocols from long-forgotten meetings held in the 1920s.[29] Not surprisingly, some of these requests did succeed in turning up compromising information. At the same time, meetings in the factories about the August show trial produced a flood of unsolicited denunciations as party members rushed to put new suspicions into writing. Korytnyi himself disappeared sometime the following year, as arrests made inroads on the Moscow city party committee. After he was convicted by the Military Collegium of the Supreme Court, his name was included on a list sent to Stalin and several other leaders for approval for execution on October 21, 1937. He won a brief reprieve when someone crossed his name off the list, but he appeared again on a second list, on December 7, 1937, and was executed shortly thereafter.[30]

INDUSTRIAL WRECKING

In the fall of 1936, the hunt for terrorists engulfed the industrial enterprises. In September, G. L. Piatakov, the deputy commissar of heavy industry, a former member of the left opposition and close associate of Trotsky's, was expelled from the Party for maintaining ties with Zinoviev and Kamenev and thereafter immediately arrested.[31] Following a grueling interrogation, he confessed to economic wrecking and sabotage. On September 23, 1936, eleven

29 TsAOPIM, f. 3, o. 49, d. 119, ll. 36–39, 54–55, 71, 125. For the initial reaction toward so-called "hidden enemies" within the local party organizations, see Goldman, *Terror and Democracy in the Age of Stalin*, pp. 86–92.

30 See http://stalin.memo.ru/spiski/tomio3.htm, Arkhiv Prezidenta Rossiiskoi Federatsii (APRF), f. 3, o. 24, d. 411, l. 232, and http://stalin.memo.ru/spiski/tomio5.htm, APRF, f. 3, o. 24, d. 413, l. 255.

31 Getty and Naumov, *Road to Terror*, pp. 286, 283.

days after Piatakov's arrest, an underground gas explosion rocked the Kemerovo coal mines in the Kuznetsk basin (Kuzbas) in western Siberia, killing ten miners and injuring fourteen more. The press did not report the accident. The problems in Kemerovo were all too common throughout the mining industry, where accidents, poor ventilation, and insufficient scaffolding were often the norm. In this instance, however, before the week was out, the Commissariat of Justice would instruct regional and local procurators to reexamine "every explosion, accident, and fire that has occurred in industry in the past three years," and Stalin would request that the Politburo replace Iagoda, head of the NKVD, with Ezhov.[32] The NKVD quickly linked Kemerovo mine managers and engineers with imprisoned former Trotskyists and implicated them in an elaborate plot to wreck the Kemerovo mines, murder workers, and commit espionage.[33] In November, the nine defendants, branded a

32 GARF, f. 8131, o. 37, d. 84, l. 108; Getty and Naumov, *Road to Terror*, p. 280.
33 Among the defendants were I. A. Peshekhonov, chief engineer of the Kemerovo mine complex, and E. P. Shtikling, a German national and chief engineer of the complex's Severnaia mine. The other defendants, who worked in the Tsentral'naia mine, where the explosion occurred, were I. I. Noskov, the mine's director; V. M. Andreev and I. E. Kovalenko, its chief engineers; N. S. Leonenko, its manager; I. T. Liashchenko, its director of ventilation; F. I. Shubin, a foreman; and M. A. Kurov, a former Trotskyist and worker. Peshekhonov had been sentenced to three years' exile in the Shakhty trial, in 1928. After serving most of his sentence in western Siberia, he was eventually appointed chief engineer of the Kemerovo mine complex. Shubin was a former Trotskyist who had participated in underground meetings held by Trotsky in 1927, before the latter's exile from the USSR. Six other men who were also implicated would be tried later, in what would become the second Moscow show trial of the "parallel Trotskyist center." They were Ia. N. Drobnis, deputy chief of construction in Kemerovo; N. I. Muralov, an old revolutionary and former Trotskyist who had been exiled to Novosibirsk in 1928; A. A. Shestov, director of a Kuzbas zinc mine; M. S. Stroilov, chief engineer of the Kuzbas Coal Trust; M. S. Boguslavskii, head of Siberian Machine Construction; and V. V. Arnol'd, a chauffeur. With the exception of Arnol'd, the reserve group were all former oppositionists. See "Protsess Kontrrevoliutsionnoi Trotskistskoi Vreditel'skoi

"counterrevolutionary wrecking group," were tried by a military "*troika*" or group of three, established after the Kirov murder to hear cases of "terrorism" and "treason." The testimony of the accused managers and engineers was deliberately framed to enrage work-ers and mobilize their support for the state. The newspapers widely quoted one defendant as having said, "Soon our workers will perish in the mines like rats."[34] The defendants, convicted on the sole basis of their confessions, were shot.[35] The trial, as reported in the national press, encouraged the public, and workers in particular, to interpret the problems of Soviet industry as the calculated work of "wreckers." Workers, deeply frustrated by hazardous, difficult con-ditions, resented managers who favored production at the expense of safety. The trial deflected blame away from the state and onto managers and former oppositionists, inviting workers to couch their complaints about safety, housing, work conditions, and food short-ages in the new language of "wrecking."[36]

The Kemerovo trial would soon prove to have been merely a rehearsal for the second Moscow show trial, which opened on January 23, 1937. Once again, reporters from all over the world were in attendance. By this time, almost a thousand economic managers were in prison, accused of deliberate sabotage.[37] The

Gruppy na Kemerovskom Rudnike," part 1, *Trud*, November 20, 1936, p. 3; part 2, *Trud*, November 21, 1936, p. 3; and part 3, *Trud*, November 22, 1936, p. 3.

34 "Protsess Kontrrevoliutsionnoi Trotskistskoi Vreditel'skoi Gruppy na Kemero-vskom Rudnike," part 1, *Trud*, November 20, 1936, p. 3.

35 "Rech' Gosudarstvennogo Obvinitelia – Zam. Prokuratora Soiuza SSR Tov. Roginskogo," *Trud*, November 23, 1936, p. 2.

36 "Soderzhanie Prigovora," *Trud*, November 23, 1936, p. 2.

37 Getty and Naumov, *Road to Terror*, 282; Oleg Khlevniuk, "Economic Officials in the Great Terror, 1936–1938," in Melanie Ilic, ed., *Stalin's Terror Revisited* (Basingstoke, Hampshire: Palgrave Macmillan, 2006).

trial was built around three interlocking conspiracies, associating sabotage in Kemerovo with wrecking on the railroads and in the chemical industry. Seventeen defendants, including Piatakov, the deputy commissar of heavy industry; K. B. Radek, editor of *Izvestiia*; and G. Ia. Sokolnikov, deputy commissar of light industry, were tried for treason, espionage, and wrecking. The defendants were also accused of creating a "parallel Trotskyist center" to serve as a reserve for the "united Trotskyist-Zinovievite center" whose members had been convicted in the August 1936 trial.[38] Allegedly motivated by a shared hatred of Stalin, the group of seventeen had supposedly conspired to undermine Soviet industry, restore capitalism, disband the collective farms, weaken the country's defense, and grant territorial concessions to Germany and Japan.[39] The defendants strongly implicated former rightists in their testimonies. Investigations of Bukharin and others were now reopened on the basis of this new evidence. The state's case, as in the August 1936 and Kemerovo trials, rested entirely upon the defendants' confessions. At the trial's conclusion, all of the defendants, with the exception of four who received lengthy prison sentences, were shot.[40]

38 *Report of Court Proceedings in the Case of the Anti-Soviet Trotskyite Center* (Moscow: People's Commissariat of Justice, 1937). Cited hereafter as *Case of the Anti-Soviet Trotskyite Center*. The defendants were G. L. Piatakov, K. B. Radek, G. Ia. Sokolnikov, L. P. Serebriakov, N. I. Muralov, Ia. A. Livshits, Ia. N. Drobnis, M. S. Boguslavskii, I. A. Kniazev, S. A. Rataichak, B. O. Norkin, A. A. Shestov, M. S. Stroilov, I. D. Turok, I. I. Grashe, G. E. Pushin, and V. V. Arnol'd. Muralov, for example, a former member of the left opposition exiled to Novosibirsk in 1928, was arrested in the spring of 1936. He refused to admit any wrongdoing, however, and held out against his interrogators until December. The defendants were grouped by industry and region: Muralov, Drobnis, Boguslavskii, Norkin, Shestov, Stroilov, and Arnol'd in western Siberia; Rataichak and Pushin in the chemical sector in the Ukraine; and Serebriakov, Livshits, Kniazev, and Turok on the southern railroads.
39 *Case of the Anti-Soviet Trotskyite Center*, pp. 6–18, 372, 574–75.
40 *Ibid.*, pp. 444–45, 51, 543.

HUNTING "WRECKERS" IN THE FACTORIES

By early 1937, the mood in the factories, and in the country more generally, had shifted decisively. The shocking and highly publicized confessions of the defendants in the second Moscow show trial, coupled with the growing threat of war, convinced many Soviet citizens that their country was being threatened by enemies both within and without. Newspapers emphasized that ordinary people had reason to be alarmed. The defendants, linked to Fascist powers, aimed to overthrow socialism, kill Stalin and other leaders, and murder ordinary people in factories, in mines, and on the railroads.[41] Following the lead of the national and factory newspapers, party organizers urged workers to identify and expose these terrorists in their own factories. An organizer in Serp i Molot wrote after the January trial, "The trial was a great lesson for us. We should now approach every accident, every breakage in a different way. It's no secret that we sometimes overlook the facts after enemy hands have acted in the factory and the shop." He advised the factory's party members to "look around closely."[42] Party organizers explained that terrorists succeeded in their plots only because workers who were rightfully suspicious "did not receive the necessary support." Workers needed to cast off their "petty-bourgeois servility" toward shop heads and managers. Urged to "reject passivity," workers in Serp i Molot signed a pledge that would be reprinted in the factory and national newspapers:

Not a single defect, not one accident, should pass by us unnoticed. We know that production complexes do not stop themselves, machines do

41 "Trotskistskie Shpiony, Diversanty, Izmenniki Rodiny," *Kirovets*, January 22, 1937, p. 4; "Sdelat' Vse Vyvody iz Protsessa," *Kirovets*, February 3, 1937, p. 2.
42 "Kakie Vyvody My Dolzhny Sdelat' iz Protsessa," *Martenovka*, February 5, 1937, p.1.

not break themselves, boilers do not explode on their own. Behind each of these acts lies some kind of hand. Is this not the hand of the enemy? This is the first question which should be asked in such cases by every one of us.[43]

The pledge was soon adopted and endorsed by workers throughout the country. Newspapers and party organizers called upon workers to seek out these hidden enemies, voice their suspicions, and not worry unduly about providing concrete proof.

Once the workers had been given this virtual carte blanche, the factories erupted into a cacophony of accusations and counteraccusations. Rational technical explanations proved a poor counterweight to allegations of wrecking, which soon offered a handy excuse for any breakdown, shortage, accident, or failure. After a fire on the Dinamo grounds, an article in the factory newspaper echoed the rhetoric of the Serp i Molot pledge: "Are these fires accidental? In the deepest night, a house does not set itself on fire, machines do not walk off the construction site themselves, and shavings do not fall into a motor from the sky. This is the hand of an enemy."[44] Shop heads, often at loggerheads with one another because low or shoddy output in one shop affected production in others, were drawn into the fray. The new emphasis on "wrecking" transformed conflicts among shops heads into political warfare. Workers and party members found the language of "wrecking" useful to redress safety hazards, challenge bosses, and pursue personal vendettas. A party member in one shop wrote, "The class enemy rules here with great energy. Not long ago we had repeated instances of oil-fueled

43 "Sdelat' Vse Vyvody iz Protsessa," *Kirovets*, February 3, 1937, p. 2.
44 "Razoblachit' do Kontsa Vsekh Vragov Naroda," *Kirovets*, May 14, 1937, p. 1.

explosions in the electric stove. Doesn't this show that class enemies are doing their evil work?"[45]

The shop heads themselves were particularly vulnerable to accusations of wrecking. In Serp i Molot, for example, Stepanova, a woman worker, tried repeatedly to get D. Sagaidak, the head of the cold rolling mill, into trouble. Angered by his highhanded manner, she complained again and again about him to others. Initially, her complaints were ignored. Yet after Sagaidak made a political error in a workers' study circle, and then a chemical accident poisoned workers in the mill, the party organization brought charges against him. In March 1937, at a long party meeting devoted to Sagaidak's case, Stepanova reiterated her accusations. Her speech, an eager and malicious attempt to demonstrate her party loyalty, epitomized the volatility of the time in an explosive mixture of class resentment, personal animosity, shop issues, and national politics. Stepanova recalled that her suspicions about Sagaidak had first been aroused when she saw how the mill's managers treated the workers:

When I first arrived at the cold rolling mill, I immediately felt that the attitude of the clerks and managers in the mill's office toward the workers was unhealthy. But I was at a dead end when I learned that the mill's boss was a Communist and that he did not seem to care about this situation. I began to look at Sagaidak.

Stepanova soon noted that Sagaidak seemed contemptuous of his fellow party members:

We had a shop meeting. All the party members gathered. But Sagaidak left to go to the shop. The party organizer went after him. He didn't find it necessary, even as a party member, to come to the meeting. The party organizer said he [Sagaidak] couldn't come because he was busy. This

45 "Ob Administrirovanii v Partiinoi Rabote," *Martenovka*, April 3, 1937, p. 1.

example shows that Sagaidak considers himself not with the Party but above it.

Next she noticed his lack of respect for the workers in the mill:

I went to a production meeting. We discussed waste. The shop makes a lot of waste. Sagaidak turned to [Dmitri] Rovnov and said, "Mitia, you rolled waste. I went to the shop and saw that you were rolling waste, but I didn't say anything to you. You are a roller. Why didn't you realize that you were rolling waste?" Sagaidak wanted to put all the blame on the workers. There was another case. There was an accident on the second machine. It was a big one. Sagaidak knew the machine had problems. I told him, but he didn't listen. The next day, he showed up at ten in the morning. The machine was already completely broken. Sagaidak yelled at the roller, "Go and think about what you will earn now that the machine is broken." A person should think about how to talk to a Soviet citizen. Is this how a Soviet engineer should speak to a worker? A worker who takes every breakdown to heart? There was a meeting about this. The meeting began. I was on the alert to see how it would go. I wanted to see if the worker got his pay. The Komsomolets [member of the Communist Youth organization], Bolotin, talked about problems in the mill. In his concluding words, Sagaidak put all the blame for the accident on this Komsomolets. How could the Komsomolets be guilty of the accident when he was on duty at the time? And Sagaidak threw phrases like this at the Komsomolets: "The cobbler should stick to his last." Criticism is being suppressed in the cold rolling mill. After this meeting, I formed a clear impression of Sagaidak as not being one of us.

On the basis of her negative impressions of him, Stepanova then denounced Sagaidak to Galkina, a member of the party committee. Galkina, however, was reluctant to get involved in petty complaints about a powerful figure in the factory. Stepanova explained:

When Galkina came to the shop, I told her that Sagaidak was not a Soviet person. He tried to buy you off. She said to me, "How could he do that?" Time passed. Sagaidak held a meeting about lowering the price of steel [in accordance with a Soviet campaign to increase production and lower costs].

He said that abroad they lowered prices at the expense of the working class. Then he talked about the great achievements in the USSR. He made it seem like our achievements were not good. I wanted to say something, but I didn't know how. I wanted to caution him. Maybe he didn't mean what he said, or it was just an accidental phrase.

Under different circumstances, Stepanova's vague resentments and garbled political criticisms might have come to nothing. Yet in the summer of 1936, all party organizations had received the secret letter from the Central Committee, urging them to uncover hidden enemies. Stepanova now pressed her claims in stronger political language, referring specifically to the letter:

They read the letter aloud in the workers' club about the uncovered Trotskyist-Zinovievite bloc. After the public reading of the letter, we had a lot of arguments in the rolling mill. I went to a worker in the steel wire shop and said that Sagaidak was not one of us, but I didn't say any more. They [party officials] said to me, "You didn't tell anyone this," but I answered that I did say something about it.

At the party meeting, Sagaidak gave a report about the Trotskyist-Zinovievite bloc. He said it supported the same policies that the Bolsheviks had supported on the eve of World War I [e.g., not to go to war with Germany]. At this time, at this moment, to say such a thing! What kind of person could come up with such language? The meeting continued, and Sagaidak tossed out that he knew Sedov [Trotsky's son] and had studied with him at school.

This was the final, damning detail that Stepanova needed to make her case. She again complained to Galkina, who was now forced to take action:

After this, I quickly went to the party committee, to Galkina, and she told me, "I will not permit you to talk about Sagaidak in this way. I will put this whole business in front of the plenum of the party committee." All these facts that I have related, this is strictly wrecking. Sagaidak is absolutely not one of us.[46]

Stepanova's accusations, like so many other people's, were a stew of inchoate complaints and baseless suspicions. Initially offended by Sagaidak's decision to skip a party meeting and by his rudeness to the workers in the mill, she then began to listen carefully to his words and consider them for evidence of wrecking. She spoke with Galkina, a member of the party committee, about her misgivings. Galkina's response was typical of those offered by many local officials. She at first tried to discourage Stepanova, but then, after Stepanova pressed her case, Galkina understood that she would be risking her own reputation if she refused to investigate. She did not want to offend Sagaidak, but neither was she willing to jeopardize her career by trying to protect him. Stepanova thus forced Galkina to take the matter to the party committee plenum. Her groundless allegations, combined with other *zaiavleniia* against him, led to serious consequences for Sagaidak.

In February 1937, before the party committee met to discuss the case, the factory newspaper became involved, in its role as a defender of worker safety. Reporting that workers were frequently being burned by splashing acid, the editor bluntly asked, "Is the hand of the enemy active in the cold rolling mill?" The article invited others to join the attack on Sagaidak, pointedly asserting, "Enemies covered by party cards should be unmasked."[47] Shortly thereafter, the party committee charged Sagaidak with "systematic nonfulfillment of orders, stoppages, concealment of the true productive capacity of the mill, poisoning of the workers, suppression of criticism, ties

46 TsAOPIM, f. 429, o. 1, d. 269 (delo renumbered as 224), ll. 16–19. On the Sagaidak case, see ll. 1–68.
47 "Na-Ruku Vragu," *Martenovka*, February 28, 1937, p. 3.

with the counterrevolutionary Fascist Sedov [Trotsky's son], smuggling in the ideas of Trotsky, and conscious wrecking." The charges against him, like those against the defendants in the Moscow trials, were an amalgam of outright lies (about his close link with Sedov, deliberate poisoning of workers, and conscious efforts to undermine production) and common industrial shortcomings (hazardous conditions, failure to fulfill the plan, frequent machine stoppages). After a lengthy interrogation, the party committee expelled Sagaidak from the party. He was arrested several months later.[48]

The Sagaidak case inflamed workers not only in the cold rolling mill but throughout the entire factory. If Sagaidak could be held responsible for the chemical accident, then perhaps other managers might likewise be found to blame for conditions within their sectors. The factory's chief engineer, L. V. Marmorshtein, fearful of being implicated in the mill's problems and accidents, frantically attempted to distance himself from Sagaidak. "I am not involved in this business," he declared at a subsequent meeting. "I didn't build those chemical baths." Marmorshtein noted that the workers were furious with him: "When I visit the shops," he said, "everyone wants to punch me in the nose." The factory newspaper responded tartly, "Could there possibly be any more serious indictment of a chief engineer than his own words that 'everyone wants to punch him in the nose?'" Sagaidak's arrest soon set off a cascade of others. The poisonous yellow fog produced by the chemical accident enveloped union, shop, and engineering personnel in a choking cloud of accusations. The inspector of labor, the local leader of the Union of Workers in Ferrous Metallurgy, and Marmorshtein were all charged

48 TsAOPIM, f. 429, o. 1, d. 269 (delo renumbered as 224), ll. 2, 68, 69.

with "betraying the interests of the workers."[49] Marmorshtein was arrested shortly thereafter.

Stakhanovism, a state-sponsored program that promised workers bonuses, prizes, and public acclaim for surpassing production norms, also induced some to press charges against their bosses. Many workers were opposed to the Stakhanovite movement, viewing it as an unsustainable form of speed-up. Others were eager to increase their wages by busting norms. Yet in order to set production records, workers needed auxiliary helpers, a steady supply of materials, and good tools. Shop heads who were either reluctant or unable to provide such support incurred the wrath of pro-Stakhanovite workers, who accused them of "suppressing the Stakhanovite movement." Conversely, shop heads, managers, and directors who criticized unrealistic production targets were said to be intentionally "lowering output" or "hiding the true productive capacity of machines."[50] To venture an honest assessment of production was to open oneself up to criminal charges, making it impossible for management to discuss output and planning in any terms other than boilerplate slogans.

Workers also used the new language of repression against one another, often trading phrases with considerable flair. When Ratkin, a machinist in Serp i Molot, tried to raise production norms by invoking the Stakhanovite movement, another worker retorted, "Ratkin is a lickspittle. He wants to earn less." Ratkin responded by calling his colleague a "malicious disorganizer of production"

49 "Glavnyi Inzhiner Zavoda Tov. Marmorshtein v Neblagovidnom Roli Advokata," "Chustvoval, chto v Nos Udariaet," "Naporistosti My Ne Proiavliali," *Martenovka*, March 17, 1937, p. 3.
50 See, for example, "Fakty i Vyvody," *Martenovka*, March 5, 1937, p. 2. On Stakhanovism and deception about productive capacity, see also James Harris, *The Great Urals: Regionalism and the Evolution of the Soviet System* (Ithaca, N.Y.: Cornell University Press, 1999), pp. 148–63.

and writing up the dispute for the wall newspaper. The volley of political insults soon attracted the attention of others. A group of the men's coworkers, furious at the prospect of the norms' being raised, resorted to the older language of the shop in warning Ratkin, "If you write anything else, we'll punch your eyes out." This faction, however, was sharply reprimanded by the factory newspaper, whose editor praised Ratkin for sending out a "very serious signal." The newspaper announced, "Only enemy elements can threaten Stakhanovites." The squabble, which began when one worker appealed to Stakhanovism in an effort to raise norms, and then another invoked the campaign against toadying in hopes of maintaining the status quo, was finally resolved in favor of increasing production. The epithet "enemy element" trumped all others, silencing everyone involved.[51]

"MASKING" AND "UNMASKING"

After the Kirov murder, party leaders became obsessed with political "masking" and "double dealing." Vyshinskii accused the defendants in the Moscow trials of masking their true beliefs, of overtly feigning loyalty to the Party and its policies while covertly plotting Stalin's demise. Party leaders were convinced that "masked" enemies lurked within the Party and the government, "hidden behind their party cards."[52] Although local party organizations within the factories were at the outset reluctant to search for enemies in their own

---

[51] "Naglaia Vylazka," "Ser'eznyi Signal," *Martenovka*, April 10, 1937, p. 1.
[52] The idea of "masked" enemies was first mentioned in Bolshevik discussions of nationalism after the revolution. See Terry Martin, *The Affirmative Action Empire: Nations and Nationalism in the Soviet Union 1923–1939* (Ithaca, N.Y.: Cornell University Press, 2001), pp. 4, 241, 247, 350.

ranks, pressure from the Moscow committee eventually compelled them to undertake a more thorough review of their membership.

The Soviet state from its inception had favored certain groups, such as workers, and discriminated against others, such as former merchants, factory owners, nobles, White Guards, priests, and members of the tsarist police. Workers were generally given preference, for example, in employment, promotions, and admission to educational institutions, yet even among the larger class of workers, there were gradations of privilege. Unemployed male workers were privileged over working-class women and peasant migrants in applying for industrial jobs in the 1920s, a period of high unemployment, as the Party strove to protect advantages for its main base of support. Later, during the first five-year plan (1929–32), when labor shortages became the bigger problem, the Party encouraged women and peasants to enter the industrial labor force. At the same time, the arrests and exile of kulaks during collectivization led the state to institute new stigmatizing policies. Kulaks and their children were initially barred from higher education and industrial jobs, then later forbidden to reside in many cities, towns, and workers' settlements. Every educational and employment application required extensive biographical information, and a "spoilt biography" – meaning one marred by kulak, noble, bourgeois, or religious connections – would severely limit an applicant's opportunities for acceptance and advancement.[53]

53 On discrimination in the 1920s, see Wendy Z. Goldman, *Women at the Gates: Gender and Industry in Stalin's Russia* (New York: Cambridge University Press, 2002), pp. 5–32. On spoilt biographies and imposture, see Fitzpatrick, *Tear Off the Masks!*; Oleg Kharkhordin, *The Collective and the Individual in Russia: A Study of Practices* (Berkeley, Calif.: University of California Press, 1999); oral history interviews in Barbara Engel and Anastasia Posadskaya-Vanderbeck, eds., *A Revolution of Their Own: Voices of Women in Soviet History* (Boulder, Colo.: Westview Press, 1997); and Sheila Fitzpatrick and Yuri Slezkine, *In the*

Many people, seeking to overcome such "spoilt biographies," concealed their origins or past activities.[54] They transformed kulak parents into poor or middle peasants, priests into village teachers, and traders into workers; they omitted any mention of service in the White army or prior membership in other parties. In other words, they "masked" their true identities with fictive ones claiming the sort of social background most favored by the Soviet system: that of workers or poor peasants. Those who wanted to join the Party had to be especially careful about how they presented themselves. On the one hand, certain biographical details could disqualify a candidate from membership; on the other hand, lying to the Party was in itself grounds for expulsion. Often candidates concealed some political or social aspect of their background in their eagerness to join. "Masking" was thus common from the early 1920s on, practiced by party members and ordinary citizens alike in order to gain acceptance and secure advancement.[55] Once the local party organizations began assiduously reviewing their rosters in 1935–36, many

Shadow of Revolution: Life Stories of Russian Women (Princeton, N.J.: Princeton University Press, 2000).

54 The poet Aleksandr Tvardovsky, for example, was the son of a kulak who hid his background and renounced his father. Orlando Figes, *The Whisperers: Private Life in Stalin's Russia* (New York: Metropolitan Books, 2007), pp. 132–36. See also the passages on Stepan Podlubnyi in Jochen Hellbeck, *Revolution on My Mind: Writing a Diary under Stalin* (Cambridge, Mass.: Harvard University Press, 2006), pp. 165–221.

55 The state's stigmatization of various social groups continued after World War II and created a vicious circle wherein people "masked" their backgrounds, which led the state to create campaigns to unmask them, which in turn led to deeper masking as more people sought to escape discovery. For a postwar example of this phenomenon, see Mark Edele's chapter on POWs, "Marked for Life," in *Soviet Veterans of the Second World War: A Popular Movement in an Authoritarian Society, 1941–1991* (New York: Oxford University Press, 2008), pp. 102–28. Paul Hagenloh also remarks on this dynamic in *Stalin's Police: Public Order and Mass Repression in the USSR, 1926–1941* (Baltimore: Johns Hopkins University Press, 2009), pp. 322–23.

members found themselves in trouble as investigations, biographical checks, and arrests of relatives revealed that they had not been completely truthful or forthcoming about their former oppositional activities or social origins. Throughout 1937 and 1938, many members were "unmasked" at meetings after their comrades came forward to expose previously hidden facts.

Meetings were held in all the shops during special "*politdeny*," or "political days," to teach people "how to recognize the aims, methods, practical wrecking, and diversionist work of foreign espionage organs and their rightist-Trotskyist agents."[56] Party organizers encouraged factory employees and party members to "unmask" (*razoblachit'*), or "tear off the masks" of, hidden enemies to expose their "true faces." Factory newspapers insisted that "masked" enemies lurked in every shop. Metaphors about "snakes," "nests," "vile bands," and "reptiles" abounded in newspaper articles as well as in official speeches delivered during party and union meetings.[57] One factory newspaper noted, "The enemy, deeply masked, still continues to act, applying devilish methods of struggle against us, double dealing, twisting like a snake."[58] Cartoons depicted strong hands wielding crowbars and swords, smashing and chopping off snakelike hands covered with swastikas.[59] The newspapers exhorted party and union officials to "overcome political nearsightedness," to "listen to the voices of the masses," and to "discern the enemy despite the

56 "Pitat' Sviashchenuiu Nenavist' k Vragam Naroda," *Kirovets*, June 24, 1937, pp. 2–3.

57 See, for example, "Zamaskirovannym Trotskist," *Kirovets*, July 20, 1937, p. 2. "Raboty Partorganizatsii na Uroven' Sovremennykh Zadach," *Kirovets*, January 6, 1938, p. 1.

58 "Razoblachit' do Kontsa Vsekh Vragov Naroda," *Kirovets*, May 14, 1937, p. 1.

59 See, for example, "Pitat' Sviashchenuiu Nenavist' k Vragam Naroda," *Kirovets*, June 24, 1937, pp. 2–3.

most carefully contrived mask."[60] Local party leaders directed their members to stop dawdling on the sidelines and join the hunt for enemies. "We still have gapers and milksops with party cards in their pockets," chastised the writer of one article.[61] The factory newspapers commanded the shop organizations and party commit- tees to apply the lessons of the recent "parallel Trotskyist center" trial, by uncovering the "enemy hidden among us" and purging the factories of the "degenerate bandit Trotsky and his hirelings."[62] Everyone needed to learn how to "recognize enemies and evil double dealers."[63]

Yet there were few clear signs by which a masked enemy could be known. Instructions were vague, and slogans provided little guid- ance: party organizers explained that one of the most confounding and heinous tricks of the enemy was to disguise himself or herself as a loyal, hardworking comrade. Unlike in Nazi Germany, where the ideological enemy – the Communist, Jew, Slav, or Roma – could be easily identified and demonized, the enemy in the Soviet Union looked identical to the respected comrade. Party members were warned that the enemy might appear in the guise of a better, more responsible version of themselves. Even worse, enemies evi- dently had the fiendish ability to "blind" those around them. "The task of every honest Soviet citizen," one newspaper editor asserted, "is to know how to unmask enemies in any mask, to discern and to prevent their insidious, traitorous activities." The newspapers, filled with accounts of the arrests of alleged spies and wreckers, fostered

60 "Sviashchennaia Ob'iazannost' Kommunista," *Martenovka,* April 22, 1937, p. 1 (reprinted from *Pravda,* April 21, 1937).
61 "Razdavat' Unichtozhit' Gadinu," *Kirovets,* January 27, 1937, p. 1.
62 "Zavodskoe Partsobranie," *Kirovets,* February 6, 1937, p. 1; "Ubiitsy Luchshikh Synov Naroda," *Kirovets,* January 1, 1937, p. 1.
63 "Ne Udastsia!" *Kirovets,* January 27, 1937, p. 1.

an atmosphere of sharp mistrust and suspicion. They cautioned their readers that enemies might go so far as to masquerade as "unmaskers," accusing others to avoid exposing themselves.[64] Even those comrades and workmates who seemed the most loyal, vigilant, and committed to the Soviet cause should not be trusted, for those very qualities often formed part of the cleverest mask.

"OVERLOOKING" THE ENEMY, "SMOOTHING OVER" ENEMY ACTIVITIES, AND "COMPLACENCY"

The factory newspapers advised employees to resist the inclination to be kindhearted or soft in dealing with suspicious coworkers or comrades. "Complacency" (*blagodushie*) became an epithet, signifying a conscious refusal to expose "wrecking" and its fatal consequences. When a group of engineers in Dinamo were arrested as "Trotskyists" and "enemies of the people," the factory newspaper blamed Dinamo's former director for his lack of vigilance. Enemies flourished in the factory, the editor insisted, because he was "infected with carelessness and complacency." Other managers and engineers would later face accusations of being "overconfident" in the director, of failing to question his authority, and of themselves exhibiting a similarly "careless and complacent" attitude.[65]

Local party officials had considerable practice in ignoring inconvenient instructions, a strategy that had long proved highly effective in tempering demands emanating from Moscow. Yet the attack on "complacency" deliberately blocked this well-trod, comfortable

---

64 "Kak Maskirovalus' Vragi Naroda na Zavode," *Kirovets*, June 2, 1937, p. 3.
65 "Otchetnoe Sobranie Partorganizatsii," *Kirovets*, April 8, 1937, p. 1.

path of least resistance. The public attack on tolerance forced even well-meaning people to begin accusing others. Everyone now had to participate actively in "hunting enemies " or risk being charged with covering for the enemy. As more people publicly assented to attacks on others and wrote denunciations of their own, the party committees were compelled to launch new investigations, and the NKVD acquired more compromising materials. In this way, a strong interlocking dynamic developed between the rank and file and party leaders at every level. Leaders pushed party members to hunt for enemies, their denunciations and accusations led to investigations, and those, in turn, led to arrests.

As more employees were "unmasked" and arrests decimated the leadership in the factories, a growing number of uninvolved bystanders were obliged to explain why they had failed to "spot the criminal activities" of the accused.[66] Managers were held responsible for the arrests of both their superiors and their subordinates. Party members took an active role in promoting guilt by association. If an official was expelled from the Party or arrested, party members would immediately attack his supervisor for "protecting an enemy." The more highly placed a manager, and the larger his network of contacts, the greater his vulnerability. When Egorov, a shop head in Serp i Molot, was implicated, the shop's party organization went after P. F. Stepanov, the factory's director, for having first appointed and then protected him. The editor of the factory newspaper declared, "The party organization demands an explanation from Comrade Stepanov about why he blindly trusted Egorov as shop head. Comrade Stepanov has not visited this shop for three years and has shown himself to be an uninterested observer of the ruin

66 "Zavodskoe Partsobranie," *Kirovets*, March 26, 1937, p. 2.

of the Stakhanovite movement in the shop."[67] Stepanov, publicly shamed, was thus forced to assume responsibility for the political reliability of all his employees, a clearly untenable proposition. His political vulnerability, like that of every other manager, was in direct proportion to the size of his associational network.

Risk percolated downward and upward through the hierarchy of the factory. If a director could be imperiled by the activities of a shop head, an employee could likewise be endangered by the supposed disloyalty or wrecking of his or her boss. After A. S. Fomin, head of the fourth instrument shop in Dinamo, was excluded from the Party as an enemy, a foreman in his shop was accused of being his supporter, and then a worker who had received a prize from the foreman also got into political trouble. "What did Fomin pay these people for?" an article in the factory newspaper asked. "Such questions should be raised by every Communist in the shop." The damage continued to ripple outward. When Balakhin, a party activist, neglected immediately to call a shop meeting to discuss the question, the newspaper's editor turned much the same persecutory zeal on him: "Why has Balakhin smoothed over this business? Perhaps he has still not given up the idiotic illness of carelessness and complacency."[68] The editor then went on to accuse Balakhin of likewise "smoothing over" (zamazat') or "overlooking" wrecking: his failure to call a shop meeting to investigate the worker's prize was held to be reason enough to mount a public attack on him. "Smoothing over" became a common code phrase for trying to protect, or failing to denounce, an allegedly guilty coworker.[69]

67 "Sabotazhnik Stakhanovskogo Dvizheniia Razoblachen," *Martenovka*, March 17, 1937, p. 2.
68 "Razoblachit' do Kontsa Vsekh Vragov Naroda i ikh Prispeshnikov," *Kirovets*, July 26, 1937, p. 2.
69 See, for example, criticism of Aleksandrov, a chief engineer in Dinamo, in "Ochistit' Nashi Riady ot Vsekh Vragov," *Kirovets*, May 24, 1937, p. 2.

After a time, having even the remotest connection to someone who had been arrested was cause for worry. At party meetings, members self-righteously called for investigations of any comrade who had a tie of any sort with an alleged enemy. "We must demand responses from party members who had contact with unmasked enemies of the people," declared one woman at a party meeting in Dinamo.[70] Such calls led to long interrogations of the coworkers of supposed enemies, which in turn produced more victims. Even casual contact with "enemies" resulted in new charges, new victims, new arrests. In meetings, suspicions escalated rapidly. Complaints of "smoothing over" or "overlooking" enemy activities easily turned into accusations of intentionally protecting enemies, which then were converted into allegations of deliberate and conscious enemy acts.

The fear of being associated with someone who either had been or might be arrested impelled people to adopt prophylactic strategies. Some tried to demonstrate their loyalty by working harder or taking on extra tasks. Yet desperate attempts like these could also backfire, as they were sometimes derided as especially clever forms of "masking." An article in Dinamo's factory newspaper, for instance, criticized one party member who had been close to a recently arrested shop head for "speechifying against waste and running around the shop." The writer asserted with cold sarcasm, "This miraculous transformation is also masking."[71] Whereas some employees offered noisy demonstrations of their own innocence in the wake of another's arrest, others tried to remain aloof, neither defending nor denouncing their coworkers and comrades. Yet factory newspapers soon made this stance untenable as well, by publicly

70 "Zavodskoe Partsobranie," *Kirovets*, March 26, 1937, p. 2.
71 "Do Kontsa Razoblachit' Vsekh Prispeshnikov Vragov Naroda," *Kirovets*, June 23, 1937, p. 2.

chiding those who did not take part for "remaining on the sidelines of this vital business."[72] As participation in the hunt for enemies became mandatory, party members had little choice but to prove their loyalty by actively "unmasking" others. The push to "unmask" rapidly became a war of each against all, a shadowy fray in which people pursued an enemy with no identifiable markers.

"LICKSPITTLES," "CRITICISM," AND "DEMOCRACY"

Mass participation in the hunt for enemies received a great boost at the Central Committee plenum held on February 22–March 7, 1937.[73] The plenum, which stressed the importance of ordinary or "little" people, was a turning point in the transition from a war on terrorism to an all-consuming terror. In their keynote speeches, Stalin, Politburo member V. M. Molotov, and A. A. Zhdanov, secretary of the Central Committee as well as the Leningrad regional and city committees, addressed the fate of Bukharin and Rykov, Trotskyism, industrial wrecking, and the upcoming elections to the soviets. The plenum delegates voted to expel Bukharin and Rykov

72 "Razoblachit' do Kontsa Vsekh Vragov Naroda i ikh Prispeshnikov," *Kirovets,* July 26, 1937, p. 2.

73 The full stenographic report was published in *Voprosy Istorii,* in installments between 1992 and 1995. Getty and Naumov provide a long excerpt in English, dealing mainly with the cases of Bukharin and Rykov, in *Road to Terror,* pp. 364–419. For discussion of the plenum, see also Gábor Rittersporn, *Stalinist Simplifications and Soviet Complications: Social Tensions and Political Conflicts in the USSR, 1933–1953* (Reading, U.K.: Harwood, 1991), pp. 114–39; J. Arch Getty, "The Politics of Repression Revisited," in Getty and Roberta Manning, eds., *Stalinist Terror: New Perspectives* (New York: Cambridge University Press, 1993); Khlevniuk, *1937-g. Stalin, NKVD i sovetskoe obshchestvo,* pp. 72–153; Roy Medvedev, *Let History Judge: The Origins and Consequences of Stalinism* (New York: Columbia University Press, 1989), pp. 364–68, on the Bukharin and Rykov cases; and Chase, *Enemies within the Gates?,* pp. 221–28, describing the effect of the plenum on the Comintern.

from the Party and to send them directly from the plenum to prison. They would both be executed a year later, in the third and final Moscow show trial of March 1938.[74] Alongside the discussion of former oppositionists, party leaders introduced two new concepts: democracy (*demokratiia*) and criticism of authority. Both would be quickly disseminated through the vast organizational pyramids of the soviets, the unions, and the Party, encouraging millions of rank-and-file members to uncover enemies among their local leaders. Stalin, Zhdanov, and N. M. Shvernik, the head of the All-Union Central Council of Trade Unions, emphasized the need for multicandidate, secret-ballot elections for posts within the Party, the soviets, and the unions.[75] Contending that the political culture had become increasingly ossified, self-serving, and bureaucratic, they invited the rank and file to reinvigorate their governing institutions. Regional party leaders assimilated this language of democracy and began to attack one another for creating private fiefdoms, ignoring the needs of the "little people," and failing to promote "criticism and self-criticism." The plenum strongly urged not only rank-and-file party and union members but also ordinary citizens to challenge their local and regional leaders and rebuild democracy from below.[76]

Although this new emphasis on democracy seemed sharply at odds with the assault on civil liberties and adoption of extrajudicial trials, the two campaigns were launched for identical reasons. Angered by the inability of local and regional officials to purge their

74 Getty and Naumov, *Road to Terror*, pp. 364–419. On the third Moscow show trial, see Hedeler, "Ezhov's Scenario for the Great Terror," in McLoughlin and McDermott, eds., *Stalin's Terror*.

75 On the paradox of combining extrajudicial arrests with elections, see Goldman, *Terror and Democracy in the Age of Stalin*, pp. 133–61, and Goldman, "Stalinist Terror and Democracy: The 1937 Union Campaign," *American Historical Review*, December 2005, pp. 1427–53.

76 "Materialy Fevral'sko-Martovskogo Plenuma," *Voprosy Istorii*, nos. 11–12 (1995), pp. 20, 14–15.

organizations of former oppositionists, party leaders mobilized the rank and file to disrupt the reigning "family circles of protection." The democracy campaign was designed to increase popular support for Stalin while at the same time emboldening the rank and file to purge and unseat regional and local elites. Party elections, mandated for June 1937, were to be preceded by "accountability" meetings in which local leaders would respond to criticism and complaints. The rank and file were instructed to "unmask, to the very last, useless and inefficient leaders and elect new people of initiative and loyalty," and expose all "violations of internal party democracy."[77]

People were encouraged to question authority and criticize their leaders in every institution and governing body. The Central Committee disseminated these instructions through the Party's hierarchy, and in response, criticism of local and regional leaders arose from the rank and file. In the factories, the party shop organizations criticized the party committees, which in turn reached beyond the factories to attack the district and city committees. National and factory newspapers played a significant role in fanning the accusatory fires. Almost daily, they headlined calls to question authority, to demand accountability, and to sharpen vigilance. Not only did they permit workers and party members to assail shop heads, managers, and other authority figures, but they even provided a ready-made vocabulary and forum for such attacks. One party member in Dinamo noted angrily, "Yesterday the secretary of the district committee spoke to us at the end of the meeting and declared that he wanted to get some criticism from our Communists, but obviously he wants to get it behind his back, because he didn't bother to show

77 "Po-Bol'shevistski Vskryt' Vse Nedostatki," *Kirovets*, March 23, 1937, p. 1;
  "Zavodskoe Partsobranie," *Kirovets*, March 26, 1937, p. 2.

up at the meeting today."[78] Party members berated their leaders for their negligence, lack of guidance, and arrogance.

As Stalin and his supporters hoped, the democracy campaign fueled the hunt for enemies. Factory employees and party members in Dinamo, as in other factories, pushed fervently for more political investigations, insisting that the "party committee is insufficiently occupied with unmasking Trotskyists." They excoriated the editors of the factory newspaper, complaining that their coverage was "too soft" and "didn't provide the needed results."[79] One party member attacked the editor of his factory newspaper "for making strong, hot speeches at meetings but not criticizing his own paper."[80] Another attacked an editor for "suppressing criticism" of the factory's director.[81] As an angry rank and file shook the pillars that held up the factory hierarchy, editors lost their bearings, unsure of what to print, whom to attack, and how far to go.

Workers and party members were initially exhilarated by their newfound freedom to criticize. Newly empowered, bolstered by the Central Committee's plenum, they vented their frustrations with officials. No matter was too trivial to be aired on the front page of the factory newspaper, and no complaint too petty. One party member in a cutting foundry wrote a front-page article claiming that Izotov, the head of his party shop organization, "was very rude." "I was sitting in the party office getting a politics lesson," he wrote, "and Izotov came in and said to me, 'Get out of here.' I answered that I was in a lesson and could not leave. Izotov answered, 'I said, get

---

78 "Zavodskoe Partsobranie," *Kirovets*, March 24, 1937, p. 1.
79 *Ibid.*
80 "Otchetnoe Vybornoe Sobranie Zavodskom Partorganizatsii," *Kirovets*, April 11, 1937, p. 1.
81 "V Partiinom Komitet s Zavoda," *Martenovka*, March 20, 1937, p. 2.

out.' The comrades from the other shops were extremely surprised at Izotov's behavior."[82] Workers picked up their factory newspapers each morning to find new attacks on shop heads, engineers, managers, and party organizers. The world of the factory was turned upside down.

Words such as *toady*, *lickspittle*, and *sycophant* (*podkhalim*), popularized by the plenum, came into daily use to describe anyone who curried favor with his or her superiors. Bold, nasty sallies against highly placed managers enlivened the front pages of the factory newspapers. "The implacable struggle against sycophancy is still not apparent in the party organization," wrote a party member dissatisfied with the lack of criticism from below. Another urged that shop heads be called to account: "The shop heads must answer the charges leveled in the factory and wall newspapers. It is the job of the wall newspapers to discuss problems in the shops."[83] In Dinamo, the factory's deputy director was singled out for "elements of sycophancy and bureaucratization," including disregard for the workers and undue deference to the head of the party committee.[84] The factory newspapers encouraged workers to expose "nests" of managers and to bust up the "family circles" of mutual protection that they created to shield their ruling groups from criticism. An article in Dinamo's newspaper pronounced T. A. Razin, a party organizer and controller in the department of technical control, "sick with arrogance," an "illness that manifests itself in extreme rudeness in his dealings with other Communists and in suppression

82 "Ob Administrirovanii v Partiinoi Rabote," *Martenovka*, April 3, 1937, p. 1.
83 "O Ne Partiinom Otnoshenii k Kritike v Pechati," *Martenovka*, March 21, 1937, p. 1.
84 "Zavodskoe Partsobranie," *Kirovets*, March 24, 1937, p. 1.

of criticism."[85] Managers were condemned for spending money on office furnishings and for "rudeness," "lordly attitudes toward workers," "carelessness," and other highhanded behaviors.[86] In Serp i Molot, the factory newspaper instructed party members to not spare the director from criticism and to renounce "the wish to get along, to please, to flatter, and to toady to those in authority."[87]

Workers were counseled to make public any complaints related to housing or safety and to name and expose the officials responsible. One worker, living in a tent of seven and a half square meters with two other families and no kitchen, demanded in the factory newspaper, "At last give us a straight answer and don't lead us by the nose."[88] An article in another factory newspaper noted, "The workers have written repeatedly to actual people about conditions in the dorms. . . . We do not understand the Olympian calm of the head of the union committee, who, knowing about all this mess, took no action."[89] Yet another article, addressed directly to the head of the sheet rolling mill in Serp i Molot, bluntly commanded: "The roof needs to be fixed. Fix it!"[90] Managers and party officials stumbled blindly over this new and unstable terrain. The radical language of democracy made it difficult for them to quash criticism or even to defend themselves, no matter how patently false or self-serving the

85 "Pochemu ne Kritikuiut Razina," *Kirovets*, March 30, 1937, p. 2.
86 "Semeistvennost', Chinonochitanie i Idiotskaia Bespechnost'," *Martenovka*, April 1, 1937, p. 2; "Zavodskoe Partsobranie," *Kirovets*, March 26, 1937, p. 2.
87 "O Ne Partiinom Otnoshenii k Kritike v Pechati," *Martenovka*, March 21, 1937, p. 1.
88 "Mesiatsami Khodiat Rabochie k Baiukovu," *Kirovets*, March 16, 1937, p. 3.
89 "O Ne Partiinom Otnoshenii k Kritike v Pechati," *Martenovka*, March 21, 1937, p. 1.
90 "Tov. Pogonchenkov ne Prislushivaetsia k Signalam 'Zagotovki'," *Martenovka*, March 28, 1937, p. 1.

accusations against them might be. Amid NKVD arrests, expulsions from the Party, and the national obsession with "wreckers," officials were also beset by criticism from below, called to account for their haughty manners and their failure to ensure better living and working conditions.

"SUPPRESSION OF CRITICISM" AND "PROTECTION OF ENEMIES"

In accordance with the new emphasis on democracy, party, state, and union leaders were expected to engage in "self-criticism," giving "accounts" of their achievements and failings to the rank and file. In the factories, the meetings devoted to such accountings quickly acquired a ritualistic pattern.[91] Party officials would typically recite a few of their more harmless failings, whereupon the audience would angrily respond that the "self-criticism had not been sufficient."[92] At one factory-wide meeting in Serp i Molot, a party member sneeringly confronted Izotov, the head of the party organization in the cutting foundry. "What did comrade Izotov talk about?" he asked sarcastically. "Everything but his mistakes." His attack precipitated others directed at the same target. "Tell about how you suppressed criticism!" one party member exclaimed to Izotov. "Why don't you talk about the insufficiencies of the party shop committee?"[93] The editor of the factory newspaper derided P. F. Stepanov, the director of Serp i Molot, for surrounding himself with unquestioning

91 On rituals of apology and self-criticism, see J. Arch Getty, "Samokritika Rituals in the Stalinist Central Committee, 1933–38," *Russian Review*, vol. 58, no. 1 (January 1999), pp. 49–70.
92 See, for example, "Otchetnoe Vybornoe Sobranie Zavodskom Partorganizatsii," *Kirovets*, April 11, 1937, p. 1.
93 "S Zavodskogo Partiinogo Sobraniia," *Martenovka*, March 30, 1937, p. 2.

"lickspittles." A member of the party committee publicly denounced Stepanov, noting, "I must say directly and openly that not only was self-criticism not valued here, but it was a completely unwelcome guest." The party committee member insolently ordered Stepanov "to reconstruct himself."[94] Rank-and-file party members also assailed A. Somov, the head of Serp i Molot's party committee, for "cursing and abusing the party organizers rather than trying to help them." Throughout the factory, workers accused their superiors of "suppressing criticism."

Local leaders and managers found themselves in an indefensible position. Any attempt to rebut criticism was simply dismissed as "suppression." Defense of others also became difficult, opening the would-be defender up to charges of "nepotism" (*semeistvennost'*), "sycophancy," or "violation of internal party democracy." Such accusations were not taken lightly. An article in one newspaper proclaimed, "Sycophancy and suppression of criticism are tools of the class enemy."[95] A leader had no choice but to admit that criticism from the rank and file was "correct"; false humility and self-abnegation were the only acceptable postures. Instructors and officials who made theoretical mistakes or unwittingly expressed incorrect political ideas were forced to apologize. When Smirnov, a party member in the Likerno-Vodochnyi distillery, suggested that new elections needed to be held because the party leadership was "blocked up," he was sharply criticized for misunderstanding the new democracy campaign. He later offered a long, groveling apology for his political error. An official from the district committee, Evteev, rudely cut him off, demanding to know, "How do you consider your

94 "O Stile Raboty Direktora," *Martenovka*, March 27, 1937, p. 2.
95 "Protiv Shumikhi i Paradnosti Usypliaiushchii Bditel'nost'," *Kirovets*, February 16, 1937, p. 1.

mistake?" Smirnov replied, "I consider my mistake a vulgar political mistake, which appears as a distortion of the decree of the Central Committee on reelections of leading party organs." Evteev pressed on, asking, "How was your mistake directed?" Smirnov answered, "It was directed against the line of the Party; it was incorrectly oriented and even a defilement of our own leading cadres."[96] This humiliating exchange, with its catechistic questions and responses, was typical of the interrogations to which members routinely subjected one another.

Refusing to accept criticism from rank-and-file members was a serious blunder, but "suppressing" a "signal" or denunciation could be deadly. If someone wrote a *zaiavlenie* about a person who was later arrested, even on different grounds, the denouncer would often take the opportunity to attack the party committee officials, claiming that they had "ignored" or "suppressed" his or her original *zaiavlenie*. Officials thus disregarded any denunciation at their own peril because no one could predict who might be arrested in the future.[97] Members of party committees were terrified of being charged with "protecting an enemy" or "suppressing criticism." Factory newspapers, which received many accusations, pushed party committees to investigate every rumor and allegation. If an official was slow or negligent in his response, the newspaper might note that he was not "attentive to signals of Communists about enemies of the people in the factory."[98] The codeword *signals* covered a multitude of possibilities, from verbal hints to written denunciations. Factory newspapers stirred up a lot of trouble, making it impossible for party committees to ignore even the pettiest salvos based on gossip, slander, and

96 TsAOPIM, f. 428, o. 1, d. 1, ll. 45–48.
97 "Zavodskoe Partsobranie," *Kirovets*, March 26, 1937, p. 2.
98 "Otchetnoe Sobranie Partorganizatsii," *Kirovets*, April 8, 1937, p. 1.

rumor. A union organizer in Dinamo, for example, spoke out against the party committee in 1937 for failing to heed his denunciation of Kreitsberg, the head of his shop. "Several times, I spoke to unmask the Trotskyist Kreitsberg in shop meetings," he complained. "My speech was transcribed in the protocols, which went to the party committee. It is obvious that the party committee did not read them or know what the rank-and-file Communists were saying." He then attacked another party member who had tried to defend Kreitsberg, calling him the shop head's "lickspittle."[99] Many shops posted their own wall newspapers, which workers used to broadcast unverified allegations.[100] Officials had little choice but to consider gossip and slander as legitimate sources of information in the crusade against enemies. Deprived of the oft-used ploy of ignoring nonsense – or allowing it, in Soviet parlance, "to marinate" (*marinovat'*) – officials found themselves spearheading investigations that further spread the terror.

"ENEMIES OF THE PEOPLE AND THEIR SUPPORTERS"

The term "enemy of the people" (*vrag naroda*), *the* signature phrase of the terror, entered the common vocabulary of ordinary citizens during the spring of 1937, after Stalin used it in his keynote speech for the February–March 1937 Central Committee plenum. Stalin, however, was not the actual author of the phrase, which in fact

99 "Otchetnoe Vybornoe Sobranie Zavodskom Partorganizatsii," *Kirovets*, April 11, 1937, p. 1.
100 In some cases, factory newspapers, hardly models of restraint, tried to impose limits on the wall newspapers, which were even worse. See, for example, "Iarche i Polnee Osveshchat' Partiinuiu Zhizn'," *Kirovets*, April 6, 1937, p. 2.

had a long history. Robespierre and other revolutionary leaders had employed it during the French Revolution, and Russian workers on factory committees had revived it in their appeals during the February 1917 revolution.[101] In the 1920s and early 1930s, the phrase had fallen into disuse, though the 1936 Soviet Constitution used it to describe those who stole public property.[102] Yet even after the Kirov murder, party leaders did not commonly utilize it to describe former oppositionists targeted for arrest. The Central Committee did not use it in either of its secret letters to the party organizations in January 1935 and July 1936, though the second of these did refer to the defendants in the upcoming Moscow show trial as "enemies of the toilers" and "enemies of the Party."[103] Vyshinskii, the state prosecutor known for his florid and vicious rhetoric, made no mention of "enemies of the people" in either the trial of the "united Trotskyite-Zinovievite center" in August 1936 or that of the "parallel Trotskyist center" in January 1937, in both of which he favored the defendants with a variety of other choice epithets.[104]

---

101 St. Just used the term in the Legislative Assembly in 1792. Marat used it in his journal, *L'Ami du peuple*, and Robespierre in his famous speech "On Revolutionary Government." George Rudé, ed., *Robespierre* (Englewood Cliffs, N.J.: Prentice-Hall, 1967), pp. 58–59. I am grateful to the French historian Katherine Lynch for these references. Boris Kolonitskii, "Anti-Bourgeois Propaganda and Anti-Burzhui Consciousness in 1917," *Russian Review*, vol. 53, no. 2 (April 1994), pp. 183–96.

102 The 1936 Soviet Constitution stated, "Persons committing offenses against public, socialist property are enemies of the people." *Constitution of the Union of Soviet Socialist Republics* (Moscow: Moscow State Publishing House of Political Literature, 1938), p. 110. This point is made by Christopher Browning and Lewis Siegelbaum, "Frameworks for Social Engineering: Stalinist Schema of Identification and the Nazi *Volksgemeinschaft*," in Michael Geyer and Sheila Fitzpatrick, eds., *Beyond Totalitarianism: Stalinism and Nazism Compared* (New York: Cambridge University Press, 2009), p. 251. Browning and Siegelbaum also note that by 1936, the state had ceased to emphasize class war, and "enemy of the people" had replaced "class enemy."

103 "Zakrytoe pis'mo TsK VKP (b)," *Izvestiia TsK KPSS*, no. 8 (1989), p. 115.

104 For example, Case of the Trotskyite-Zinovievite Terrorist Center, pp. 120, 122.

Neither did party leaders commonly use the phrase in their speeches about the trials. At a vast open-air meeting of thousands of workers in Red Square, called to explain the verdict in the January trial, N. S. Khrushchev, head of the Moscow party committee, described the defendants as "traitors to the toilers," "agents of fascism," "hired murderers," "wreckers," and "diversionists," but never as "enemies of the people."[105]

Although the phrase was known, it was thus not in widespread currency either in print or in the speeches of party leaders and orga-nizers. Newspapers used it only occasionally in articles about the first Moscow show trial, in August 1936. It made isolated appearances in the labor newspaper *Trud*, first in late August, in connection with the arrest of a group of former Trotskyist union officials in Rostov – said to be "enemies of the party and the people" – and then in November, during the Kemerovo trial, in a reference to Trotskyists as "brutal enemies of the people."[106] Party organizers read aloud some of these articles, including *Pravda*'s lead piece on the August trial, "Enemies of the People Caught Red-Handed," to tens of thousands of workers. A few workers repeated the phrase in their comments at public meetings about the trials, though they, like the local party officials, were more likely to call the defendants "counterrevolutionaries," "class enemies," or just "enemies."[107]

After Stalin used the phrase in his speech to the plenum, how-ever, it entered the common lexicon of party leaders and ordinary people. Stalin asked, "Why have our leading comrades been so naive

105 TsAOPIM, f. 30, o. 50, d. 5, ll. 1–13.
106 "Trotskistskie Posledyshi v Rostovskom Dvortse Truda," *Trud*, August 22, 1936, p. 4. "Prigovor Ozverelym Vracham Naroda," *Trud*, November 23, 1936, p. 1.
107 "Vragi Naroda Poimany s Polichnym," a lead editorial in *Pravda* on August 15, 1936, was read throughout Moscow factories to workers. See TsAOPIM, f. 3, o. 49, d. 129, ll. 1–44.

and blind that they could not make out the face of these enemies of the people?"[108] Soon after the plenum, the term began popping up everywhere: in speeches, newspapers, and meetings. Functioning as simple shorthand, it replaced more cumbersome tags such as "unprincipled band of wreckers, diversionists, spies, and murderers," "spying and diversionist terrorist agents," and "Zinovievite-Trotskyist bloc." Newspapers urged people to "exterminate enemies of the people like mad dogs, burn them out with a red-hot iron."[109] Party members and ordinary citizens were soon using the epithet to describe anyone who had been arrested or was under suspicion. Associates of these "enemies of the people" were known as "helpers" or "supporters" (posobniki), a status that in itself could also lead to arrest.

The phase became popular not only in deference to Stalin but because, like so many idioms, it answered the needs of the moment. By the spring of 1937, people were being arrested for many different reasons, only one of which was former oppositional activity. More often than not, the specific reason for an individual's arrest would remain a mystery to his or her coworkers, relatives, and friends, as the judiciary, the NKVD, and prison officials provided no justification for their actions, even to frantic family members. Soviet citizens, baffled as to precisely why people were disappearing, groped for explanations. Some believed that while the vast majority of those arrested were guilty, the arrest of their particular friend or relative must be a mistake that the authorities would soon rectify. Others reasoned that enemies had taken control of the NKVD or that Stalin himself was unaware of how widespread the arrests were.[110] The phrase "enemy

108 "Materialy Fevral'sko-Martovskogo Plenuma TsK VKP (b) 1937 goda," Voprosy Istorii, no. 3 (1995), p. 3.
109 "Razoblachit' do Kontsa Vsekh Vragov Naroda i ikh Prispeshnikov," Kirovets, July 26, 1937, p. 2.
110 On the thinking of ordinary people at the time, and their belief that spies and terrorists posed a genuine threat to the state, see Figes, Whisperers, pp. 261–71;

of the people" was useful because it economically expressed a political situation in which hundreds of thousands of people, arrested and sentenced by extrajudicial bodies, simply vanished. The term encompassed many possible offenses and required no concrete proof of wrongdoing. As an accusation, it demanded no evidence of an actual crime or knowledge of previous factional debates. Unlike "Zinovievite," "Trotskyist," or "rightist," all of which pointed to the victim's earlier adherence to a specific oppositional program, "enemy of the people" was not associated with any prior political position. In this sense, it was the perfect figure of speech for a plenum that popularized repression by involving the rank and file in a mass campaign against authority. N. S. Khrushchev would make a similar point in his speech to the Twentieth Party Congress, in 1956. Claiming that Stalin had coined the phrase, he explained:

This term automatically made it unnecessary that the ideological errors of a man or men engaged in a controversy be proven. It made possible the use of the cruelest repression, violating all norms of revolutionary legality, against anyone who in any way disagreed with Stalin, against those who were only suspected of hostile intent. . . . The concept "enemy of the people" actually eliminated the possibility of any kind of ideological fight or the making of one's views known on this or that issue, even [issues] of a practical nature. On the whole, the only proof of guilt actually used, against all norms of current legal science, was the "confession" of the accused himself. As subsequent probing has proven, "confessions" were acquired through physical pressures against the accused.[111]

By the spring of 1937, the term was so common that people considered its meaning self-evident. It quickly became a tautology, the

---

Lydia Chukovskaya's 1939–1940 novel, *Sofia Petrovna* (Chicago: Northwestern University Press, 1988); and Evgeny Tsimbal's 1989 film, *Defense Counsel Sedov*.

111 For the full text of Khrushchev's speech, see http://www.marxists.org/archive/khrushchev/1956/02/24.htm.

ideal linguistic expression of wide-ranging and unchecked repression. Who was an "enemy of the people"? Any person who was arrested. Why had this person been arrested? Because he or she was an "enemy of the people." Two short Russian words, *vrag naroda*, thus became both a description and an explanation of a victim's fate.

CONCLUSION

The Kirov murder was a catalytic event. Coupled with fears of social discontent, foreign spies, and unrepentant oppositionists, it proved, in the words of one NKVD official, "fatal for the country and the Party."[112] Beginning with a search for Kirov's murderer, the investigation steadily widened as each confession spawned new fears of conspiracies among former oppositionists. By early 1937, the targets included former Zinovievites, Trotskyists, rightists, industrial "wreckers," and leaders of the military, cultural organizations, and other institutions. The Party initiated a self-cleansing program, the 1935 review and exchange of documents, which soon turned into an internal witch hunt. Under pressure from higher party officials, local party organizations began examining their records for members who had concealed biographical or other compromising information. Coerced confessions, the Moscow show trials, and news about wrecking panicked ordinary citizens.

A vast linguistic machine, fueled by party meetings, national and factory newspapers, and *"besedchiki"* in the shops, generated new words and phrases for ordinary people to use in conceptualizing

---

112 "O Tak Nazyvaemom 'Antisovetskom Ob"edinennom Trotskistsko-Zinov' evskom Tsentr'," *Izvestiia TsK*, no. 8 (1989), p. 88.

events. "Wrecker," "lickspittle," "enemy of the people," "masking" and "unmasking," and "suppressing criticism" all entered the daily parlance of factory employees, lending import, purpose, and direction to daily resentments and workplace quarrels. Workers used "wrecking" charges, for example, to draw attention to neglected problems of safety, housing, and consumption. Subordinates seized upon "suppression of criticism" to attack their bosses, and shop heads and workers employed "lickspittle" and other political epithets in conflicts over production and resources.

The transition from an assault on alleged terrorists to an all-encompassing terror had a clear internal logic. Investigations led to arrests and coerced confessions, which in turn fed the paranoia of party leaders and inspired ever more insidious and elaborate visions of conspiracy. At the February–March 1937 Central Committee plenum, party leaders deliberately enlisted rank-and-file party members and ordinary people in the hunt for enemies by launching a democracy campaign to shake up local and regional centers of power. The plenum proved extraordinarily successful in extending the hunt for enemies to local party organizations, workplaces, unions, and soviets. Military units were likewise consumed by accusations against and criticism of officers. In June 1937, following a secret trial known as the "Case of the Trotskyist Anti-Soviet Military Organization," Marshal M. N. Tukhachevsky and seven other military commanders would be convicted of conspiracy and espionage and executed.[113] Beginning in July of the same

113 Roger R. Reese, *The Soviet Military Experience: A History of the Soviet Army, 1917–1991* (London: Routledge, 2000), pp. 52–92; Reese, *Red Commanders: A Social History of the Soviet Officer Corps, 1918–1991* (Lawrence, Kans.: University Press of Kansas, 2005); and Reese, "The Red Army and the Great Purge," in Getty and Manning, eds., *Stalinist Terror*, pp. 198–214.

year, the mass and national operations targeted new groups of victims in mass police sweeps. Yet Stalin and party leaders were not the only ones responsible for the terror. At the local level, party members embraced the new language, writing *zaiavleniia* about comrades and coworkers, accusing one another in meetings, and transforming the state's targeted campaign against former oppositionists into a war of each against all.

Why did employees in the factories turn against their colleagues? Was it fear that drove them to adopt as their own the language and ideas disseminated by the state? Or were they trying somehow to draw official attention to their difficult working and living conditions, to win technical arguments, or to pursue personal vendettas? Did they truly believe that they were exposing "enemies"? It is difficult, if not impossible, to know what people at the time were actually *thinking* when they used these phrases. Yet it is possible to reconstruct how they *behaved:* what words they uttered, what actions they took, and how they treated their friends, their relatives, and their coworkers. Obviously, words alone did not launch the terror, and disembodied phrases were not responsible for mass arrests. As Soviet leaders themselves were so fond of saying, "Behind every act is a human hand." Yet this language became a critical element in the political culture, achieving a weight and force of its own in shaping behavior. Step by step, the state's campaign against terrorism itself became a mass terror. Comrades and coworkers turned against one another as interrogation and denunciation became familiar aspects of everyday life.

2: Comrades and Coworkers

ON A FREEZING NIGHT IN JANUARY 1937, A FIRE SWEPT through the scrap shop of Dinamo, an electrical-machine-building factory in the Proletarskii district of southeastern Moscow. The shop was covered by a wooden scaffold, which went up like dry kindling, sending sparks high into the night sky. Leaping over the rickety wood structure and rapidly devouring the makeshift roof, the flames lit up the yards, illuminating the high drifts of dirty snow and discarded equipment, the darkened barracks, the factory's redbrick building, and the spur railway line that ran to and from its loading lock.

Hundreds of people, roused by the blaze, scurried in panic through the factory yards, carrying their meager belongings. Huddling in small groups, they stared at the fire. The yards were full of home-less peasants who slept in improvised shelters, dugouts, and tents, hoping for housing and jobs. Recent migrants from the countryside, they lived on the factory grounds, cooking over small open-air fires, smoking hand-rolled cigarettes, and heating their rude dwellings with unreliable homemade stoves. No one – not the factory's direc-tor, not the head of the party committee, not the chairman of the union – knew exactly how many people were camped in the yards.

Thousands of peasant migrants arrived daily in Moscow to look for work and a place to live. The city's great factories, short of labor, were quick to offer employment, but housing had failed to keep pace with the headlong expansion of industry. Almost seven thousand people worked in Dinamo, which manufactured industrial electric locomotives for use in mines and factories, along with trams, trolley buses, electrical equipment for cranes and trains, specialized switches, graphite electrodes, high-voltage traction motors, and heavy-lifting magnets. Dinamo was critical to the government's industrialization drive, for it was the only plant in the country that produced these items, which had previously had to be imported at great cost. The factory had expanded significantly during the 1930s, more than doubling its number of machines and quadrupling its grounds.[1]

The shoddy roof of the scrap shop, like the migrants' cobbled-together housing, was a testament to the nationwide shortage of building materials. Dinamo, like every other factory in the Soviet Union, lacked lumber. The state provided for only a fraction of its construction needs, and roofing materials were worth almost their weight in gold on the black market. The scrap shop, which doubled as a warehouse, was piled high with goods of all sorts: consumer items due to be distributed to Dinamo's workers were haphazardly

1 A. I. Efanov, ed., *Istoriia zavoda 'Dinamo'* (Moscow: Izdatel'stvo VTsSPS Profiz-dat, 1964), vol. 2, pp. 137–300. This three-volume set recounts the history of Dinamo from the prerevolutionary period to the 1960s; it was published in 1964 as part of the de-Stalinization effort under Khrushchev. The trilogy resurrected the reputations of many engineers and managers who were arrested in 1937–38. It was written under the direction of A. I. Efanov, who headed the factory committee (*zavkom*) in July 1937 and was twice elected secretary of the party committee, in January and April 1938. Efanov lived through the terrible period of arrests and executions. He participated in many meetings in which his comrades were denounced, and survived to tell the truth about the men and women who contributed so much to Dinamo in the 1920s and 1930s.

heaped among electrical machines and equipment awaiting shipment to defense plants. Here as in factories and on construction
sites everywhere, there was also a desperate shortage of stevedores
and freight cars. Now workers watched in horror as the red inferno
devoured consumer goods, defense orders, and the shop's wooden
scaffold. Someone ran to call the fire brigade, but it would arrive
only after a gang of workers, frantically hauling and hurling buckets
of water, had finally extinguished the blaze.

Early the next morning, the factory's higher-ups arrived to inspect
the damage. The workers had already stripped the smoking shop of
its charred goods, tools, and timber. Anything that might be put
to use had been carried off. As the news spread through the other
shops, the same question was on everyone's lips: Had wreckers set
the fire? The second great show trial, involving the members of the
"parallel Trotskyist center," was scheduled to open in Moscow the
next day, and the newspapers were filled with articles reporting on
the "wrecking" activities of the defendants. Had a hidden enemy
now shown its hand in Dinamo?

The day after the trial began, Dinamo's party committee met to
discuss the fire. Among those in attendance were V. G. Starichkov,
the young, ambitious head of the party committee; M. E. Zhukov, the
factory's ailing director; Bakhmutskii, an aggressive party organizer;
N. A. Mikhailov, the editor of Dinamo's daily newspaper, *Kirovets*;
and Shashkin, in charge of the "special department," which dealt
with politically sensitive personnel issues. In a grave voice, Zhukov
addressed the meeting. Like many directors, Zhukov was a loyal
party member possessed of both great intelligence and considerable
organizational energy. He had joined the Party in 1918 as a young
worker and received some training in engineering. Still just forty-
one in 1937, but in ill health, he had the look of a much older man.

Zhukov explained that the scaffolding over the scrap shop had burned, incinerating special defense orders and consumer goods worth almost 300,000 rubles.[2] He then got directly to the point: "The cause of the fire was arson," he said bluntly. "This was a sally by the class enemy – there was deliberate destruction and wrecking of defense orders even before the fire. They were piled in the warehouse to make it easier to burn them all together rather than ruin them one item at a time. Moreover, this class enemy exploited our weakness, the absence of class vigilance." He paused. "Of course, we have class vigilance," he corrected himself, "but not enough." Zhukov insisted that it could not have been accidental: "To think that the fire could have started by itself, or because someone threw away a lighted cigarette, is impossible. The warehouse closes at four p.m., and the fire began hours after that. Also, the fire could not have started in the electrical wiring because the entire system had been checked beforehand." The party committee members stared at Zhukov, slowly absorbing his statement.

In the discussion that followed the director's unequivocal announcement, no one disputed that the fire had been caused by "wrecking," though several speakers brought up underlying problems that had contributed to the damage. A. I. Efanov, head of the union committee responsible for the social welfare of the workers, noted, "We have a shortage of factory guards because we have no housing for them." Basurmanov, head of the main machine shop, urged the party committee to rescue what remained of the scrap shop, put up a temporary roof, and heat the building so it could continue to

---

2 Starichkov, secretary of the party committee, later put the value of all the goods destroyed at 13 million rubles, including two months' worth of the factory's output. Tsentral'nyi Arkhiv Obshchestvenno-Politicheskoi Istorii Moskvy (TsAOPIM), f. 432, o. 1, d. 176, l. 25.

function. "Unfortunately," he reminded the party committee, "we have no material for a roof." He added that one shift had not shown up for work before the fire, and a few workers had subsequently taken advantage of the disaster to try to bargain for higher wages during the cleanup. "We need to look seriously at how people related to the fire," he advised. Wrecking nevertheless provided the easiest explanation. Bakhmutskii, eager to assign blame, demanded that an investigation be undertaken of several highly placed managers and shop heads, including V. I. Baronskii, head of the technical bureau of traction machines; D. B. Lipshtein, head of the technical department; and A. A. Tolchinskii, the factory's technical director. "There are facts indicating wrecking," Bakhmutskii categorically declared. "We have a group of wreckers. This was a defense order that burned: magnets wrapped in rubber and then in linen. Someone unwrapped the linen, cut the rubber, and then rewrapped the magnets. We have wheels with shavings in the bearings. The foundry produces only waste; 60 to 70 percent of its production is waste. Now we need to look at certain people – at Baronskii, Lipshtein, and particularly Tolchinskii, who has been seen around town but has not shown up in the factory since January first." Mikhailov, the editor of *Kirovets*, seconded Bakhmutskii's suggestion. "We must hold shift meetings and discuss the fire with all the workers," he insisted. "Vigilance in everything is lacking. Our guards are poorly trained. Mukhanov and I crawled through a window into the courtyard, and the guard never even noticed. Tolchinskii was connected with the Trotskyists, and when the party committee discussed the question of the electric locomotive shop, he – the technical director – did not even bother to come to the meeting. He was drinking with Kreitsberg and Prokhorov instead. Also, Baronskii and Lipshtein never participated [in meetings about] or spoke openly of the current trial of the Trotskyists. There is evidence showing that they are linked to the Trotskyists."[3]

The party committee quickly arrived at a consensus: wreckers had deliberately set the fire, and Tolchinskii, Baronskii, and Lipshtein, along with Kreitsberg, head of the second instrument shop, and A. Prokhorov, head of the experimental station of mobile prototypes, were most likely responsible. This group would soon find itself the target of an NKVD investigation. The party committee then unanimously resolved to order the homeless migrants off the factory grounds, assign night watchmen to the shops, organize night patrols of party members, reorganize the factory guards, and rebuild the roof of the scrap shop. They agreed, "The facts of the fire show that it was undoubtedly the act of class enemies. . . . The fire started on the eve of the trial of the Trotskyists. It was unquestionably a demonstration by enemies in response to the trial."[4]

Notwithstanding the unequivocal conclusion reached by the party committee, its own members had provided considerable evidence that the fire could also have been caused by a smoldering cigarette, a faulty stove, or an electrical malfunction. The scaffolding did not keep out rain and snow, and the wiring could easily have been damaged by moisture. The consumer goods and defense orders had been stockpiled in the scrap shop not because, as Zhukov indicated, wreckers wanted to "burn them all together," but because of the chronic shortages of storage space, stevedores, and freight cars. Yet "wrecking" was certainly the most convenient explanation. It kept Zhukov from having to answer hard questions about why the building had not had a real roof in the first place, or why special

3 TsAOPIM, f. 432, o. 1, d. 179, ll. 20–22.
4 *Ibid.*

orders for defense equipment, as well as desperately needed consumer items, were stockpiled in a leaky shop amid Dinamo's scrap. No one had to take responsibility for the homeless workers and peasants who were living in primitive conditions in the yards, or for the guards' own lack of housing. The "wrecking" charges deflected blame from all those in attendance at the meeting, while allowing the fervent, virtuous Bakhmutskii to pursue his campaign against Tolchinskii and other highly placed managers.

The fire continued to cause damage in Dinamo long after it was extinguished. Soon NKVD officers were swarming over the factory grounds, interrogating anyone even remotely connected to the scrap shop. Over the next few months, they would arrest a number of shop heads and managers. But the matter would still not be settled. The arrests of those connected with the fire would reverberate through the factory as their associates were then arrested in turn. By summer, Dinamo's leadership would be decimated by a chain of events touched off, in all likelihood, by a single smoldering cigarette carelessly discarded by a freezing migrant peasant who also lacked a real roof over his head.

DINAMO: THE FACTORY

Only a few years earlier, Dinamo's employees had been heady with success and hope for the future. The factory was a central element in the country's first and second five-year plans and figured in its most fabled industrial projects. In 1933, in conjunction with two other factories, it produced the first electric trolley bus, designed to revolutionize public transportation in urban areas. One year later, staff from Dinamo helped to dig tunnels for the new Moscow metro. Sleeping in the shop, toiling day and night, a group of young workers and

engineers, including Prokhorov, assembled the metro's first passenger locomotive. Zhukov, the factory's director, and Tolchinskii, its
technical director, boarded this first metro car when it was rolled out
amid great public fanfare in October 1934. (All three of these men
would later be arrested.) In 1936, Dinamo employees developed and
produced new and complex hydroelectrical equipment to be used in
the construction of the storied Moscow-Volga canal. By 1937, the
factory had eighteen separate shops, a research bureau, an experimental station, and its own spur railroad line.[5] Of the factory's total
workforce, three quarters were workers, with the remainder comprising engineers, technicians, and service and administrative personnel. About one fifth of the workforce was female, and more than
one third was under the age of twenty-four.[6] Its workers belonged to
the Union of Workers in the Electrical Machine-Building Industry.

Dinamo was distinguished from most other Soviet enterprises by
its central location in Moscow, its long revolutionary history (dating back to 1903), and its unique, important, and highly publicized
products.[7] Yet during the industrialization drive, the factory also
shared many problems with other, less favored enterprises, including

---

5 "Zavod v Tret'eu Piatletke," *Kirovets*, July 29, 1937, pp. 2–3.
6 As of April 1937, Dinamo had 6,991 employees; see TsAOPIM, f. 432, o. 1, d.
176, l. 6. By March 1938, the number had decreased to 6,328; see TsAOPIM,
f. 432, o. 1, d. 193, l. 25.
7 The Dinamo electrical engineering factory opened in 1897 and soon had a strong
Bolshevik organization, formed in 1903. During the Civil War, it contributed a
large contingent to its Moscow district's Red volunteer force. It was nationalized
in 1918, but old equipment and fuel shortages forced it to close briefly in 1919.
Dinamo resumed production in 1920, and its fortunes revived in 1921, when
it began manufacturing equipment for new power stations. During the 1930s,
it expanded to become one of the Soviet Union's largest electrical engineering
plants. It is still in operation today. A. M. Sinitsyn et al., *Istoriia rabochikh
Moskvy 1917–1945 gg.* (Moscow: Nauka, 1983), pp. 111, 114; Efanov, *Istoriia
zavoda 'Dinamo'*, vol. 2, pp. 36–41, 65–68.

a high turnover rate among employees, irregular deliveries, transport bottlenecks, and persistent shortages of construction materials and fuel. Its workers had to endure a lack of consumer goods, housing, dining halls, kitchen facilities, baths, and laundries. As was the case in most Soviet factories, Dinamo's leadership was drawn from three disparate groups: "bourgeois" specialists; revolutionaries and Civil War veterans; and younger, Soviet-trained workers who still had machine oil under their fingernails. This motley group took on new challenges in production, designing and manufacturing complex machines of the sort that the state previously had to import from abroad. Enthusiasm, creativity, and a collective spirit abounded, as did production conflicts, disorganization, and accidents. Workers and engineers frequently worked around the clock to design, test, and produce the specialized locomotives, passenger cars, and electrical machines the country needed. Like many of their fellow citizens, they were proud of the Soviet Union's stunning industrial accomplishments and hopeful that daily life within its borders would eventually become easier and more prosperous.

Unlike its smaller, less important peers, Dinamo had a large party organization dating back to 1903. In 1936, Dinamo had 1,030 party members and candidates, a testament to the factory's size, location, history, and important role in industrialization. About one out of every seven employees was either a party member or a candidate to become a member. By April 1937, however, the total number had dropped by roughly 29 percent, to 739 (561 current members and 178 candidates). In the understated words of the party committee secretary, "Our ranks dwindled significantly during this time."[8] A year later, in April 1938, current membership had decreased even

8 TsAOPIM, f. 432, 1, 176, ll. 8–9.

further, from 561 to 532, though the overall total had grown slightly, from 739 to 761, due to an increase in the number of candidates.[9] These numbers reflected, among other factors, the considerable impact of party expulsions and arrests, as well as the recruitment of new candidate members to offset those losses. Between 1936 and 1938, the size of the party organization shrank by about one quarter, a marked reduction.[10]

Dinamo's party members, like their comrades nationwide, enjoyed rapid upward mobility in the 1930s. Thanks to the industrialization drive, leadership positions opened up within every enterprise and institution. Industry was desperate for foremen, shop heads, engineers, technicians, managers, bookkeepers, and economic planners. In 1928, almost all of Dinamo's Communists worked in production.[11] By 1937, the majority were in administrative posts, with less than one in four still being employed in production. Fully 94 percent of party members came from working-class backgrounds, and some 12 percent were women.[12]

The vast majority of engineering and technical personnel, party members included, were not far removed in either time or educational attainment from previous jobs in production. Out of Dinamo's 679 engineering and technical employees, less than half (42 percent) held diplomas, about one third had been foremen and were trained in the shops, and the remaining quarter could claim some brief technical training. In other words, almost 60 percent of Dinamo's engineering and technical personnel had been promoted from the

9 TsAOPIM, f. 432, 1, 193, l. 109.
10 These numbers are not an exact reflection of exclusions and arrests because new party members also entered and left the factory for reasons unconnected to the terror.
11 Efanov, *Istoriia zavoda 'Dinamo'*, vol. 2, p. 173.
12 TsAOPIM, f. 432, o. 1, d. 176, l. 9.

shop floor, without diplomas. A little over one quarter of the engineering and technical personnel were party members.[13]

Each shop in Dinamo had its own party organization, headed by an elected committee, and one or more officially designated "organizers" who were responsible for propaganda and other political activities within the shop. The larger shops were divided into groups, each with its own organizer. As of 1937, the Party had seventy-four group and shop organizers spread out among Dinamo's various sectors and shops.[14] A party committee of ten to fifteen members, elected by the general membership every two to three years, supervised party work within the factory. Its members came from every employment level and included workers, shop heads, managers, engineers, and the director. The party committee met twice a month to go over both political and production issues, and it wielded a good deal of power not only in setting but in enforcing policy.

SECRET DENUNCIATIONS

In the summer of 1936, Dinamo was shaken by the first tremors of the terror, set off by the August trial of the "united Trotskyist-Zinovievite center." Like their counterparts in other factories and workplaces, party organizers in Dinamo convened mass meetings of workers in the shops to review and discuss the proceedings. Horrified by what they read and heard, party members and workers responded publicly with fervent support for Stalin and the government, then privately with a flurry of secret *zaiavleniia* detailing the suspicious activities of their comrades, colleagues, and coworkers.

13 TsAOPIM, f. 432, o. 1, d. 193, l. 126.
14 TsAOPIM, f. 432, o. 1, d. 176, l. 9.

Such accounts were sent to shop, party, district, or city committees, to the NKVD, or directly to A. Ia. Vyshinskii, the prosecutor
of the trial.[15] At the time, only the officials who actually received
the *zaiavleniia* knew about the accusations; the letter writers' targets were not told that they were the subjects of complaints, and
the authors' identities remained confidential. In a few cases, pairs
of close coworkers even wrote to the authorities about *each other*,
then continued to work together, side by side, blithely unaware
of their mutual denunciations. People's motives for writing varied,
ranging from conflicts between or within shops to long-simmering
professional differences, pointed personal vendettas, and the genuine belief that the accused really was a hidden enemy. The electric
locomotive shop, for example, proved to be a hotbed of recriminations connected to failed designs, with some technical specialists' feeling so strongly about their own prototypes that they recast
design disagreements as evidence of their rivals' wrecking. Others,
spurred on by the volatile atmosphere surrounding the trial, eagerly
informed the authorities about the suspect political backgrounds
of their comrades. In the 1920s, many left-wing oppositionists had
been active in the shops. One party member later explained, "The
Trotskyists ran everything everywhere.... In our shop there was a
whole group of Trotskyists: Maksimov, Kuz'min, Rumiantsev. They

---

15 See Starichkov's report, TsAOPIM, f. 432, o. 1, d. 176, ll. 13–14. On work-
    ers' responses to the trial, see Wendy Z. Goldman, "Terror in the Factories,"
    in Donald Filtzer, Goldman, Gijs Kessler, and Simon Pirani, eds., *A Dream
    Deferred: New Studies in Russian and Soviet Labour History* (Bern: Peter Lang,
    2008), pp. 193–218. On denunciations, see Sheila Fitzpatrick, "Signals from
    Below: Soviet Letters of Denunciation of the 1930s," *Journal of Modern History*,
    vol. 68, no. 4 (December 1996), pp. 831–66. Matthew E. Lenoe, *The Kirov
    Murder and Soviet History* (New Haven, Conn.: Yale University Press, 2010),
    pp. 453–54, notes that the Kirov murder set off an "ecstasy of denunciations"
    among ordinary citizens.

distributed proclamations to every worker's box, and you could find leaflets on all the joiners' machines."[16] By the early 1930s, however, these former oppositionists had either quit the Party or abandoned their oppositional activity. Those who remained had close personal and professional ties both to one another and to other party members. Then Kirov's murder, the review and exchange of documents that began in May 1935, and the August 1936 trial revived long-forgotten antipathies toward the left.[17]

The first in the factory to come under attack were a quartet of prominent managers: Tolchinskii, the technical director; Baronskii, head of the technical bureau of traction machines; Kreitsberg, head of the second instrument shop; and Prokhorov, head of the experimental station of mobile prototypes. All four men were the subjects of numerous *zaiavleniia* in the summer and fall of 1936. Their troubles began during a shop meeting in July, when Kreitsberg was accused of Trotskyism by Kotiuchenko, a party member in his shop. Kotiuchenko would later complain that no one heeded his denunciation: "The Party didn't listen to the voices of the lower masses. I spoke out and said that Kreitsberg had been an ardent Trotskyist in the past and remained one now. I gave examples, but they were ignored."[18] The motivation for Kotiuchenko's attack is not clear. He may genuinely have believed Kreitsberg to be a political threat, or he may simply have resented him as head of his shop. In any case, his first attempt to implicate his boss had little effect.

In August, amid intensifying anxiety over the first Moscow show trial, two other divisions of Dinamo were beset by a crossfire of

16 TsAOPIM, f. 432, o.1, d. 179, l. 75.
17 See, for example, the case of Torbeev, TsAOPIM, f. 432, o. 1, d. 179, l. 15.
18 TsAOPIM, f. 432, o. 1, d. 176, l. 39.

denunciations. Khvedchen, an engineer and party organizer, wrote a *zaiavlenie* charging Tolchinskii, Prokhorov, and Kreitsberg with wrecking. Khvedchen had worked directly under Prokhorov for three years in the experimental station, and now he accused the three managers of undermining the engineers there and in the electric locomotive shop. A commission was set up to look into his allegations. Starichkov, secretary of Dinamo's party committee, later noted that he had forwarded Khvedchen's *zaiavlenie* to both the NKVD and Dinamo's "special department," which was responsible for investigating employees.[19] Almost simultaneously, Tolchinskii himself submitted a joint *zaiavlenie* that he had written with I. S. Khailov, head of the technical department of mobile prototypes, to Vyshinskii, prosecutor of the Moscow show trial. Their *zaiavlenie* described technical design arguments within the electric locomotive shop and singled out various engineers and technicians as "wreckers." The engineers and the managers thus denounced one another at exactly the same time. Khailov, for his part, had unwittingly made an all but fatal mistake in linking his name to Tolchinskii's: after the latter's arrest the following spring, Khailov would be excluded from the Party and himself arrested for "wrecking, aiding wreckers, and failing to speak up and unmask Tolchinskii," Then and later, when the party committee interrogated him, he would try to defend himself by denouncing others, including Starichkov, secretary of the party committee. He denied that he had ever had a relationship with Tolchinskii or any of the other alleged Trotskyists in the factory and claimed that he had even written a *zaiavlenie* against them.

19 TsAOPIM, f. 432, o. 1, d. 179, ll. 51, 90. In the spring of 1938, Khvedchen was accused of "discrediting honest Communists" and arrested by the NKVD. "Razvernut' Bol'shevistskuiu Samokritiku na Otchetno-Vybornom Sobranii," *Kirovets*, April 7, 1938, p. 1.

Evidently, sometime after signing the joint letter of complaint with Tolchinskii about the engineers in the electric locomotive shop, he had turned against him and written another *zaiavlenie* denouncing *him*. When Khailov was called to account for association with Tolchinskii, he attempted to deflect the blame onto Starichkov, accusing him of "marinating" his *zaiavlenie* against Tolchinskii and failing to act on the information it contained. Khailov's defense provoked a sharp rebuff from other party members, who assailed him for "failing to speak up in meetings during which enemies were unmasked." One member dismissed his professions of innocence with contempt, saying, "You're sitting there like a little Christ and not helping the party organization."[20]

The conflict between the engineers and the managers was not the only matter that drew the attention of the NKVD to Dinamo's workforce. In September of 1936, the factory's party committee sent a list of alleged Trotskyists and other suspicious employees – including Tolchinskii, Prokhorov, Baronskii, and Kreitsberg – to the district party committee. That same month, whether as a result of the list or of Khvedchen's *zaiavlenie*, or both, Prokhorov was briefly detained and then released by the NKVD. In many cases party officials, repelled by the unsupported accusations piling up on their desks, initially took no action at all on them. M. S. Iakovlev, Dinamo's chief mechanic and a member of the district party committee, tried to cling to the distinction between rumor and evidence. There were no facts to support the charges against Tolchinskii, he maintained, and "everything was fine." Yet despite Iakovlev's best efforts to quench them, the accusatory fires continued to burn. After Tolchinskii was arrested, in March 1937, Iakovlev got into trouble for ignoring the earlier allegations. He was sharply criticized by a party member who furiously proclaimed, "Already, there were facts demanding Tolchinskii's exclusion. . . . They did not pay attention to the signals from below."[21]

Tolchinskii's position as technical director left him vulnerable to numerous accusations. He had been sent to America in 1935 by the Party to study electrical moving bodies, a trip that would later invite speculation that he was a spy. He worked closely with Dinamo's director, shop heads, and technical personnel, including I. S. Sheinin, deputy director of economic and administrative affairs. Sheinin considered Tolchinskii a friend, yet in the fall of 1936, he, too, wrote a *zaiavlenie* questioning his relationships with various "enemies of the people" within the factory. Sheinin, as second in command in Dinamo, was likely aware that Tolchinskii's name was on the list of alleged Trotskyists sent to the district party committee, and he must have submitted his *zaiavlenie* in hopes of protecting himself in the event of his friend's arrest. Such preemptive or self-protective *zaiavleniia* were not uncommon. Once a person realized that a workmate or colleague was in political trouble, he or she would often attempt to gain some distance from the victim by penning a denunciation. Of course, the preemptive *zaiavlenie* served only to compound the plight of the victim by adding new suspicions to his or her file. Sheinin thus exacerbated Tolchinskii's difficulties and contributed to his downfall, as Tolchinskii himself had done with the engineers.

If Tolchinskii was both denouncer and victim, Sheinin likewise played conflicting roles in Dinamo's unfolding drama. He denounced Tolchinskii, yet at the same time he tried to protect

21 TsAOPIM, f. 432, o. 1, d. 176, l. 54.

him: in the fall of 1936, besides writing a *zaiavlenie* about his friend, he also advised him to leave the factory and find a new post elsewhere. In the meantime, Sheinin had his own political problems to deal with at home. Several members of his family had been arrested and exiled on charges of Trotskyism, and he had been regularly sending them food parcels and other needed items. Within six months, Sheinin himself would be arrested and expelled from the Party for concealing the arrests of his relatives and aiding them.[22] What Sheinin did was both deeply contradictory and entirely comprehensible. His first impulse was to protect himself at Tolchinskii's expense, but he also warned Tolchinskii and secretly supported his own exiled relatives. His behavior, though not easily classified, was typical of the reactions of many people in the same situation: he attempted to assist the victims he was closest to, even as he also helped to spin the web of terror that would ultimately entangle him and many others. Sheinin was a party member, yet his willingness to disobey the Party's rules suggests he never believed that Tolchinskii or his relatives were really "enemies." He seems to have understood quite early on that innocent people were being arrested, and to have acted mainly out of an instinct for self-preservation. Tolchinskii, too, denounced some coworkers and tried to save others. He wrote *zaiavleniia* claiming that certain engineers were wreckers, but he also defended some former Trotskyists in the factory, declaring, "These people are valuable; they contribute much that is useful; and we must protect them."[23] Many people under threat behaved in a similar fashion, torn between shielding their comrades and saving themselves.

22 B. Voronov, "Kak Maskirovat' Vragi Naroda na Zavode," *Kirovets*, June 2, 1937, p. 3.
23 *Ibid.*

In the first months of 1937, as winter gave way to spring, party members inadvertently let slip more information about their actions the previous fall. Many had "written" to the party committee, the NKVD, or both at one time or another to protect themselves. Even at this early stage, the line between victims and denouncers was hardly clear. Both Sheinin and Tolchinskii had written *zaiavleniia* against others. Sheinin had acted as both denouncer and supporter of the very same person: Tolchinskii. And Tolchinskii himself had played a double role, protecting some people in the factory while attacking others. Khailov had partnered with Tolchinskii to write one *zaiavlenie* and then had turned against him and written another accusing him of Trotskyism. After the August 1936 meeting, many hastened to denounce others, either out of a misguided sense of loyalty or in a preemptive attempt at self-protection. The net effect of all of these *zaiavleniia* was to heighten the atmosphere of fear and mistrust and pave the path to prison for countless victims.

FIRE AND TRIAL

The fire in the scrap shop in January 1937, coupled with the great national propaganda campaign focused on the second Moscow show trial of the "parallel center," intensified fears in the factory. *Kirovets* published daily reports on the trial, couched in harsh, lurid language. "The parallel center has been unmasked by the NKVD," one article proclaimed. "They organized spying, wrecking, and diversionary acts to weaken defense."[24] Dinamo's employees were urged to take action: "We must not be calm," warned the editor. "Every honest

---

24 "Trotskistskie Shpiony, Diversanty, Izmenniki Rodiny," *Kirovets*, January 22, 1937, p. 4 (reprinted from *Pravda*, January 21, 1937).

citizen should think about what these despicable traitors are preparing to do to us and our beloved country."[25] Dinamo's workers, like others throughout the Soviet Union, were given detailed information about the trial and about the defendants' alleged wrecking in the mines, in the chemical industry, and on the railroads. The defendants had supposedly set "wrecking norms" for freight cars, which prohibited them from carrying full loads. Dinamo, like most other factories, had experienced all of the problems that were attributed in the trial to wrecking. Indeed, the goods destroyed by the fire in the scrap shop had been stockpiled precisely because of a shortage of freight cars.

More than six thousand Dinamo employees attended a series of huge, raucous meetings held in the shops to endorse a death sentence for the defendants. Vyshinskii's closing argument, reprinted in the national and factory newspapers, was read aloud. Party organizers encouraged their audiences to link the traitorous activities of the defendants to wrecking in their own shops. One worker, expressing the sentiments of many, wrote to Kirovets that the trial had shown everyone "that the enemy is hidden among us."[26] On February 3, Kirovets announced that the defendants had been convicted and shot. The paper advised workers "to draw the proper conclusions." The defendants had been able to wreck industry because "the voices that drew attention to wrecking did not receive the necessary support." Dinamo's employees were urged to take the pledge written by workers in Serp i Molot, vowing to search for "the hidden hand" behind every stoppage, shortage, and accident.[27] Seeking to

25 "Razdavat' Unichtozhit' Gadinu!," Kirovets, January 27, 1937, p. 1.
26 "Ubiitsy Luchshikh Synov Naroda," Kirovets, January 27, 1937, pp. 1, 3.
27 "Sdelat' Vse Vyvody iz Protsessa," Kirovets, February 3, 1937, p. 2. The pledge was also published in Pravda. See chapter 1 for its full text.

forestall any hesitation workers might feel about challenging authority or reporting their suspicions, the factory newspaper reminded its readers that the writing of a *zaiavlenie*, whether substantiated or not, was an act of patriotism.

The January trial and the fire prompted a careful review of Dinamo's shops. Starichkov, head of the party committee, spoke out strongly against "whitewashing" (*ochkovtiratel'stvo*), the common practice of misrepresenting spoiled products as quality output. Shop heads frequently counted unfinished, defective, or ruined output toward their production quotas, passing the problem off to the next shop in the production chain. The tool shop, for example, habitually distributed unusable tools. A. M. Kiselev, the head of that shop, and Bogatyrev, one of its employees, were both accused of whitewashing. Bogatyrev immediately tried to shift the blame onto his boss: "I gathered material for two months against Kiselev," he protested, "but all the same, none of this came out." The party committee warned Kiselev that if the quality of his shop's work did not improve, he would be severely reprimanded. In addition, several party members in the tool shop, including Bogatyrev, received reprimands of their own for squabbling and whitewashing instead of taking action to clean up the mess.[28]

In early February, hundreds of party members crowded into the workers' club for a boisterous, two-day-long meeting organized by the Moscow party committee. The meeting had no set agenda. Instead, party members were encouraged to voice any general concerns or suspicions they might have. After some brief introductory remarks by Starichkov and some district and city party officials,

28 TsAOPIM, f. 432, o. 1, d. 179, ll. 27–31.

the meeting quickly degenerated into an unmoderated free-for-all, an eventuality that the Moscow party committee had undoubtedly anticipated. Seventy-four people signed up to speak on the first day alone. A palpable sense of excitement, anxiety, and fear animated the audience as party members "harshly criticized" party and factory officials, claiming that technical problems, combined with an absence of vigilance, "were creating the possibility of wrecking by enemies in the factory." Bakhmutskii, once again taking the lead, denounced the party leadership for its failure to promote "internal party democracy," and the factory administration for its lack of accountability. S. P. Kulikov, a party organizer in the foundry, seized the opportunity to complain about M. A. Kogan, head of that shop, in the first of a series of attacks that would ultimately culminate in Kogan's arrest.

The main business of the meeting, however, was to consider the cases of Baronskii, Tolchinskii, and Prokhorov, who were brought to the front of the great hall to defend themselves against hostile questions from the floor. After vainly attempting to head off the onslaught with a righteous call to unmask enemies in the factory, Baronskii faced a concerted attack as various party members revealed that a relative who lived with him, also a party member, had recently been arrested for Trotskyism. He was forced to admit to having sent food and money to the prisoner. Like Sheinin, Baronskii had concealed his relative's arrest from the Party. He, too, was living a double life, racked by worry over his family by night, making hot speeches against alleged enemies by day. Party members also sharply criticized Tolchinskii and Prokhorov for their friendships with alleged Trotskyists in the factory, including Kreitsberg, former head of the second instrument shop, who had already been arrested by this point. The party committee agreed to "completely purge the factory of the bandit degenerate Trotsky and his hirelings" and to investigate the accusations against Baronskii, Tolchinskii, and Prokhorov.[29]

The subsequent investigation quickly led to the electric locomotive shop, where all three men were involved in the design of an industrial electric locomotive. The shop, beset by long-running feuds over the locomotive and its motor, had been the source of numerous denunciations since the previous August. A shipment of electric locomotives, ordered from Italy and destined for Soviet steel plants, had proved faulty, causing the shop significant embarrassment. The managers and engineers fought bitterly over responsibility for the debacle. Tolchinskii and Khailov had denounced the engineers; Khvedchen, an engineer, had denounced Tolchinskii, Prokhorov, and Kreitsberg; and Khailov had then denounced Tolchinskii.[30]

The party committee's investigation was swiftly concluded. By March 1937, Tolchinskii, Baronskii, Prokhorov, Kreitsberg, and Sheinin had all been arrested, brought down by a combination of technical and political allegations. Tolchinskii was arrested on March 10. On June 14, his name appeared on a list of people to be judged by the Court of the Military Collegium of the Supreme Court, which was forwarded to Stalin, Molotov, and Voroshilov for their approval. Of the 132 alleged Trotskyists on the list slated for execution, Aron Anatol'evich Tolchinskii was number 72. Sentenced by the court on June 16 for his participation in a counterrevolutionary terrorist organization, he was shot the next day. His body

29 "Zavodskoe Partsobranie," *Kirovets*, February 6, 1937, p. 1.
30 Efanov noted in 1964 that the Italians had actually been responsible for the defects. See *Istoriia zavoda 'Dinamo'*, vol. 2, p. 242.

was dumped in the Donskoi cemetery in Moscow. He was thirty-three years old.[31] Sheinin was arrested and then excluded from the Party for a long list of "crimes," including arson, sabotage of housing construction, violations of labor safety, double dealing, and failure to unmask his relatives. Sheinin's prominent position as deputy director of Dinamo, and the existence of his "enemy" relatives, guaranteed the party committee a wide selection of justifications for expelling him from the Party after his arrest.[32]

The prosecution of this highly placed managerial circle deprived the factory of its technical director, its deputy director, and three shop heads. Shock waves would reverberate through the factory for months. Not only did the arrests leave important posts vacant, but they also goaded party members into zealously going after one another in an effort to expose anyone who had worked with or defended the arrested men. In the late spring of 1937, Lipshtein, Baronskii's successor as head of the technical bureau of traction machines, was attacked for being "a friend to Tolchinskii" and for "not helping to unmask enemies in his shop." After Kreitsberg was arrested, an employee of the second instrument shop, formerly headed by him, called for an investigation of those who had "protected Kreitsberg and the system of whitewashing." The same worker also accused another party member of having criticized Kreitsberg

31 Memorial maintains a Web site devoted to the victims of Stalinist terror, containing more than one million names culled from numerous sources and archival documents. See http://Stalin.memo.ru/spiski/index.htm and http://lists.memo.ru/index19.htm. The list bearing Tolchinskii's name is in Arkhiv Prezidenta Rossiiskoi Federatsii (APRF), f. 3, o. 24, d. 409, l. 194. Tolchinskii was rehabilitated on May 15, 1955.

32 TsAOPIM, f. 432, o. 1, d. 179, ll. 54–55. Tolchinskii, Baronskii, and Kreitsberg were later rehabilitated and praised for their enormous contributions to the Soviet Union's industrial development. See Efanov, *Istoriia zavoda 'Dinamo'*, vol. 2, pp. 300, 166, 170.

"toothlessly and incorrectly."[33] The first arrests touched off a new round of denunciations, as party members charged their comrades with failing to unmask those now in prison.

Kirovets assumed a major role in promoting such accusations, relentlessly pursuing connections among recently arrested employees and their coworkers. Embracing the principle of guilt by association, it traced Baronskii's, Prokhorov's, and Tolchinskii's ties to others in the electric locomotive shop. The newspaper accused V. Viktorov, a young engineer who had designed an award-winning motor, of "following Baronskii." Similarly, *Kirovets* blamed the failure of the "SK," an experimental locomotive, not only on Tolchinskii and Prokhorov but on "a whole group of lickspittles who extolled the 'SK.'" It charged one party member and engineer with failing "to unmask those lickspittles," and other engineers with "nepotism" (*semeistvennost'*). The paper also initiated an investigation into M. A. Kogan, head of the foundry, noting that Tolchinskii had been "Kogan's great protector." Devoting an entire page to Kogan's poor leadership, the editor derided the foundry for producing too much waste and pronounced Kogan's "objective explanations" for production problems, including electrical blackouts, unacceptable. Making a determined effort to stir up the foundry employees against Kogan, *Kirovets* asked pointedly in an editorial, "Are the hands of the class enemy active in the foundry?"[34] These attacks provoked sickening fear among the newspaper's targets, and at least one

33 TsAOPIM, f. 432, o.1, d. 176, ll. 39–40.
34 "Protiv Shumnikhi i Paradnosti Usynliaiushchii Bditel'nost'," "Razgul'dlistvo ili Vreditel'stvo," and "Spes' i Zaznaistvo Meshaiut Koganu," *Kirovets*, February 16, 1937, pp. 1, 3. "SK" stood for Sergei Kirov. Many of the model locomotives carried the initials of party leaders.

engineer went to Starichkov, head of the party committee, in hys-
terics after being criticized in its pages.[35]

By the spring of 1937, in addition to Tolchinskii, Kreitsberg,
Prokhorov, Baronskii, and Sheinin, the NKVD had arrested A. P.
Khliupov, head of the scrap shop, and Muravin, an employee in
the shop of machines of alternating current, in connection with the
January fire. The Party excluded both men from its ranks after their
arrests, Khliupov for associating with recently arrested Trotskyists,
and Muravin for committing arson and concealing his social origins (he was allegedly the son of a prosperous trader). The NKVD
also arrested V. I. Romanov, head of the research bureau and controller's administration; Ia. I. Menis, Romanov's replacement; and
K. P. Mashkin, head of the electrical shop, thus eliminating another
significant share of the factory's leadership. Zhukov, Dinamo's director, received permission from the Party to resign from his position
due to illness. Yet in the end, not even his resignation and ill health
could save him: he, too, would later be arrested.[36]

SILENCE: THE LAST REDOUBT OF DECENCY

As Dinamo's leadership disappeared into prison, fear permeated the
factory. Throughout the spring, alarming revelations about earlier
denunciations spilled out in party meetings. Those who had written
zaiavleniia began to understand that they themselves might have
been the targets of others. Reluctant to trust anyone, people became
increasingly guarded in their conversations. Party members adopted

35 TsAOPIM, f. 432, o. 1, d. 179, l. 49.
36 Efanov, Istoriia zavoda 'Dinamo', notes that Zhukov was arrested and then
   rehabilitated, vol. 2, p. 300.

carefully constructed public personae, mouthing newspaper slogans and demonstrating their "loyalty." No one could voice doubts about arrests and expulsions without being accused of "protecting the enemy." Silence became the last redoubt of decency.

Soon enough, though, even that choice was lost, a casualty of the Party's organizational response to the mounting arrests. An imprisoned "enemy" could obviously not be allowed to remain in the Party. Each arrest of a party member in good standing was a highly visible, humiliating indication of the local organization's failure adequately to identify the enemies within and purge them from its ranks. The party committee had to find some reason to expel those members who had been arrested and to explain why it had "overlooked" them during the membership review. Khliupov, Sheinin, Mashkin, and Muravin, for example, were all expelled on charges concocted after they were arrested. Beginning in February, these peculiar expulsions of phantom members became a familiar aspect of party life. For complicated reasons, including the fact that the real basis for many members' arrests was unknown, the party committee sought its own justifications for excluding the victims.

Yet what *had* these people done to justify their expulsion? In the absence of substantive evidence, the simplest reason for excluding a victim after his or her arrest was "silence," or a lack of participation in unmasking others. This was the case, for example, with Mashkin, head of the electrical shop, after the NKVD arrested him. Mashkin had first joined the Party in 1915, when he was twenty. In 1937, this forty-two-year-old veteran of World War I, the revolution, and the Civil War was arrested for his alleged ties to M. P. Tomskii, former head of the All-Union Central Council of Trade Unions and a "rightist" in the party debates of 1929–30. The party committee excluded Mashkin for being a "rightist enemy," but the main evidence against him was his "silence." In discussing his expulsion, the committee members said nothing about Mashkin's rightist activities; instead, they complained that he had not spoken out in the factory-wide party meeting held during the August 1936 Moscow trial, and had later denounced "enemies of the people" only in order to avoid being "unmasked" himself.[37] The party committee also excluded Ia. I. Menis, head of the research bureau, for his silence. After his arrest, party members charged him with protecting his former boss Romanov, failing to unmask Trotskyists, abstaining from the vote to exclude Tolchinskii, and refusing to denounce publicly the "Trotskyist-Zinovievite and rightist enemies of the people." Menis, too, had failed to participate actively in the hunt for enemies.[38] Both men were excluded not for what they did, but for what they did *not* do.

These ex post facto exclusions based on the "failure to unmask" or the "failure to speak out against enemies" sent a chilling message to all remaining party members: party organizations would now construe silence at meetings as evidence of enemy sympathies. No matter how repugnant a party member might find the spectacle of a group attack, everyone would have to join in the baying of the pack. This injunction, reinforced through fear, exclusions, and arrests, greatly widened the terror's scope, converting it from a phenomenon of isolated, targeted arrests by the NKVD into a broader and collective process.

It was but a short step, of course, to proceed from utilizing the charge of "silence" to expel members who were already in prison to using it against those in good standing. Party members soon began

37 TsAOPIM, f. 432, o. 1, d. 179, ll. 54–55.
38 TsAOPIM, f. 432, o. 1, d. 179, l. 56.

hurling this charge at one another. The case of I. F. Marek, a technician in the fourth instrument shop, marked this new phase in the terror's reach. Marek, a party member since 1932, was first denounced
by Chereshnev, another employee in his shop, in one of the many
zaiavleniia sent to the party committee during the August 1936 trial.
Chereshnev's *zaiavlenie* claimed that Marek was friendly with M. F.
Agureev, a thirty-four-year-old Komsomol organizer in Dinamo and
an alleged Trotskyist. At this time, there was no evidence that
Agureev really was a Trotskyist, and Marek's acquaintance with
him held little interest for the party committee. As they did with
many other baseless *zaiavleniia*, officials let this one "marinate."[39] In
December 1936, however, Agureev was arrested, and officials were
compelled to reexamine the relationship between the two men.[40]

At a meeting of the party organization in the fourth instrument
shop in late February 1937, Marek was forced to respond to Chereshnev's charges. During the ensuing debate, Marek's comrades claimed
that he had "hidden his ties to Agureev" and had "shied away from
discussions of the August trial, hidden in some corner somewhere,
and read the newspaper." Marek did not deny being friendly with
Agureev, nor did he refute the accusation that he had "failed to
unmask" him. In fact, he flatly stated that he had never hidden his
friendship with the other man. Excluded by his shop organization
for "concealing his social origins and his friendship with Agureev,
betraying the Party, and not unmasking Agureev and other Trotskyists," Marek was called before the party committee two days later.

39 TsAOPIM, f. 432, o. 1, d. 179, l. 62.
40 http://lists.memo.ru/index1.htm. Agureev was given a five-year sentence by
the special board (*Osoboe Soveshchanie*) of the NKVD on May 23, 1937, for
counterrevolutionary terrorist activity. He was sent to a camp in Vorkuta, from
which he was released on October 12, 1944.

His interrogation provided a lesson for all party members about the necessity of demonstrating one's vigilance through denunciation. The proceedings began with Marek's opening statement:

Marek: I did not conceal that I had a close tie to Agureev. I got to know him when he came to the shop to work with us. I invited him to my apartment, and I went to his. I also spent time with him at Rafalovich's, and Briunin was there, too. I saw Agureev in September, after vacation, when I was very ill. I wrote him a letter asking him to help me get to the hospital. He came to visit me in a car and took me to the hospital. I met with him after he was excluded from the Party. He complained to me about being excluded. I myself was not a Trotskyist, and I was connected with Agureev only as a friend. I warned him several times not to get involved with Trotskyists.

Starichkov (head of the party committee): Why didn't you speak out when Agureev was unmasked at the general party meeting about the Trotskyist-Zinovievite center?

Marek: I made a mistake then.

Terushkin (first machine storage shop): Did you sympathize with Trotsky at some time?

Marek: No.

Nikitin: I am surprised that so many Trotskyists are working in responsible positions. Marek worked as a technician for the adapters. This was a small sector. He hid behind the fact that he was a party organizer... he did little planning. . . . He was closely tied to Agureev; he never spoke during the unmasking of the Trotskyists and of Agureev in particular. We should exclude him as an "enemy of the people" and as a Trotskyist.

Razin (controller in the department of technical control): Marek committed two crimes: he hid his social origins from the Party, and he hid his ties to Trotskyists up to this time. Exclude him.

Starichkov: I have no doubt that [he is] a Trotskyist, judging from the fact that [he] knew Agureev was a Trotskyist and had ties to Trotskyists. Exclude him.[41]

41 TsAOPIM, f. 432, o. 1, d. 179, ll. 62–63.

Marek was excluded by the party committee for "concealing his ties to Trotskyists, for refusing to unmask Trotskyists before the Party, and for exhibiting an anti-Soviet attitude in meetings." Starichkov cited Marek's own admission, "I warned him several times not to get involved with Trotskyists," as proof that he had *known* that his friend had Trotskyist contacts. In fact, it was unlikely that Marek or even Agureev and his associates were "Trotskyists." The left opposition had collapsed in 1927, and its adherents had long since abandoned their former activities. Yet the August 1936 and January 1937 Moscow show trials turned "Trotskyist" into a broad epithet to be applied not only to active oppositionists but to anyone even tenuously connected with the long-vanquished left opposition. Marek's real fault was that he had failed to betray Agureev in advance of his arrest. The party committee had initially used charges of "silence" and "failure to unmask enemies" to exclude those members who had already been arrested, but Marek was a party member in good standing. If the "failure to unmask" someone who was subsequently arrested was grounds for expulsion, then a significant percentage of loyal members were at risk. Moreover, it was an offense that was all but impossible to avoid committing – for how could anyone predict who would be arrested next?

ASSOCIATIONAL TIES

All managers, including Tolchinskii, Baronskii, Prokhorov, and Kreitsberg, maintained a wide network of contacts and relationships throughout the factory. Long after these four managers were arrested, their associational ties would continue to entangle and destroy their coworkers. Throughout the spring and summer of 1937, the NKVD arrested many shop heads on the mere basis of their connections to earlier victims. In May, G. N. Fridman, Prokhorov's replacement as head of the experimental station of mobile prototypes; M. A. Kogan, head of the foundry; and I. S. Khailov, head of the technical department of mobile prototypes, were excluded from the Party for their ties to Tolchinskii, Prokhorov, and others who had already been arrested. Fridman, born in 1911 to a working-class family, had joined the Party in 1931. Too young to take an active part in the revolution, he was nevertheless among the first generation of Soviet workers to reap its educational benefits. Smart and able, he first began tinkering with electric locomotives while still a worker. He received some training in electrical engineering in the early 1930s, helped to design and produce Dinamo's electric locomotives, and took over Prokhorov's job after the latter was arrested. In March, this talented twenty-six-year-old engineer was attacked in *Kirovets* for his connections to Tolchinskii, Prokhorov, and Kreitsberg. Fridman, who had attended engineering school with Prokhorov and worked closely with him in the experimental station, retained faith in his boss even after the NKVD began its investigation. He told coworkers that he strongly doubted Prokhorov was a Trotskyist. The comment would come back to haunt him. After Tolchinskii's arrest, a commission was appointed to investigate the electric locomotive shop. It reviewed the shop's documents and blueprints, found no papers bearing Tolchinskii's signature, and promptly charged Fridman with destroying evidence.[42] (Eventually, the widening circle of blame would encompass the investigative commission as well: a year later, in 1938, E. S. Avatkov, its chairman, was himself arrested.) In May, the party committee interrogated Fridman, who defended himself by insisting that he had been the first to expose wrecking

42 "Do Kontsa Razoblachit' Fridmana," *Kirovets*, March 26, 1937, p. 2.

in the experimental station. How could he, a denouncer of others, be guilty? Like Tolchinskii and Khailov, Fridman admitted that he, too, had written a *zaiavlenie* to Vyshinskii in 1936. He swore that he had no ties to Tolchinskii and had never discussed anything other than work-related matters with him. Other party members challenged Fridman's statements. They claimed that he formed a "*troika*" with Kreitsberg and Prokhorov, that he had failed to speak out against them when they were first unmasked, and that he had ordered the faulty locomotives from Italy. Fridman's protestations of innocence counted for little. He was excluded from the Party as a "supporter of enemies of the people."[43]

The fate of this young engineer served as a warning to party members and others, who quickly learned to conceal their reservations and attack those in political trouble. To defend a comrade or even to express doubt about his or her purported guilt was to risk one's future. Each expulsion inculcated and reinforced certain behaviors in those who remained. Witnessing the destruction of others taught people not to question the actions of the NKVD, not to suggest or even so much as hint that an accused person might be innocent, and most of all, never to trust a comrade or coworker. The law of the jungle now reigned: hunt or be hunted.

Associational ties also brought down Kogan, head of the foundry. Trained as a metallurgical engineer, Kogan was about a decade older than Fridman, but the two shared a similar career trajectory. Born in 1899, Kogan joined the Party in 1930, and like Fridman, he, too, had worked closely with Tolchinskii. The foundry produced a lot of waste, and in 1936, Kogan asked Tolchinskii to lower the

43 TsAOPIM, f. 432, o. 1, d. 179, ll. 127–128. Efanov, *Istoriia zavoda 'Dinamo'*, praises Fridman as a "talented engineer" and ranks him and Avatkov among "the best employees of the factory," vol. 2, pp. 170, 241.

production target so that the shop could focus on improving quality while still meeting its quota. After Tolchinskii's arrest, Kogan was charged with "retarding the productive power of the shop" and excluded from the Party for "assisting enemies of the people."[44] If Tolchinskii's arrest redounded on Kogan, Kogan's exclusion in turn hurt others. Rassadin, Kogan's replacement, soon came under fire for his failure to "liquidate the consequences of wrecking" by purging the foundry of employees who had been close to Kogan. Mikhailov, the editor of *Kirovets*, led the attack with a *zaiavlenie* against Rassadin at a party committee meeting. Refusing to accept Rassadin's claim that there was no longer any wrecking occurring in the foundry, he called for an end to "self-complacency" in the shop. "They need to struggle now with the consequences of wrecking," Mikhailov declared. "The hunt for enemies in the foundry must continue."[45] Others also fell victim to associational ties with those who had been arrested. A. A. Aleksandrov, Dinamo's chief engineer, was strongly criticized for "smoothing over the wrecking" of Tolchinskii, Mashkin, and others.[46] The appetite for investigation and purge seemed insatiable: the destruction of each new victim appeared only to whet the group's desire for another.

The ties of the Tolchinskii group extended not only downward into the shops but upward to include Zhukov, the former director. Zhukov, who had wisely resigned because of illness, was heavily compromised by the arrests. Born in 1896, he had joined the Party at the young age of twenty-two, in 1918, and had taken part in the Civil War. He became Dinamo's director in 1929, proudly presiding over the factory's design and production achievements of the early

44 TsAOPIM, f. 432, o. 1, d. 179, ll. 128–31.
45 TsAOPIM, f. 432, o. 1, d. 179, l. 131.
46 "Ochistit' Nashi Riady ot Vsekh Vragov," *Kirovets*, May 24, 1937, p. 2

1930s. Surrounded by talented young engineers and skilled workers whom he had promoted to managerial posts, Zhukov led the team that produced the country's first electric locomotive, named "VL" for Vladimir Lenin, in 1932. Several team members, including Kreitsberg and Fridman, were feted and awarded prizes.[47]

Beginning in the summer of 1936, Zhukov became the target of numerous *zaiavleniia*. By February 1937, the young engineers and workers he had promoted had disappeared into prison, and Zhukov himself was sick and exhausted. Yet even after he resigned, many in the party organization insisted that he must bear responsibility for the "wrecking" of Tolchinskii and others. Party members brought charges against him at a general meeting on March 6, criticized him again at a general meeting on March 26, and forced him to present an account of his leadership on April 8. Zhukov, allegedly "infected with carelessness and complacency," became the scapegoat for the party committee's failure to expel a number of shop heads and engineers before they were arrested.[48] By mid-April, the charges against Zhukov had been amplified from "carelessness" to "protection of enemies of the people," a far more serious accusation.[49]

On May 12, party committee members charged Zhukov with having allowed enemies to take control of the factory. In a long and painful meeting, they questioned him closely about his relationships with Tolchinskii, Baronskii, and others who had been arrested.[50] Much of the interrogation focused on the electric locomotive shop and the faulty locomotives purchased from Italy. Zhukov, well schooled in survival, fought back. Using the common defensive

47 Efanov, *Istoriia zavoda 'Dinamo'*, vol. 2, pp. 166–67.
48 "Otchetnoe Sobranie Partorganizatsii," *Kirovets*, April 8, 1937, p. 1.
49 "Pod Znakom Bol'shevistskoi Samokritiki," *Kirovets*, April 22, 1937, p. 1.
50 TsAOPIM, f. 432, o. 1, d. 179, ll. 114–117.

strategy of shifting blame to a superior, he invoked no less a lumi-
nary than G. K. "Sergo" Ordzhonikidze, the former commissar of
heavy industry, who had committed suicide that February. (At
the time, party leaders had announced that Ordzhonikidze had
suffered a heart attack, and gave him a hero's funeral.) Zhukov's
testimony imparted some sense of the complex technical squab-
bles that Ordzhonikidze had routinely adjudicated. Zhukov claimed
that he and Tolchinskii had both appealed to Ordzhonikidze in a
dispute over the electric locomotives, and that each of them had
tried to use politics to discredit the other. Zhukov said that he
had told Ordzhonikidze that Tolchinskii was politically suspect,
and Tolchinskii had told the commissar that Zhukov bore him a
personal grudge. Ordzhonikidze had then ordered Zhukov to keep
Tolchinskii on and to stop pursuing "personal vendettas." Zhukov
thus cleverly deflected responsibility for Tolchinskii's presence in
the factory to Ordzhonikidze. He further explained that he had
been closely connected not only to "Comrade Sergo" but also to
N. S. Khrushchev, secretary of the Moscow party committee. He
insisted that he had informed Khrushchev about the managers who
were later arrested, including Romanov and Sheinin. Zhukov thus
dared the party committee to censure him for retaining personnel
sanctioned by the commissar of heavy industry and the head of
the Moscow party committee. Citing these two powerful patrons,
Zhukov declared that an attack on his judgment was, by extension,
an attack on *them*. No one was willing to challenge Zhukov's defense.
His strategy ultimately prevented his expulsion from the Party, but
it did not shield him from the lesser charge of "political blindness."
I. G. Kabanov, a member of the party committee, responded carefully, "You seem to have lost your instinct. Of course, it is impossible
to say that you are a wrecker and a Trotskyist, but you lost every

instinct; you didn't understand what to do, you didn't master Stalin's speech, and your Bolshevism is not worth a kopek. You didn't even know what we had accomplished in the factory, and all this was the result of your political blindness. They worked under your nose, they did whatever they wanted, and I think all this should result in a severe party reprimand." Razin, a controller in the department of technical control and organizer in the first instrument shop, also attacked Zhukov: "I want to say that Zhukov has a high opinion of himself. It is impossible to tell him anything. Indeed, Zhukov knew that Romanov was a Trotskyist, and he promoted him to a high post. When Romanov crawled into the leadership, the promotions extended down the line. Romanov promoted Agureev, Telushkin, and Grinev [all arrested for Trotskyism] even though they were all barely more than unskilled workers and did not have any kind of qualifications. They all ended up in leadership." Numerous other party members spoke against Zhukov as well.[51] The former director escaped with a reprimand and notation in his personal party file, but he was unable to elude the NKVD.[52] After Zhukov left Dinamo, he served briefly as director of the First State Watch Factory. He was arrested on July 17, 1938, and sentenced by the Military Collegium on August 29 for participating in a counterrevolutionary terrorist organization. Shot the same day, he was buried in Kommunarka, a mass grave about two miles from Moscow. He was forty-two years old.[53]

Lipshtein, head of the technical bureau of traction machines, was the next to suffer for his association with Tolchinskii, Baronskii, and others. In March 1937, at a large, factory-wide party meeting, Lipshtein was attacked for failing to help the Party "unmask the

51 TsAOPIM, f. 432, o. 1, d. 179, ll. 114–117. Interpolation mine.
52 Efanov, *Istoriia zavoda 'Dinamo'*, vol. 2, p. 300.
53 http://lists.memo.ru/index7.htm. Zhukov was rehabilitated in May 1955.

work of wreckers," for encouraging nepotism (*semeistvennost'*) in his department, and for not taking the lead in self-criticism.[54] In April, he was accused of overlooking wrecking, "pretending that nothing had happened and, as before, remaining careless and complacent."[55] *Kirovets* noted, "Lipshtein worked for a long time with enemies of the people – Tolchinskii, Baronskii, and Lipshits – and did not help unmask them or discuss his relations with them with the necessary sharpness. This was not accidental." The article continued, "Lipshtein had close relationships with these enemies of the people and directly and actively supported several of them." He was also charged with "playing no small role in the wrecking of the electric locomotives."[56] In May, the party organization again devoted much time to considering Lipshtein's "friendships with enemies."[57] In July, *Kirovets* announced, "Tolchinskii did not act alone but had the help of Fridman, Lipshtein, Prokhorov, and others." Lipshtein, born in Łódź in 1898, was arrested in November 1937 and sentenced in September 1938 for active participation in a Trotskyist counterrevolutionary organization. He was shot immediately after sentencing, then buried in the mass grave at Kommunarka.[58] The head of the party committee, Efanov, later lauded *Kirovets* for unmasking many enemies of the people, and specifically for providing the information that led to the exclusion and arrest of Lipshtein.[59]

54 "Zavodskoe Partsobranie," *Kirovets*, March 24, 1937, p. 3, and same title, *Kirovets*, March 26, 1937, p. 2.
55 "Otchetnoe Sobranie Partorganizatsii," *Kirovets*, April 8, 1937, p. 1.
56 "O Sviaziakh Lipshteina s Trotskistami" and "O 'Tochke Zreniia' Lipshteina," *Kirovets*, May 15 and 20, 1937, pp. 2, 1.
57 "Ochistit' Nashi Riady ot Vsekh Vragov," *Kirovets*, May 24, 1937, p. 2.
58 See http://stalin.memo.ru/names/index.htm and http://lists.memo.ru/index12 .htm. Lipshtein was rehabilitated in May 1955.
59 "Razoblachit do Kontsa Vsekh Vragov Naroda i ikh Prispeshnikov," *Kirovets*, July 26, 1937, p. 2; TsAOPIM, f. 432, o. 1, d. 188, l. 46.

Throughout the spring of 1937, *Kirovets* acted as a self-anointed avatar of the terror, promoting the hunt for enemies in Dinamo's shops and administration. The paper ran articles on Mashkin and Kreitsberg, the former heads of the electrical and second instrument shops, respectively. Both men had already been arrested, but the editor now accused Mashkin of "wrecking" and Kreitsberg of "overpaying" workers, a common practice among managers who wanted to boost productivity. In both cases, *Kirovets* also criticized their replacements, for failing "to liquidate the consequences of wrecking." Article after article derided a seemingly endless parade of party members, shop heads, and managers for being sycophants, "covering up messes," and toadying. The tone was vicious and irresponsible, with one writer's suggesting, for instance, that Sheinin's former secretary, K. Prytkov, "tried to get in wherever he did not have to work."[60] As part of the campaigns for "criticism and self-criticism" and "party and union democracy," popularized by the February–March plenum of the Central Committee, the newspaper encouraged every self-styled crusader to step forward and expose abuse. The pressure on the remaining shop heads intensified greatly as arrests cut their number and *Kirovets* shamed them before the entire factory.

By summer, *Kirovets*, swollen with power and self-importance, was directing shop organizations to unmask specific people. Basing its directives on associational ties, the paper printed instructions about who should unmask whom. It singled out Minaev, a foreman in the electrical shop, as "a double dealer" and "sycophant who treated the workers only with insolence and rudeness" and was "loyal to

60 "Net Bor'by Protiv Doplat" and "Vyvody Eshche Ne Sdelany," *Kirovets*, March 23, 1937, p. 3. "Podkhalimy v Zavodoupravlenii," *Kirovets*, February 22, 1937, p. 3.

the unmasked Mashkin," the shop's former head. The editor called on the shop's party organization to investigate Minaev "as a supporter of a class enemy."[61] When Gostev, a former mechanic in the electrical shop, was arrested as a Trotskyist, *Kirovets* noted that he was a denizen of "the asp's nest" built by Mashkin.[62] Ongoing arrests by the NKVD reinforced the paper's investigations into associational ties. After Zil'berman, a dispatcher, and D'iakova, an economist, were imprisoned, the editor traced their connections with A. S. Fomin, former head of the fourth instrument shop. The newspaper also attacked Dodevo, former head of the technical bureau of cranes, and Tregubov, former head of the sales department.[63] Its writers had earlier accused the talented engineer Viktorov of having a connection to Baronskii, but now they went further, openly seeking out his destruction. Viktorov had begun his career in Dinamo as a worker, then trained in the factory, designed a specialized trolley-bus motor in the early 1930s, and won a prize for his work on the electric locomotives. A *Kirovets* article accused Viktorov of protecting Tolchinskii and other "enemies of the people" in the electric locomotive shop, and of having "a sick love of glory." The writer demanded that he "be held responsible for his activities."[64] The paper also urged party members in the foundry "to root out" those who were still loyal to Kogan, the former head of that shop, and asserted that "nepotism and

---

61 "Nerazoblachennyi Oruzhenosets Vraga Naroda," *Kirovets*, June 5, 1937, p. 1.

62 "Zamaskirovannym Trotskist," *Kirovets*, July 20, 1937, p. 2; "Razoblachit' do Kontsa Vsekh Vragov Naroda i ikh Prispeshnikov," *Kirovets*, July 26, 1937, p. 2.

63 "Kak Velos' Vreditel'stvo v Proizvodstve Elektrooborudovaniia," *Kirovets*, June 8, 1937, p. 1.

64 Efanov, *Istoriia zavoda 'Dinamo'*, vol. 2, pp. 240–41. "Posobnik Vragov Naroda," *Kirovets*, August 5, 1937, p. 2.

sycophancy still reigned" in the party organization of the factory administration. Hectoring headlines called on workers to "unmask to the end all remaining masked enemies of the people and their supporters."[65] Each arrest thus triggered its own small witch hunt, as the party committee investigated the victim's coworkers, superiors, and subordinates. *Kirovets* pushed for investigations within the shop organizations, shaming committee members who seemed reluctant to investigate associational ties. Arrests fed investigations, which in turn prompted more arrests. The alternating links between investigations and arrests were replicated through 1937 and 1938 in ever-lengthening chains. The iron logic of guilt by association pulled entire chains of coworkers into prison.

STRATEGIES OF SURVIVAL

Everyone in the factory was vulnerable to accusations based on associational ties. Over time, people came up with ways to insulate themselves from guilt by association. Unfortunately, these defensive strategies, though somewhat useful to the individual, increased the danger for the wider group. One of the simplest strategies was to distance oneself from a victim, either in a relatively benign manner, by breaking off all contact, or in a more malignant fashion, by denouncing him or her publicly or secretly. The case of Mashkin, head of the electrical shop, provides an example of this dynamic and its harmful effects. Before Mashkin was arrested, S. Mironov, a technician in the shop, respected and worked well with his boss. The two men had much in common: almost the same age, they had both joined the

---

65 "Razoblachit' do Kontsa Vsekh Vragov Naroda i ikh Prispeshnikov," *Kirovets*, July 26, 1937, p. 2.

Party at the beginning of World War I. Both were veterans of that war, the revolution, and the Civil War. Mironov, the son of a party member and Dinamo worker, had followed his father into the factory at the age of fourteen. Mashkin also came from a working-class family. In 1936, Mironov had served on a commission charged with investigating waste in the shop. The commission had concluded that Mashkin was an effective shop head and exculpated him from any wrongdoing. Within several months, however, Mashkin got into political trouble for his alleged ties to former "rightists." In this light, the commission's conclusions now looked like an attempt to protect an enemy. Mironov, desperate to distance himself from both the commission and his boss, promptly denounced Mashkin. The Party praised Mironov for "unmasking Mashkin," and Mashkin was arrested.

Mironov's stratagem of distancing himself from Mashkin by means of a *zaiavlenie* was initially effective in dispelling any accusations of a close tie between the two men. Yet *Kirovets* soon took an active role in exposing Mironov. In June 1937, an article in the paper suggested that Mironov was stomping around and decrying waste in the electrical shop in an effort to demonstrate his loyalty. "This miraculous transformation is also a form of masking," the writer maliciously noted. Moreover, the paper criticized the shop's party organization for its "incomprehensible sluggishness in investigating Mironov's ties to Mashkin," a barely veiled order for the Communists in the shop to begin such an investigation immediately. The editor urged the shop's party members "to unmask thoroughly all friends and accomplices of Mashkin and his supporters who remain in the factory." In February 1938, about a year after Mashkin's arrest, Mironov was excluded from the Party for his connections to Mashkin and other alleged Trotskyists. One party member testified about Mironov that "he persistently covered for Mashkin. Mironov refused to unmask Mashkin. Mironov surrounded himself not with honest Communists, but only with those who are now enemies of the people."[66] In the end, Mironov could not escape his association with Mashkin. Ironically, his initial denunciation had deepened Mashkin's political difficulties and contributed to his arrest, making him an even more dangerous person for Mironov to have ties to.

Mironov's behavior was not unusual. At the first hint of a political problem, people would try to shift blame, recast former ties, and "unmask" their coworkers. In attempting to demonstrate their own reliability, they often managed to stir up more political trouble. When Prokhorov, head of the experimental station, was arrested in February 1937, Khvedchen, an engineer in the electric locomotive shop, got caught up in the perilous aftershocks. Khvedchen had denounced Prokhorov, Tolchinskii, and Kreitsberg the previous August, but he had also worked closely with Prokhorov for three years. Khvedchen feared he would be linked to Prokhorov, despite his earlier *zaiavlenie* against him, because he had not publicly criticized him during the general party meeting in February 1937, in which Tolchinskii, Baronskii, and Prokhorov were attacked. Many people had signed up to speak, but Khvedchen was not among those selected. He now claimed that Moscow party officials had been denied the opportunity to hear the "full story," and that Starichkov, the party committee secretary, had rigged the agenda and prevented

66 Mironov appealed his case and was reinstated in 1938. Thus, within eighteen months, he turned in dizzying succession from protector into denouncer, and from victim into rehabilitated party member. TsAOPIM, f. 432, o. 1, d. 179, l. 55, "Obshchezavodskoe Partiinoe Sobranie," *Kirovets*, March 28, 1937, p. 2. "Do Kontsa Razoblachit Vsekh Prispeshnikov Vragov Naroda," *Kirovets*, June 23, 1937, p. 2; "Razoblachit do Kontsa Vsekh Vragov Naroda i ikh Prispeshnikov," *Kirovets*, July 26, 1937, p. 2.; TsAOPIM, f. 432, o. 1, d. 194, l. 24.

him from speaking. He wrote several *zaiavleniia*, charging Starichkov with "suppressing criticism" and accusing Zhukov, former director of the factory, and Romanov, former head of the research bureau and controller's administration, of various transgressions. The NKVD paid close attention to the *zaiavleniia* of "unmaskers," and Khvedchen's denunciations may have contributed to Romanov's subsequent arrest.[67] Such preemptive *zaiavleniia*, like pellets spewed from a shotgun, were most often intended to cover their authors from potential attacks. In his desperation, Khvedchen took aim at numerous people, adding to their problems in the hope of lessening the danger to himself.

"Distancing" and the preemptive *zaiavlenie* were not the only strategies employed during this period by those hoping to save themselves. A person accused of having associational ties to an "enemy" might also endeavor to "dilute" the blame by involving other people. Every expulsion from the Party required an interrogation. Victims were often quick to name names and implicate others. When Fomin, head of the fourth instrument shop, was attacked at a party meeting for having ties to "enemies," he immediately tried to spread the blame. Fomin had worked in Dinamo since the 1920s, circulating over the years through several shops in which the left opposition had once been active. The fourth instrument shop had been a particular hotbed of oppositional activity, and Fomin was politically and socially connected to several former oppositionists and others who had been arrested. Fomin had also worked with the recently arrested Romanov, head of the controller's administration. Romanov had left the factory before his arrest, and Fomin had attended his farewell party. When the party committee questioned

67 TsAOPIM, f. 432, o. 1, d. 179, ll. 48–51.

him about the gathering, Fomin eagerly asserted that Aleksandrov, Dinamo's chief engineer and recently appointed deputy director, had also been present. Here Fomin tried another common defensive tactic, dropping the name of Aleksandrov, a highly placed official, in the hope of neutralizing his own association with Romanov. Why should he, Fomin, suffer for having attended a social function that had included more prominent people than himself? This gambit, however, also pulled more people into troubled waters. A victim's impulse to prove that his or her social activities had been harm-less by identifying others involved often had the contrary effect of multiplying guilt rather than bestowing innocence. In this case, the party committee decreed that "Fomin had close ties to Trotskyists who have now been arrested.... They met regularly and invited him to join them. Fomin portrays all these meetings as having been either accidental or purely social occasions. Fomin did not help his party organization to unmask them. He concealed his meetings with them. *He never wrote a* zaiavlenie *about any of them*.... He is excluded for aiding Trotskyists, participating in their gatherings, hiding these ties from the Party, and not unmasking Trotskyists."[68] Fomin's expulsion for "failure to unmask" reinforced the message that only a preemptive *zaiavlenie* could ensure protection from guilt by association. This encouraged people "to write," but in doing so, it also expanded the terror.

Throughout the spring of 1937, the political terrain became ever more dangerous and difficult to negotiate. Party members construed silence as evidence of enemy sympathies, demanded public criticism of victims as a demonstration of loyalty, employed the preemptive *zaiavlenie* as an insurance policy, and named their superiors in an

68 TsAOPIM, f. 432, o. 1, d. 179, ll. 75–79. Emphasis mine.

attempt to deflect blame for their own associations with "enemies." They learned and adopted all of these strategies quickly. Yet the very behaviors that offered some measure of protection for the individual served only to implicate ever-larger numbers within the group. Fear rose like water in the hold of a sinking ship. The factory's employees were caught in treacherous and unpredictable currents that pulled them forward, swept them back, and sent them crashing into one another. And the more disoriented and frightened they became, the wilder their behavior in lashing out at others. Like drowning people, they tried to save themselves by struggling atop the bodies of their comrades and frantically pushing them underwater.

EACH AGAINST ALL

In late March, officials from the Moscow city and district committees called a factory-wide meeting to brief Dinamo's seven hundred party members and candidates on the Central Committee plenum's new campaign for democracy, featuring multicandidate, secret-ballot elections in the Party, the soviets, and the unions.[69] Similar meetings were held in workplaces throughout the country. Party members were already familiar with the plenum's keynote speeches, which had been reprinted in the newspapers, and Dinamo's rank and file deftly picked up the new slogans. Repin, an organizer in the welding shop, declared that the party committee was "divorced from the masses"; Kulikov, a party organizer in the foundry, was incensed by "violations of internal party democracy"; and another member noted that

---

69 See Wendy Z. Goldman, *Terror and Democracy in the Age of Stalin: The Social Dynamics of Repression* (New York: Cambridge University Press, 2007), pp. 133–62.

some comrades displayed "a lordly attitude toward workers." All of these themes and phrases had been popularized by the plenum.[70]

The democracy campaign ignited a firestorm of criticism directed against the factory's leaders. Numerous party members asserted that officials had ignored their complaints and *zaiavleniia*. Mikhailov, editor of *Kirovets*, and Starichkov, head of the party committee, became frequent targets. The responsibility they had assumed for purging Dinamo of "enemies" exposed them to charges of having ignored "signals" from below. At the paper, Mikhailov controlled the floodgates across the turbulent river of denunciations that poured into his office. His ability to decide what to print gave him enormous power, but it also left him vulnerable to accusations that he had suppressed information or protected enemies. Starichkov, for his part, wielded great influence over investigations and the appeals of party members who had been excluded by their shop organizations. Among Mikhailov's loudest critics was P. P. Khorikov, later to become the factory's third director, who lambasted him for defending Prokhorov prior to his arrest. Another party member went after the editor for failing to publish a *zaiavlenie* he wrote about Tolchinskii's wrecking, then assailed Starichkov for ignoring his complaints. "When they didn't print my note," he said, "I took it to Comrade Starichkov. He didn't encourage me. He said, 'Wait. I don't have time for this.'" His account inculpated both men in the offenses of "suppressing criticism," "smoothing over enemy activities," and "protecting wreckers." Popov, an engineer, attacked Mikhailov for not being tough enough on his subjects. "*Kirovets* is occupied with 'soft criticism,'" he said. "And this does not provide the necessary

---

70 "Zavodskoe Partsobranie" and "Obshchezavodskoe Partiinoe Sobranie," *Kirovets*, March 24 and 25, 1937, pp. 1, 2.

results."[71] Here as in other arenas, party members demonstrated their loyalty by portraying themselves as committed "unmaskers" who had been spurned by higher officials.

The Central Committee plenum severely undermined the established lines of authority. Criticism now flew in all directions: no one in the factory was immune to attack. The rank and file charged Baiukov, the new deputy director who had replaced the recently arrested Sheinin, with "elements of sycophancy and bureaucratization." An article in *Kirovets* noted, "He is willing to do a lot for Starichkov, but workers can't get him to respond to even the smallest request."[72] Lautov, an engineer, was taken to task for his own sycophantic and "loathsome behavior" toward the factory's leaders. Dinamo's union organization (*zavkom*) also received its share of complaints. Party member Glushenkov tattled on Gladkov, a union organizer, for bringing vodka to the leader of the union. It was not made clear whether Gladkov's offense lay in having brought drink to the meeting in the first place or in offering it only to the union head.[73] In any case, a union official tossed the blame back onto the party committee for "poor leadership of the unions." Barkanov, a party educator in the workers' barracks, attacked his boss for "not attending to the political education of his staff." In the foundry, Kulikov, a welder and party organizer, accused a fellow party member of toadying to Kogan, their shop head. Kogan, himself the victim of previous attacks, assailed another party organizer for her poor propaganda work. His remarks were a payback for an earlier affront when she had allegedly squelched his complaints, telling him, "Do what you were told. Otherwise we will make note

71 *Ibid.*
72 *Ibid.*
73 *Ibid.*

of it." All who spoke sought to portray themselves as righteous avengers, victimized by their bosses' efforts to "suppress criticism." Party members quickly grasped that the Central Committee plenum not only encouraged but even required them to criticize their superiors. Il'ina complained that M. V. Iasvoin, the factory's new director; Baiukov, his deputy; and Aleksandrov, the chief engineer, all continued to defend Zhukov, the former director, and "smooth over the facts about wrecking."[74] By demanding further interrogations, party members kept the motor of terror humming. In this "world turned upside down," the dual imperatives of attack and defense transformed the meeting into a name-calling free-for-all. All the strategies of survival – preemptive criticism, blame shifting, and the avenging of past slights – were vividly enacted. Blaming others was at once a shield and a weapon, wielded more or less aggressively by all.

Nor did the attacks and criticism remain a private matter within the Party. *Kirovets* reported extensively on party meetings, quoting both attackers and victims by name and printing long excerpts of party members' speeches. Dinamo's entire workforce was thus familiarized with the humiliations heaped on various shop heads and officials. By broadly publicizing the mudslinging within the Party, the paper spread the criticism campaign to the workers and further undermined the leaders' authority.[75]

Throughout the spring and summer of 1937, *Kirovets* continued to foment fear in the shops. After an article accused Razin, a controller in the department of technical control and organizer in the first instrument shop, of being "sick with arrogance," Razin

---

74 *Ibid.*
75 *Ibid.* "Mesiatsami Khodiat Rabochie k Baiukovu," *Kirovets*, March 26, 1937, p. 3.

chased the editor home and confronted him. The paper's next article chided, "Razin will never correct his shortcomings if he can't stand criticism." The relentless printed attacks targeted one official after another, from Aleksandrov, the chief engineer, to Kiselev, head of the tool shop.[76] *Kirovets* further complicated the already fraught political situation by revealing that a number of the employees who had been arrested had themselves previously denounced others: Sheinin, for example, had provided compromising information about Tolchinskii. The paper crowed that all these "wreckers" were presently sitting in prison. By divulging that many people, either now under arrest or still at work, had submitted damning *zaiavleniia*, *Kirovets* fomented an atmosphere of gnawing anxiety and suspicion. Dinamo's employees began to realize that the factory was a snake pit of reciprocal denunciations. Who had denounced whom? What information did the party committee or the NKVD possess? Who would be the next victim? "Enemies are so clever," one article in *Kirovets* suggested, "that they even masquerade as unmaskers."[77] If even active "unmaskers" might be enemies, then no one could be trusted.

Although the paper played a critical role in spreading the terror in Dinamo, it did not represent any identifiable faction or stratum within the factory. It printed attacks on managers, shop heads, and party organizers, but most of these were penned by people of similar rank. *Kirovets* furnished a platform from which accusations could be hurled, but the accusers were indistinguishable from the victims, and over time, some accusers actually became victims themselves. Those who contributed articles to the newspaper did not constitute a

76 "Otchetnoe Sobranie Partorganizatsii." *Kirovets*, April 8, 1937, p. 1.
77 "Kak Maskirovalis' Vragi Naroda na Zavode," *Kirovets*, June 2, 1937, p. 3.

special group, impervious to criticism or invulnerable to attack. The factory's leaders, with some help from the workers, often used the pages of *Kirovets* to slander one another.[78] The various wall newspapers, written and posted in the individual shops, were even more defamatory than their factory-wide counterpart. Aimed at their own shop heads, technical personnel, and party organizers, they routinely published rumors and malicious accusations. Here again, there was little practical difference between those who composed the attacks and their victims. The political atmosphere in the shops became so toxic that even *Kirovets*, itself hardly a model of fair journalism, printed an article chastising the editors of the wall newspapers, asserting that "they have gone too far in criticizing because they are not checking or reporting facts."[79]

CHAOS

By the summer of 1937, the factory had exploded into chaos. The party committee's only activities now consisted of considering *zaiavleniia*, launching investigations, and hearing accusations and counteraccusations. Authority within the factory collapsed. Why should anyone take orders from a manager or shop head who might soon be exposed as a wrecker? Following Zhukov's resignation, in February, Iasvoin had replaced him as director, but his own troubled tenure would be abruptly cut short by his arrest that same July. During his five months in the post, he was battered by unremitting

---

78 See, for example, the following articles in *Kirovets*: "Pochemu Ne Kritikuiut Razina" and "Ne Zaglushat', a Smelei Razvertyvat' Samokritiku," March 30, 1937, pp. 2, 1; "Bezotvetstvennost' Kiseleva i Litvaka," April 3, 1937, p. 1; and "Volokitchiki" and "Partkom Zabyl o Partgruppakh," April 5, 1937, pp. 3, 2.

79 "Iarche i Polnee Osveshchat' Partiinuiu Zhizn'," *Kirovets*, April 6, 1937, p. 2.

criticism, unable to make even the simplest move without being attacked by either *Kirovets* or the party committee. Yet in order to run the factory effectively, the director had to act decisively. Numerous shop heads, engineers, managers, and technical employees had been arrested; new, inexperienced employees desperately needed direction; managers had lost their power over workers; and technical personnel were terrified of making decisions. Problems with the electric locomotives remained unresolved, the foundry was still producing too much waste, and two accidents on Dinamo's railroad spur lines had resulted in several fatalities.

Iasvoin's political troubles multiplied in proportion to his organizational and technical challenges. The party committee refused to support his leadership, and he soon sank into a leaden depression. Perhaps he sensed that his arrest was imminent. In April, the party committee censured him for failing to "liquidate the consequences of wrecking." Dinamo had fallen short of its production goals for March and April, as a result of the chaos created by the terror. Engineers in the electric locomotive shop were at loggerheads over a new prototype, the factory was still unheated, and labor safety had deteriorated. Iasvoin was upset because the shop heads were all at one another's throats, each blaming the next for the production problems. "The shop heads think only about their own shops," he told the party committee, "but all the shops here are tied to one another." He begged the party committee for help "in eliminating these moods."[80]

In June, Starichkov, head of the party committee, confirmed that Iasvoin had once again failed to meet Dinamo's production quota, and the party committee called the director to account for

80 TsAOPIM, f. 432, o.1, d. 179, ll. 102–4, 108.

"violations in the system of leadership." Baiukov, Sheinin's replacement as deputy director, was now under attack as well, and Iasvoin promoted I. Nikitin, head of the bureau of the engineering technical sector, to fill the post. Nikitin, though he had worked in Dinamo since 1931, was a new party member. The party committee was angered by Iasvoin's choice, complaining that he had selected for the job someone whom "nobody knew." Iasvoin was so cowed that he begged the party committee's pardon. "I didn't know who was supposed to select cadres, me or the party committee," he humbly explained. The committee reprimanded him for a variety of mistakes and then noted of him, "First of all, he has to eliminate his pessimistic attitude toward work."[81] Yet with labor discipline plummeting, production decreasing, and arrests being made on every side, it is difficult to imagine where Iasvoin might have looked for sources of optimism.[82]

Within a month, Iasvoin himself was placed under arrest. *Kirovets* announced in July that the director was "a masked wrecker" who had ruined labor discipline and "covered his wrecking with the slanderous claim that he had eliminated the consequences of wrecking in what he said was a short time."[83] In August, the editor accused Iasvoin of having caused a "great turnover" of employees, while also discouraging shop heads from establishing stronger labor discipline among their workers. Between January and July 1937, 1,558 people had left the factory, out of a workforce of almost 7,000. Several shops, including the foundry and the hard insulation shop, experienced 100 percent turnover. Although Dinamo's turnover rate was

81 TsAOPIM, f. 432, o. 1, d. 179, ll. 150–51.
82 *Ibid.*
83 "Razoblachit' do Kontsa Vsekh Vragov Naroda i ikh Prispeshnikov." *Kirovets*, July 26, 1937, p. 2.

not especially high in comparison with that of industry as a whole, the party committee nevertheless put the blame for it on Iasvoin and his fellow "wreckers."[84] Iasvoin was arrested sometime early in the summer of 1937 and remained in prison through the fall. On December 7, 1937, a list of 270 people proposed for execution was sent to Stalin, Molotov, and Zhdanov for their approval. Iasvoin's name was on the list, and he was shot shortly thereafter.[85] His position at Dinamo was filled by P. P. Khorikov, the factory's third director in less than seven months. Khorikov, too, stepped into a snake pit: at least two party members, including Sorokin, a member of the bureau of the engineering technical sector, and Nikitin, still the deputy director, wrote *zaiavleniia* to the Moscow party committee in an attempt to derail his appointment. Sorokin was later arrested by the NKVD.

During the fall of 1937, *Kirovets* stopped printing denunciations and articles about wrecking. By this time, however, the arrests and exclusions had already done terrible damage. Between April 1937 and April 1938, sixty-four party members were expelled for being "enemies of the people," for being associated with such enemies, or for other political reasons. Of these, forty-four were arrested.[86] Thus approximately 11 percent of the factory's party members in 1937 were excluded for political reasons, and 8 percent were arrested. Nearly one in every ten party members in Dinamo was sent to prison during that one year, a ratio that created and then perpetuated a poisonous atmosphere of anxiety and fear. It is worth noting,

---

84 TsAOPIM, f. 432, o.1, d. 188, l. 34; "Po-Bol'shevistski Borot'sia za Likvidatsiiu Posledstvii Vreditel'stva," *Kirovets*, August 21, 1937, p. 2, cites a slightly lower figure for those leaving.
85 http://stalin.memo.ru/names/index.htm, APRF f. 3, o. 24, d. 413, l. 260.
86 TsAOPIM, f. 432, o. 1, d. 188, l. 9.

moreover, that these figures do not take into account the considerable number of arrests and expulsions antedating April 1937. The Party had already expelled 143 members who worked in Dinamo during the review and exchange of party documents (*proverka* and *obmen*) of 1935–36.[87] All of those excluded from the Party lost their jobs.

Managerial staff was hit hard by the expulsions and arrests. Between 1936 and 1938, the factory lost a significant share of its shop and department heads, engineering and technical personnel, party organizers, and administrators. In the cynical words of Margolin, a party member, "They are shooting all the intelligent ones and leaving all the fools."[88] Margolin himself was arrested.[89] Out of Dinamo's eighteen shops, research bureau, and experimental station, at least eight, or almost half, lost their heads – in some cases more than once – to arrest or exclusion. Among those imprisoned, expelled, or both were Denisov, head of the crane shop; Fomin, head of the fourth instrument shop; Prokhorov, head of the experimental station of mobile prototypes; Fridman, Prokhorov's replacement; Khailov, head of the technical department of mobile prototypes and the department of safety; Khliupov, head of the scrap shop; Kogan, head of the foundry; Kreitsberg, head of the second instrument shop; and Mashkin, head of the electrical shop. At the shop level, where production actually took place, the leadership was crippled.

In addition, numerous department heads, managers, engineering and technical personnel, and party officials were arrested or

87 In April 1937, Dinamo's party organization had 561 members (plus 178 candidates). One year later, it had 532 party members (plus 229 candidates). See TsAOPIM, f. 432, o. 1, d. 176, l. 9, f. 432, o. 1, d. 193, l. 109, f. 432, o. 1, d. 188, l. 1.
88 TsAOPIM, f. 432, o. 1, d. 179, l. 142.
89 TsAOPIM, f. 432, o. 1, d. 188, ll. 26–27.

excluded, among them Zhukov, Dinamo's director, and Iasvoin, his immediate successor; Sheinin, the deputy director; Tolchinskii, the technical director; Avatkov, head of the bureau of the engineering technical sector; Baronskii, head of the technical bureau of traction machines, and his replacement, Lipshtein; Lipshits, head of the planning transport group; Romanov, head of the research bureau; Tregubov, head of the sales department; A. G. Koliad, deputy secretary of the party committee and member of the Moscow party committee; P. N. Sokolov, a former party committee secretary; D'iakova, an economic planner; Khvedchen, an engineer in the experimental station of the electric locomotive shop; Marek, a technician in the fourth instrument shop; Okunev and Torbeev, members of the department of chief mechanics; Sorokin, a member of the bureau of the engineering technical sector; Viktorov, an engineer in the electric locomotive shop; and Zil'berman, a dispatcher in the fourth instrument shop. All of these men, too, had critical functions within the factory. Still others were also excluded and arrested, including Agureev, a Komsomol organizer; Gorchakov and Mikhailov, employees of the bureau for rationalization and inventions (BRIZ); Gorshko, Mironov, and Gostev, skilled workers in the electrical shop; Iosilevskii, a member of the fourth instrument shop; Korneev, a Komsomol member and worker in the electric locomotive shop; and Muravin, a worker in the shop of machines of alternating current.

CONCLUSION

The publisher of the English translation of Eugenia Ginzburg's famous memoir of the terror, *Krutoi Marshrut*, retitled her book *Journey into the Whirlwind*. The image captured the shock, fear, and destruction that upended Soviet life in 1937–38.[90] If events in Dinamo were representative, however, the title may be more apt as a descriptive rather than an analytical metaphor. The terror did not descend on Dinamo like a tornado from above; rather, the actions and reactions of employees were integral to events that transpired within the factory. The terror itself was composed of people who were swept up in the "whirlwind" of NKVD arrests, but these same people also helped, both individually and collectively, to create the whirlwind they experienced. In fact, the actions of the state cannot easily be separated from those of the workers and managers who brought terror into the factory by writing denunciations, politicizing shop conflicts, and recasting accidents and chronic production problems as wrecking.[91]

The terror in Dinamo began in the summer of 1936 with a flurry of denunciations inspired by the first Moscow show trial. Managers, engineers, and party members wrote unsolicited *zaiavleniia* to Vyshinskii, the state prosecutor, to officials on the Party's shop, factory, district, city, and regional committees, and to the NKVD. The existence and extent of these denunciations would be revealed only later, as party members desperately tried to portray themselves as loyal "unmaskers." A very partial and incomplete list of denunciations shows wide participation in the development of the terror.

90 Eugenia Semenovna Ginzburg, *Journey into the Whirlwind* (New York: Harcourt Brace Jovanovich, 1967). A more precise translation of the Russian title would be "The Steep Path."
91 Christian Gerlach and Nicholas Werth note, "If denunciations, generally speaking, were indeed commonplace and if political accusations, in particular, were embedded within the same culture of petitioning and complaint, this suggests that political participation and the violence that emerged were closely intertwined. . . . " "State Violence – Violent Societies," in Michael Geyer and Sheila Fitzpatrick, eds., *Beyond Totalitarianism: Stalinism and Nazism Compared* (New York: Cambridge University Press, 2009), p. 175.

In July 1936, Kotiuchenko, a worker in the second instrument shop, denounced Kreitsberg, the shop's head, for "Trotskyism." In August, Khvedchen, an engineer in the experimental station, denounced his boss, Prokhorov, along with Kreitsberg and Tolchinskii, the technical director, for wrecking. That same month, Tolchinskii and Khailov, head of the technical department of mobile prototypes, denounced the engineers and technicians in the electric locomotive shop for wrecking, and Fridman, later to replace Prokhorov as head of the experimental station of mobile prototypes, denounced Tolchinskii. In the fall, Khailov and Sheinin, the deputy director, both separately denounced Tolchinskii. Numerous employees denounced Zhukov, Dinamo's first director; and then Iasvoin, its second; and finally Khorikov, its third. Zhukov and Tolchinskii denounced each other to Ordzhonikidze, the commissar of heavy industry. And Khvedchen, who had earlier denounced Prokhorov, Kreitsberg, and Tolchinskii, moved on to attack Zhukov, Starichkov, head of the party committee, and Romanov, head of the research bureau and the controller's administration. This brief accounting, culled from stenographic reports of party meetings and from articles in the factory newspaper, undoubtedly represents the mere tip of a very large iceberg.

The behavior of Dinamo's employees gave the state-sponsored terror its own internal, self-generating logic. The initial flurry of denunciations in the summer of 1936 exposed longstanding technical, political, and personal quarrels among the factory's workforce. In the early fall, Starichkov sent a list of politically suspect party members to the district committee. A few highly placed party members in Dinamo, knowing the political histories of their comrades, deduced who might be named on the list. At this point, several hastened to denounce Tolchinskii and others in a preemptive effort to distance themselves from political trouble. Ongoing arrests by the NKVD heightened the intensity of workers' and managers' responses as fear pervaded the factory. "Silence" and "failure to unmask," terms initially used by the party committee as catchall justifications for expelling party members who had already been arrested, soon began to be applied to members in good standing. Once silence itself could be interpreted as a sign of enemy sympathies, everyone was forced to participate actively in the search for enemies. The factory newspaper, *Kirovets*, was inundated with written accusations from employees. The newspaper's ability selectively to publish this "informational material" greatly expanded its power, transforming it from a tool of managers and party officials into an arbiter of their fates. A denunciatory fever swept through the factory as each individual sought to protect himself or herself. Guilt by association pulled many people into prison. Collective meetings in the shops, departments, unions, and party organizations taught members severe and repeated lessons, which influenced their subsequent behavior. Yet over time, it became more and more difficult to distinguish the pupils from their teachers. People tried to protect themselves through tactics that served only to increase the risk to their comrades and coworkers. The strategies of writing preemptive *zaiavleniia*, naming names, and diluting blame all fattened the dossiers of the NKVD.

The events in Dinamo raise important questions about the relationship between denunciations and arrests, suggesting that the terror cannot be understood solely as a form of excisionary violence from above. Rather, it involved an entire political culture built on NKVD actions and local participation. Did local investigations, accusations, and denunciations influence NKVD officials when they were compiling their lists of victims? The complete answer to this question is still hidden in the archives. Yet the microhistory of

Dinamo demonstrates that factory employees played an active role in promulgating a terror against their comrades and coworkers.[92] By 1937, people's behavior had assumed deeply destructive patterns as individual responses, aimed at self-protection, set in motion a deadly group dynamic.

92 Other descriptions confirm that events in Dinamo were similar to those that occurred in other workplaces and institutions. On the factories, see John Scott, *Behind the Urals: An American Worker in Russia's City of Steel* (Bloomington, Ind.: Indiana University Press, 1989); Victor Kravchenko, *I Chose Freedom* (New York: Charles Scribner's Sons, 1946); James Harris, *The Great Urals: Regionalism and the Evolution of the Soviet System* (Ithaca, N.Y.: Cornell University Press, 1999); Sergei Zhuravlev, "Terror against Foreign Workers in the Moscow Elektrozavod Plant, 1937–8," in Barry McLoughlin and Kevin McDermott, eds., *Stalin's Terror: High Politics and Mass Repression in the Soviet Union* (Basingstoke, Hampshire: Palgrave Macmillan, 2003), pp. 225–40.

3: Family Secrets

MARGOLINA, A PARTY MEMBER IN TREKHGORNAIA MANU-faktura, a textile factory, hurried home from work at the end of a chilly spring day in April 1937. The snow was melting, and for the first time in many months, it was possible to glimpse the topmost railings of the park benches poking through the drifts. Picking her way through icy slush and puddles, Margolina entered the vestibule of her building, where she checked the dented, rusty metal mailbox. Pulling out a postcard, she stared at its single scrawled line. The card seemed to be written, in Margolina's words, "in a sort of code." The cryptic message, signed by her brother in Kharkov, stated that Vera, their married stepsister, "was alone." Margolina knew what that meant, but she was unsure what to do. Anxious not to conceal information from the Party, she showed the postcard to Makarevich, a member of her factory's party committee. Makarevich scanned its message quickly. Now Makarevich faced a choice of her own: she could order Margolina to bring the postcard to the attention of the party committee and trigger an investigation, or she could let the matter drop. Makarevich did not discuss the card with Margolina. Making a swift decision, she told her that she must not correspond further with either her brother or her stepsister, "and that she knew this." In their brief exchange, significant mainly for what was left unsaid, both women revealed that they grasped the full import of the message, and they tacitly agreed to ignore it. In going to Makarevich, Margolina had done what the Party required: she had reported receiving the information. Makarevich, for her part, took a political risk in providing Margolina with the small protection of negligence.

Margolina did not write back to her brother, and for months, she heard nothing more. In November, she finally got a letter from him, confirming what she suspected: Frid, her stepsister's husband, had been arrested. Her brother wrote not a word about himself. Three days later, Margolina's case came up before a party committee meeting, and her family's problems tumbled out. Not only had Frid been arrested, but new information revealed that her brother had been excluded from the Party for his connection to him. "I had nothing in common with this Frid," Margolina told the committee members. "I visited them only once in the past year, for several hours." "Why such caution about receiving a postcard?" someone slyly asked. It was a question fraught with danger: if Margolina were to admit that she had had suspicions about Frid's arrest in April, she would open herself up to further interrogation about her failure to report it to the party committee. Now she chose her words carefully: "This is a very sharp moment," she replied, "and something seemed not right." A barrage of questions followed:

Question: Did you have any tie to Frid?

Margolina: I already explained this.

Question: Do you know anyone at the airport?

Margolina: No.

Question: Who were your parents?

Margolina: My stepfather was a trader; my father was a glazier.

Question: Did your stepfather own a house?

Margolina: He had his own house.

Question: Did you mention your stepfather when you filled out the questionnaire required to enter the Party, and during the purge [review and exchange of documents]?

Margolina: I spoke about him during the purge.

Question: Did your brother conceal his social origins?

Margolina: Judging from the information, he did.

Question: How old is your brother? What is his education? Whom does your mother live with?

Margolina: Alone.

Question: Do you have relatives who are still in the Party or have been excluded from the Party?

Margolina: I have another brother who is a party member.

Question: Do you have any relatives living abroad?

Margolina: My other brother.

Question: Where does your brother work?

Margolina: In Kharkov somewhere – I don't know where.

Question: Has your brother who lives abroad ever sent you anything?

Margolina: He bought a bicycle for his wife. She died. He sent it to me.

Question: Were you ever in any other party before?

Margolina: No.

Question: How long have you worked in the factory?

Margolina: Since 1930.

Question: Why did you end up in Moscow?

Margolina: I was acquainted with Baranov, and I went to him, and then I entered the Communist Academy.

Question: Why do you have a juridical education?

Margolina: I graduated from the Institute of the National Economy in Kharkov.

Question: Where and with whom did Baranov work?

Margolina: Somewhere in the south – exactly where, I don't know.

Question: What does your sister's husband do?

Margolina: He's a writer.

Question: Do you have relatives living in Moscow?

Margolina: My sister and her husband.

Question: Did you have any old acquaintances who helped you to settle in Moscow?

Margolina: No.

Question: Where are your mother's relatives living and registered?

Margolina: In Kharkov.

The questions continued: "Is there information about your brother?" "Why were you interested in Frid?" "Where and in what factory does your brother work?" "Why did you leave things in your brother's room?" "Why did you receive a bicycle?" "How is it that *we* never knew you liked bicycling?" In the end, the party committee instructed Makarevich to correspond with all the institutions and organizations involved in the case, including the Kharkov NKVD and city party committee and the party organizations to which Frid and Margolina's brother belonged. The party committee now launched the investigation that the two women had hoped to avoid, and it resolved to reconsider the case in the light of any new information it gathered.[1]

The party committee closely questioned Margolina about her relatives and contacts – her siblings and their spouses, her mother, her

1 Tsentral'nyi Arkhiv Obshchestvenno-Politicheskoi Istorii Moskvy (TsAOPIM), f. 369, o. 1, d. 173, ll. 41–44. Jochen Hellbeck, *Revolution on My Mind: Writing a Diary under Stalin* (Cambridge, Mass.: Harvard University Press, 2006), p. 34, notes that by the mid-1930s, social origin had lost its "original significance as a polluting influence. From now on all instances of impurity could only emanate from individual souls." Yet in party meetings within the factories, questions about social origins remained an important part of interrogations and membership reviews through the 1930s.

mother's relatives, her father and stepfather, her mentor Baranov, her acquaintances, her airport contacts – as well as her education and the gifts she had received from abroad. Frid's arrest had already led to her brother's expulsion from the Party. Would the latter event now affect Margolina? Like a subterranean detonation, her brother-in-law's arrest made waves that rolled from Kharkov to Moscow and back again, engulfing Margolina's relatives, mentors, and friends. Although she was circumspect in her answers, tersely supplying only the minimum information required, her entire family circle could expect to be investigated and interrogated in turn.

THE IRON RULES OF THE GAME

Margolina and thousands of other party members were ensnared by rules common to local party organizations in every workplace and institution. These rules had been in place and in use for years, with few negative consequences. Yet between 1936 and 1938, as arrests mounted and the search for hidden enemies intensified, they pulled many party members into the vortex of the terror. The Party required its members to write *zaiavleniia* if they received information about enemies or had contact with people who were politically suspect. If a relative, coworker, or friend was arrested, for example, a party member had to inform his or her local party organization of this fact immediately, and in writing. Beginning in 1936, many loyal Communists were forced to confront family members' arrests. Some had brothers or sisters who were rounded up among former left or right oppositionists. Others lost relatives to the mass operations launched in the summer of 1937 against priests, former kulaks, and various "untrustworthy" national groups. And many more had relatives who were branded as "enemies" for reasons no one could fathom. Each of these devastating losses demanded a confessional *zaiavlenie*.

Yet the decision to adhere to party rules and write a *zaiavlenie* was neither simple nor easy. Every party member who was compromised by the arrest of a relative had to struggle with the choice between writing and not writing. Both alternatives carried grave consequences. On the one hand, writing a *zaiavlenie* generally meant that a lengthy investigation would be forthcoming. The party committee would request detailed information about the writer's voting record at meetings, and past political activities, and would scrutinize the political histories of his or her relatives, friends, coworkers, and contacts. Those who wrote *zaiavleniia* about the arrests of family members could expect to be interrogated by their shop committees, by their party committees, and sometimes also by hundreds of fellow party members in factory-wide meetings. At best, the interrogations were intimidating and difficult; at worst, they resulted in expulsion and arrest. By 1937, most party members had attended enough meetings to understand just how much damage a confessional *zaiavlenie* could do to them and those around them. Honesty was not always the best or the safest policy. Not writing, on the other hand – that is, having information but choosing not to submit a *zaiavlenie* – could open a party member up to charges of concealment, which in itself was grounds for expulsion and possibly even arrest. Expulsion alone had serious implications: excluded party members lost their jobs and factory housing and frequently found it impossible to get hired anywhere else. With no way of supporting themselves and nowhere to live, they often had no other recourse than to rely on relatives, who might well be unable or afraid to register them in their own living quarters or to offer them job contacts or financial assistance.

Throughout 1937 and 1938, party members, torn between their duty to the Party and their growing fear of being investigated, struggled with this painful dilemma. As members' past activities and ties came under closer scrutiny, relatives became a source of ever-increasing risk. The investigations that followed *zaiavleniia* invariably resulted in widening circles of repression. Party members faced excruciating choices about whether to reveal or conceal the fate or the very existence of suspect relatives. They also agonized over the Party's orders that they renounce spouses, children, siblings, and parents who were labeled "enemies," and spurn the needy children of arrested relatives. The family became both a critical vector in the spread of terror and the locus of a searing choice between party loyalty and human relationships.

THE SOVIET FAMILY

By 1937, Soviet families had endured and been shaped by two decades of upheaval, demographic cataclysm, geographic dispersal, and upward mobility. For centuries, the members of the typical multigenerational peasant family had lived together in a single dwelling, under the control of a patriarch (*bol'shak*), and tilled a plot of land, producing and consuming in common. This kinship form was destroyed by collectivization, which consolidated village lands and substituted the collective farm for the household as the primary unit of production. In the great migration from village to town inspired by the industrialization drive of the late 1920s, rural relatives frequently moved in with family members in the city. Housing was in short supply, and people divided and subdivided houses, apartments, and even single rooms. *Kommunalki*, or communal apartments, carved from grand prerevolutionary mansions, sheltered many families, each inhabiting a single room with the use of a common kitchen and toilet. Several generations of a family might even occupy a "corner," an official unit of space in a room divided into four. People shared beds and slept in corridors, kitchens, and closets.

Real wages dropped by half in the early 1930s, and few families could get by on the earnings of a single breadwinner.[2] Millions of women entered the workforce during the first and second five-year plans (1929–37), constituting the largest such influx into the waged labor force in so short a time in any country ever. Between 1933 and 1937, women comprised the sole source of new, incoming workers. Peasant women took waged work in towns and cities, as did working-class housewives seeking to supplement their husbands' income. Families with small children and elderly dependents relied on a combination of waged and unwaged labor to survive. Grandmothers played an indispensable role in family life, queuing in long lines for food and consumer items, doing the cooking, washing, cleaning, and mending, and caring for their grandchildren while their adult children worked for wages. The number of available places in childcare centers was limited, especially in newer towns and settlements, and the centers themselves were overcrowded and unhealthy. Women and men worked long hours, and the difficulty of obtaining food and other consumer items in overstrained, poorly organized state retail stores made queuing and shopping a full-time, albeit unpaid, occupation. For most single mothers, their own mothers' help was a critical factor in their ability to work and care for their children.[3]

For their part, older women also needed the help of their adult children. Millions had lost their husbands to the demographic

2 Wendy Z. Goldman, *Women at the Gates: Gender and Industry in Stalin's Russia* (New York: Cambridge University Press, 2002), pp. 76–82, 265–72.

3 On women's roles and life cycles, see Barbara Engel and Anastasia Posadskaya-Vanderbeck, eds., *A Revolution of Their Own: Voices of Women in Soviet History* (Boulder, Colo.: Westview Press, 1997); David Ransel, *Village Mothers: Three Generations of Change in Russia and Tartaria* (Bloomington, Ind.: Indiana University Press, 2000); Sheila Fitzpatrick and Yuri Slezkine, *In the Shadow of Revolution: Life Stories of Russian Women* (Princeton, N.J.: Princeton University Press, 2000).

catastrophes of the early twentieth century, from World War I and the Civil War to epidemics, famine, dekulakization, and other upheavals. Widowed and alone, they found a place in the families of their sons and daughters, themselves overburdened and desperate for assistance. The shortage of housing, coupled with the need to pool wages, obliged extended families to live together in small spaces. Although not all young adults had mothers who were both willing and able to pitch in, many if not most families included a single grandmother.[4]

Even as disruptive historical forces encouraged family closeness, however, they also drove relatives apart. Families were repeatedly shattered under the blows of successive social upheavals. War, revolution, and famine created vast refugee populations. The demographic imbalance of the 1920s made it difficult for older women to marry, even as liberal divorce laws permitted men to abandon their older wives and children in favor of younger, single women.[5] In the early 1930s, more than 380,000 so-called kulak families, numbering over 1.8 million people, were exiled from their native villages in the struggle over collectivization. Settled in wastelands without shelter or food, tens of thousands died; others escaped to build new lives for themselves under fictive identities. Men were often separated from their families.[6] Millions of peasants left elderly parents and young children behind in the village to seek waged work in steel

4 Beatrice Farnsworth and Lynne Viola, eds., *Russian Peasant Women* (New York: Oxford University Press, 1992); Gijs Kessler, "A Population under Pressure: Household Responses to Demographic and Economic Shock in the Interwar Soviet Union," in Donald Filtzer, Wendy Z. Goldman, Gijs Kessler, and Simon Pirani, eds., *A Dream Deferred: New Studies in Russian and Soviet Labour History* (Bern: Peter Lang, 2008).
5 Wendy Z. Goldman, *Women, the State and Revolution: Soviet Family Policy and Social Life, 1917–1936* (New York: Cambridge University Press, 1993), pp. 101–43.
6 Lynne Viola, *The Unknown Gulag: The Lost World of Stalin's Special Settlements* (New York: Oxford University Press, 2007), p. 196.

mills, chemical complexes, dams, hydroelectric stations, mines, and railroads. Young peasants and workers crowded the railroad stations, moving from city to city in search of jobs and housing.

The pressing labor shortage created new, exciting educational and career opportunities. There was an enormous demand for unskilled and skilled workers, technicians, engineers, agronomists, teachers, doctors, and numerous other kinds of professionals. The state set up short training courses in every workplace, urging workers to acquire additional expertise and increase their wages. Young people flocked to institutes and universities, from which they graduated to jobs in growing industries in dire need of their newly minted skills. Sons and daughters of illiterate peasants became skilled workers and managers. The Party sent off its members to fill positions all over the country, splitting up married couples for long periods. Many people lost contact with distant relatives or kept in touch with them only sporadically, by mail. They might write and visit occasionally, but mass migration, constant transfers, and the difficulties of daily life made it hard to nurture family ties across great distances, over poor roads, and through frequent changes of address.

Revolutionary ideas about the family also influenced people's behavior and attitudes. Early on, the Bolsheviks had believed that the family would eventually "wither away." People would continue to fall in love and live together, but dining halls, day-care centers, and laundries would eliminate women's unpaid domestic labor, free them to enter the workforce on an equal basis with men, and render superfluous the legal obligations of marriage. The first Family Code, of 1918, had legalized divorce, abolished the legal concept of "illegitimacy," and encouraged spouses to become financially independent. Divorce, almost impossible to obtain in the tsarist period, now became commonplace. A husband or wife could secure a divorce simply by signing a form in a registry office, leaving his or her spouse to be informed of the news by postcard. By 1926, more than half of all marriages in Moscow were ending in divorce, as were two thirds of those in Leningrad. Even peasants, bound to the household through common land holdings, availed themselves of the new laws. Although the simplified divorce procedure gave Soviet citizens an unaccustomed degree of personal freedom, the revolutionary ideals of "free love" frequently had a negative impact on women and children. Abandoned wives flooded the courts in the 1920s and early 1930s to press alimony and child-support suits. The common family configuration of a grandmother's living with her adult child and caring for her grandchildren was the combined result of easy divorce, large numbers of widows, and a demographic imbalance between the sexes.[7]

By 1936, the state had reversed its earlier view that the family would and should "wither away," and enacted stricter divorce and alimony laws in an attempt to foster stronger family ties. Men who left their families without providing for child support now faced criminal penalties. Divorces became harder to obtain, and parents were made legally responsible for the criminal actions of their minor offspring. The state, unable to cope with the massive numbers of homeless and unsupervised children, the high juvenile crime rate, and the burden of impoverished single mothers, attempted to force men to shoulder their responsibilities. Abortion, legalized in 1918, became illegal again, as part of a pronatalist campaign intended to increase the birth rate and strengthen the family.

In its emphasis on a "strong, socialist family," the state was more interested in creating a stable unit of social discipline and financial

7 Goldman, *Women, the State and Revolution*, pp. 106–8; see also Christine Kaier and Eric Naiman, eds., *Everyday Life in Early Soviet Russia: Taking the Revolution Inside* (Bloomington, Ind.: Indiana University Press, 2006); Elizabeth Wood, *The Baba and the Comrade: Gender and Politics in Revolutionary Russia* (Bloomington, Ind.: Indiana University Press, 1997).

support than in fostering intense emotional ties. State campaigns and popular culture in the 1930s celebrated those who contributed to building the new socialist society: Stakhanovite workers who set production records, female brigade leaders, Arctic explorers who discovered new lands, aviators, engineers, inventors, even children who informed on their "enemy" parents. The state tacitly encouraged children to shift their primary loyalty from the family to political organizations such as the Young Pioneers and the Komsomol. In 1932, a major campaign extolled Pavlik Morozov, a peasant boy who had allegedly denounced his father for forging identity documents and selling them to "enemies of the state." His father, sentenced to ten years in a labor camp, was later executed. According to the myth constructed by the state, young Pavlik was a hero who fought for collectivization and was murdered by his relatives for his efforts. He became a martyr to the Soviet cause: youth groups took his name, and statues were erected in his memory. His example, and the cult that grew up around it, urged children to inform on their parents if they suspected them of wrongdoing.[8] This prospect excited fear within families, freezing discussion and obliging parents to keep their political doubts or dissident opinions to themselves. Party members in particular were constantly reminded that their first loyalty must be to the Party. Political activism and assignments took precedence over the needs of the family.[9] When Petukhova, head of the party committee in the Likerno-Vodochnyi distillery, tried to refuse reelection to that position in 1938, she explained that she had three children at home, the youngest then only three months old.

8 Historians later discovered that almost everything about the official version was false. See Yuri Druzhnikov, *Informer 001: The Myth of Pavlik Morozov* (Piscataway, N.J.: Transaction, 1996); Catriona Kelly, *Comrade Pavlik: The Rise and Fall of a Soviet Boy Hero* (London: Granta Books, 2005).

9 Cynthia Hooper, "Terror of Intimacy: Family Politics in the 1930s Soviet Union," in Kaier and Naiman, *Everyday Life in Early Soviet Russia*, pp. 61–91.

A male party member testily responded that Petukhova's reasons were "unimportant": many other comrades also had three children, he noted, and Petukhova's mother could take care of her kids.[10] His attitude was not unusual.

By 1937, the Soviet family had thus changed dramatically as a result of the social upheavals and revolutionary experiments of the previous two decades. Subject to the centrifugal forces of divorce and sexual freedom as well as those of war, collectivization, industrialization, and rapid upward mobility, families were torn asunder, and their members scattered across vast geographical and hierarchical distances. At the same time, however, this very disruption and dislocation encouraged people to cling more tightly to whatever shreds of family remained to them. The overwhelming responsibilities and sheer number of single, widowed, and working women provided grandmothers with an essential household role. Scarce housing, low wages, poor childcare institutions, long lines, and constant shortages of food and consumer goods induced relatives to pool their resources and reinforced the structure of the multigenerational family. The twin forces of disintegration and bonding, so contradictory on their face, would become even fiercer and more tightly intertwined as the terror, yet another cataclysmic upheaval, shook the family unit to its roots.

THE TERROR'S IMPACT ON THE FAMILY

As the terror unfolded, the state targeted a succession of political, social, and national groups, ranging from former oppositionists to kulaks to immigrants from hostile border countries. Although these

10 TsAOPIM, f. 428, o. 1, d. 1, ll. 123, 1230b.

target groups appeared to be separate and distinct, their members were invariably connected to others outside the group through family ties. It was not uncommon for a loyal party member and factory worker to have, for example, a so-called "kulak" uncle, a former Trotskyist sister, or a Latvian husband. The family united people through the most intimate of bonds, forming a single entity made up of individuals of differing ethnic and social origins and varied political beliefs and backgrounds. Family members with no risk factors of their own might be pulled into the vortex of terror by the arrest of a relative who belonged to a persecuted group. From the vantage point of the family, the primary social unit for most people, the terror was experienced not as a series of separate, targeted campaigns but as an ongoing and amorphous threat. The orders for the mass and national operations, for example, were not made public at the time, but kept secret by the state. Ordinary citizens often had no idea why their relatives had been arrested. People received little information from the NKVD, prison officials, or the judiciary about the fate of arrested relatives. Most victims of the terror had families whom they lived with and loved, and it was this small circle of intimates that absorbed both the initial impact and the aftershocks of an arrest.

Overall, women constituted only a small percentage of those arrested, executed, or sent to the camps for political crimes during the terror, but they suffered greatly as family members dealing with the consequences of such dispositions.[11] Historians have calculated that between 24,000 and 34,000 women were executed in 1937–38,

---

11 See, for example, Lydia Chukovskaya's fictional depiction of a mother whose beloved son is arrested, *Sofia Petrovna* (Evanston, Ill.: Northwestern University Press, 1988); Cathy A. Frierson and Semyon Samuilovich Vilensky, *Children of the Gulag* (New Haven, Conn.: Yale University Press, 2010), pp. 136–232;

comprising some 4 to 5 percent of the total number of executions. The largest group of these women was composed of nuns and other religious personnel, who tended to be older, single, and childless. A smaller group had been active in suspect political parties such as the Mensheviks and Socialist Revolutionaries, or in oppositional factions within the Bolshevik Party.[12] Several prominent party leaders and heads of state, including V. M. Molotov, head of the Soviet of People's Commissars, and M. I. Kalinin, head of the central executive committee of the Congress of Soviets, lost their wives to the camps. These women were well-known party leaders in their own right. Other women, such as Anna Larina, Bukharin's wife, were arrested after their husbands were imprisoned or executed.

Although a far greater number of men than women were arrested and executed, women were members of all of the different groups targeted by the state. In the immediate wake of the Kirov murder, for example, thousands of former aristocrats, clergy, and other "former" people (*byvshie liudi*) were expelled from Leningrad with their families – a total of 11,072 people.[13] In May and June of 1937, former oppositionists who had been excluded from the Party were exiled

---

Melanie Ilic, "The Great Terror in Leningrad: A Qualitative Analysis," unpublished paper presented at the Conference on Stalinist Terror, University of Leeds, August 2010.

12 There is a considerable body of work on women and Stalinist repression, both memoir and history. See Melanie Ilic, "The Forgotten Five Percent: Women, Political Repression and the Purges," in Ilic, ed., *Stalin's Terror Revisited* (Basingstoke, Hampshire: Palgrave Macmillan, 2006), pp. 116–39; an excellent discussion of these preliminary statistics may be found on pp. 131–34. See also Ilic, ed., *Women in the Stalin Era* (Basingstoke, Hampshire: Palgrave Macmillan, 2001), and Ilic, "The Great Terror in Leningrad: A Quantitative Analysis," *Europe-Asia Studies*, vol. 52, no. 8 (2000).

13 Golfo Alexopoulos, "Stalin and the Politics of Kinship: Practices of Collective Punishment, 1920s–1940s," *Comparative Studies in Society and History*, vol. 50, no. 1 (2008), p. 104.

from key cities along with their families.[14] Women also fell victim to the mass and national operations, being included among the former kulaks, recidivist criminals, former aristocrats, priests, White Guards, and Polish, Latvian, Korean, and German immigrants successively singled out for arrest. An internal memorandum dated July 3, 1937, ordered NKVD units to compile lists of the family members of those sentenced by the Military Collegium of the Supreme Court from the time of the Kirov murder. The families were to be sent to camps. The Politburo affirmed the memo two days later, adding the stipulation that children under the age of fifteen should be taken to orphanages, while the fate of older children would be decided individually. All children of "enemies" were to be prohibited from living in regime cities such as Moscow, Leningrad, and Kiev. The following month, on August 15, Ezhov, head of the NKVD, signed order 00486, specifically addressing the wives of convicted Trotskyists and rightists. The order mandated that these women (including common-law wives and divorcees), regardless of their beliefs or prior activities, be confined to labor camps for a period of five to eight years. Their children, meanwhile, were to be sent to children's homes, labor colonies, or camps, depending on their ages and attitudes. The NKVD would establish special camps for wives and collect extensive data on the relatives of the repressed. Wives who denounced their husbands were exempted from the

---

14 "Spetssoobshchenie N.I. Ezhova I.V. Stalinu ob Iskliuchennykh iz VKP (b) Trotskistakh i Pravykh, Prozhivaiushchikh v Moskve," "Postanovlenie Politbiuro TsK VKP (b) o Vyselenii Semei Trotskistov i Pravykh," and "Zapiska I.V. Stalina o Vysylke Zhen Osuzhdennykh Rukovoditelei," in V. N. Khaustov, V. P. Naumov, and N. S. Plotnikova, eds., *Lubianka. Stalin i glavnoe upravlenie gosbezopasnosti NKVD, 1937–8: Dokumenty* (Moscow: Izdatel'stvo 'Materik', 2004), pp. 186, 216, 226. (Hereafter cited as *Lubianka.*) These cities included Moscow, Kiev, Leningrad, Rostov, Taganrog, and Sochi.

order.[15] The wife of M. V. Iasvoin, a director of Dinamo, was among
those affected by this NKVD action. After her husband was arrested,
Frida Iasvoin-Merlas followed him into prison, and after he was
shot, in December 1937, she was sentenced to eight years in the
Akmolinsk Labor Camp for Wives of Traitors to the Motherland
(ALZhIR), as the wife of an enemy of the people.[16] By October
1938, when the order was revised to include only those wives who
were convicted of enemy activities in their own right, about 18,000
women had already been arrested under its terms.[17]

The arrests of all these targeted groups had a considerable impact
on party members and employees in the factories. Shop and party
committees were occupied almost solely with reviewing denunciations and confessional *zaiavleniia* regarding the arrests of relatives. In
textile factories such as Trekhgornaia Manufaktura, where women
made up a large percentage of the workers and party members, party
organizations devoted countless meetings to discussing the intimate
and painful details of the arrests of husbands, children, and relatives. In some cases, the women concerned submitted their own
zaiavleniia about these arrests; in others, coworkers brought them to

15 On order 00486, "On the Repression of Wives of Enemies and Traitors of
the Motherland, of Members of Right Trotskyist Espionage Sabotage Organizations Sentenced by the Military Collegium and by Military Tribunals," see
"Postanovlenie Politburo TsK VKP (b) 'Vopros NKVD'," *Lubianka*, p. 238;
Frierson and Vilensky, *Children of the Gulag*, pp. 156–62; Alexopoulos, "Stalin
and the Politics of Kinship," pp. 104–5; Corinna Kuhr, "Children of 'Enemies
of the People' as Victims of the Great Purges," *Cahiers du Monde Russe*, vol. 39,
nos. 1–2 (1998), p. 212; Ilic, "The Forgotten Five Percent," pp. 126–30; Nikita
Petrov and Arsenii Roginskii, "The Polish Operation of the NKVD," in Barry
McLoughlin and Kevin McDermott, eds., *Stalin's Terror: High Politics and Mass
Repression in the Soviet Union* (Basingstoke, Hampshire: Palgrave Macmillan,
2003), pp. 158–59, 180–81.

16 http://lists.memo.ru/index30.htm. Frida Iasvoin-Merlas was released in August
1942.

17 Ilic, "The Forgotten Five Percent," p. 129.

the attention of the local party organization. Women showed no more inclination to protect one another than men did, and they were not shy about exposing their female comrades. Murasheva, a female party member in Trekhgornaia Manufaktura, stood up at a factory-wide meeting of more than five hundred party members in March 1937 and loudly announced, "Shtrul and Ignat'eva should not be leading party activities or even be in the Party at all, because their husbands are Trotskyists."[18] Shtrul suffered the attack silently; her husband had not yet been arrested or expelled, and he would defend himself against the charge of Trotskyism later in the meeting. Yet just as the arrest of an employee affected his or her coworkers, subordinates, and superiors, the arrest of a relative hurt the entire family. In this instance, Murasheva called for the expulsion of two female comrades from the Party because their husbands were in political trouble. In families as with coworkers, guilt by association extended the reach of the terror beyond the groups marked by the state.

A party member who lost a spouse to prison was required by the Party to denounce and sever all contact with him or her. Not all party members were willing to obey this injunction. Varvara I. Torbeeva, a timekeeper in Dinamo's first instrument shop, was excluded from the Party because she expressly refused to renounce her husband, Torbeev. At a factory-wide meeting in August 1936, Lavrent'ev, another party member, accused Torbeev of Trotskyism. Lavrent'ev's accusation was a typical preemptive denunciation: both men had been friendly with Kliukvin, an alleged Trotskyist in Dinamo who had been arrested. Lavrent'ev hoped to distance himself from the arrested Kliukvin before anyone had a chance to mention their

18 TsAOPIM, f. 369, o. 1, d.171, l. 48.

friendship. His denunciation of Torbeev hinged on a single occasion on which the two of them had visited Kliukvin and gotten drunk. Lavrent'ev claimed that Torbeev and Kliukvin had engaged in "counterrevolutionary conversations." By informing on Torbeev, Lavent'ev bought a measure of protection for himself. Torbeeva, for her part, was simply stunned by the accusation. She herself had also been there when the men got drunk, and she adamantly denied Lavrent'ev's version of events. Later, after her husband had been excluded from the Party and arrested, Torbeeva declared, "I will not sever relations with Torbeev. I will go with him and help him, even if he is exiled. They are wrong to exclude him. I was at that one meeting at Kliukvin's house where they drank." In the end, however, Torbeeva's protestations not only failed to help her husband but badly hurt her as well. The row of dominoes fell in smooth succession: Kliukvin's arrest precipitated the denunciation by Lavrent'ev, which led to Torbeev's exclusion and arrest, which in turn triggered the interrogation and exclusion of Torbeeva, his wife.

Starichkov, head of Dinamo's party committee, opened the meeting on Torbeeva's case with a motion to exclude her from the Party. "She doesn't have the correct view of Trotskyism," he announced. "She does not consider her husband a Trotskyist, and until the end of his trial, she did not consider him guilty." Torbeeva doggedly insisted on her right to her own opinion of her husband, independent of the state, the Party, and the NKVD – a stance the party committee could not countenance. She spoke bravely and honestly in his defense, asserting, "I am still not sure why they arrested my husband. They did not provide any information." The party committee members were quick to challenge her:

Question: Why didn't you vote to exclude your husband at the general party meeting?

Torbeeva: I don't know.

Question: Did you tell Lavrent'ev that you had now calmed down?

Torbeeva: I never said this.

Question: What do you think about Lavrent'ev's speech?

Torbeeva: Up to this past summer, Lavrent'ev treated my husband as a comrade.

Question: What kind of contact do you have with your husband now?

Torbeeva: I went to the prison and left some money for him there. Nothing more. They promised me a meeting with him, but it hasn't happened. I lived with Torbeev for eleven years, and he always urged me to study.

Question: How do you view the fact that you wish to go to the prison to meet with a Trotskyist?'

Torbeeva: You know, I have two children, and he is their father.

Torbeeva's poignant refusal to disavow her husband, the man who had "urged her to study" and fathered her children, infuriated the party committee members. Lavrent'ev, she reminded them, had been friendly with her husband up to the time he denounced him. Why was Torbeev alone guilty, when both she and Lavrent'ev had also visited Kliukvin? Razin, a controller in the department of technical control, responded angrily, "Torbeeva thinks that her husband has been slandered, that he is not guilty, that he is not a Trotskyist. She says that she and Lavrent'ev were also at Kliukvin's and that they drank, but she doesn't say what else they did." Mikhailov, the editor of *Kirovets*, added, "Torbeeva knew that her husband visited Kliukvin, but she tried to cover it up. The decision of the shop organization to exclude her is correct. We must affirm it." And

Bakhmutskii, known for his zealous denunciations of others, noted, "At the factory-wide party meeting on August 17, I sat next to Torbeeva. When they called her husband's name, she said, 'This is nonsense, he is not guilty.' I was very interested in Torbeev. He denied everything, but Torbeeva herself testified that her husband would disappear from the house and say he had an assignment from the party committee. They invited Torbeeva to Kliukvin's in order to mislead her [otvesti glaza], and also when they drank, so they could have counterrevolutionary conversations." Bakhmutskii now turned to Torbeeva and addressed her directly: "Torbeev carried on subversive work here in the factory and deceived you." Starichkov summed up the discussion: "Torbeeva is not convinced of the Trotskyism of her husband. Torbeeva spoke one way at one time, and now speaks another way. We must show everyone: this is how weak Communists view the Party. Torbeeva visited Kliukvin, which was useful to her husband, who deceived her. Torbeeva now declares that she has not severed her relationship with him, and she takes money to him in prison. She fell under his influence and became his footstool [skamalas]." Torbeeva again protested that there was little justification for either her husband's arrest or her own pending expulsion. In exasperation, she explained, "I was with him at Kliukvin's because when Lavrent'ev arrived to pick him up, I would not allow him to go, and they said, 'Come with us' and gave me the address, and I went. When I got there, they were already drunk. Then some time passed, and I met Kliukvin's wife on the street. She told me that her husband had been arrested. I never met her again after that." The party committee expelled Torbeeva for "knowing that her husband had attended a Trotskyist meeting in Kliukvin's apartment," abstaining from the vote on his exclusion, failing to unmask him, hiding his Trotskyist activities, and maintaining ties to him after he was arrested.[19] What emerges from these charges is the all-too-common plight of a loyal wife tired of her husband's leaving her alone to get drunk with his friends. Kliukvin's arrest and Lavrent'ev's preemptive denunciation had transformed an ordinary bout of drinking into a singular tragedy for the Torbeev family.

An outright refusal to admit a husband's guilt, as in Torbeeva's case, was rare. Most wives were merely stunned, unable to comprehend the arrest or its consequences. Sharova, a textile worker and party member in Trekhgornaia Manufaktura, came before the party committee in December 1937 to announce that her husband had been arrested. "I have lived with him for sixteen years," she began. "He worked as a switchman on the railroad, and then as a watchman at the fourth station post. During his watch, there was a dense fog. A train came, but its semaphore was shut off, and he did not use the flag. I did not know about any of this at the time, but when he did not come home, I went to the railroad station, and there I learned that he had been arrested and was in Taganka prison. They gave me a summons to take to the railroad procurator, who gave me his things. The procurator told me I had permission to say good-bye to my husband, but he did not put it in writing, and then he left. I was not able to say good-bye. They searched my apartment, and they took some of my husband's papers and correspondence with his relatives. I thought there would be a trial on October 9, 1937, but there was no trial. They called it a 'preinvestigation.'" Sharova, a worker with little education, had only the dimmest understanding of what had happened. Like many other women in the same situation, she rushed from one office to another, unable to obtain even the most

19 On Torbeeva's case, see TsAOPIM, f. 432, o.1, d. 179, ll. 14–15.

basic facts about the charges, the court date, or her husband's fate. The party committee grilled her:

Question: Why did your husband know German?

Sharova: I don't know where he learned it.

Question: What kind of books did your husband read?

Sharova: I don't know. I am barely literate.

Question: Did your husband have relatives?

Sharova: He has a sister in Leningrad, but we didn't write to her.

Question: When will the trial be?

Sharova: I don't know.

Question: What did they do in the search, what were they looking for? Obviously, they weren't looking for nuts.

Sharova: They took his certifications and the letters from his sister and nephew.

Question: Did your husband read the letters to you?

Sharova: He read a bit, but not everything.

Question: Do you have children?

Sharova: No.

Question: Parents?

Sharova: My father died.

Question: What was your husband's mood?

Sharova: I never noticed a poor mood.

Question: What kind of opinion do you have of your husband?

Sharova: I can't say anything now, and I don't understand.

Question: Whom did your husband visit?

Sharova: I don't know, and I also don't know his comrades.[20]

20 TsAOPIM, f. 369, o.1, d. 173, ll. 52–55.

The party committee resolved to follow up with NKVD officials in the railroad station where Sharova's husband worked, and to revisit the case once more information was available. If the train accident led to a charge of wrecking, Sharova would be forced to choose between her husband and the Party. If she denounced and divorced him, she could remain a member, but if she refused to disavow him, she would lose her party membership, her job, and her factory housing. At the meeting that day, Sharova was but one in a long line of party members who came forward to announce the arrests of their relatives. The party committee attended to no other business beyond listening to these heartbreaking *zaiavleniia*.

By 1938, the interrogations had intensified, and comrades were tearing one another apart. Party members were no longer satisfied with a wife's repudiation of a husband who had been arrested. Now they demanded to know why she had failed to unmask him. How was it possible to live with someone and not realize that he was an enemy? Even the most committed of Communists were affected by the arrests. Bykhovskaia, the sole woman on Dinamo's party committee and its "cultural propagandist," worked in the electrical shop. It was her particular misfortune to have not one but *two* husbands arrested: her current one, Pavlinov, and her former husband, Pechernikov. Her comrades suggested that the arrests, at the very least, raised serious doubts about Bykhovskaia's choice in men. Her shop organization excluded her for having a "tie to an enemy," but the party committee reversed the shop's decision and reinstated her with a reprimand for her "lack of vigilance." In February 1938, Bykhovskaia's case came up again before a factory-wide party meeting attended by more than 550 people. The agenda consisted of a long list of comrades who were to be considered for expulsion. Bykhovskaia was charged with "failing to unmask" her second husband, Pavlinov, a party member who had been

expelled and arrested as an "enemy of the people." Bykhovskaia
readily accepted a measure of blame, in the hope that she would
be allowed to remain in the Party: "I showed a total lack of vigilance," she admitted to the audience. But she denied having any
connection to her former husband: "I broke with my first husband,
Pechernikov, more than five years ago. I am not responsible for
him. Pavlinov, my current husband, was arrested on January 16th
[1938], and I informed the party organization on January 17th." The
discussion that ensued revealed the absurd demands party members
now made of one another. Mazurov, a leader of the factory guards,
announced, "This business is not clear to me. Bykhovskaia is a politically developed person. When she lived with Pechernikov, he was
not isolated from her. In a nutshell, perhaps it was possible for her
to unmask him." Mazurov wondered, in effect, why Bykhovskaia
had not "unmasked" her first husband in 1932 – at which time no
campaign to "unmask" had even existed, and Pechernikov himself
was a party member in good standing. Reasoning thus, Mazurov concluded, "It is not accidental that her second husband is an enemy of
the people. I think she should be excluded." Many party members
had worked in Dinamo for a number of years and knew one another
well. Batsheev, an employee in the shop of direct current, came
to Bykhovskaia's defense: "Mazurov is wrong that Bykhovskaia is
pretending," he said flatly. "She is very alert, and that is why she
survives so well. I was a witness to the fact that when she was with
Pechernikov, they were at loggerheads. She did not have discussions with him; she tried to leave him. I didn't know her second
husband, but her grave mistake was to overlook an enemy of the
people." A coworker of Bykhovskaia's in the electrical shop likewise defended her, noting that she had actively denounced others
in their shop. Still others agreed with Mazurov. A member of the
factory administration declared, "I support Mazurov. It is impossible

to believe that a wife doesn't know her husband, what he conceals in his heart. She deserves a more severe punishment." Now Mazurov himself intervened once again. Aiming thoroughly to discredit Bykhovskaia, he asked her if her husband had supported the rightists in the early 1930s. Bykhovskaia, however, skillfully flung his insinuation back at him. "I knew this," she said. "But Mazurov knew it even better than I did, because he worked closely with my husband in the factory, and I myself did not work here at that time." The head of the party committee, alarmed by the spreading accusations, nervously called for a vote. Two anonymous denunciations had already been passed to the podium. He asked that members please "sign their names if they want to write." In a split vote, the party committee moved to give Bykhovskaia a reprimand rather than exclude her.[21]

The cases of Torbeeva, Sharova, and Bykhovskaia impart some sense of the range of responses of female party members to their husbands' arrests. Torbeeva stood by her husband, refusing to disavow him. Sharova was stunned by what had transpired and reacted passively to the party committee's demands. Bykhovskaia publicly broke with both of her husbands and conceded that she had shown a "lack of vigilance." Both Torbeeva and Bykhovskaia defended themselves by accusing their accusers. Bykhovskaia followed the rules by providing a *zaiavlenie* immediately after her second husband's arrest, yet even her compliance could not shield her from a nasty interrogation. She was lucky to escape with only a reprimand, because many other people, including her husband, were excluded and arrested for the same infraction – namely, having a "tie to an enemy of the people." Bykhovskaia was saved in part by her denunciation of others in the electrical shop: before becoming a victim

21 TsAOPIM, f. 432, o. 1, d. 194, ll. 25–27.

herself through her second husband's arrest, she had been an active perpetrator. Nor did she hesitate to counter the accusation that her husband had once had rightist inclinations. Pointing out that Mazurov's relationship with him had predated her own, she implied that her accuser had himself failed to recognize her husband as an enemy, and that perhaps he, too, had been involved with rightists in the factory. Party organizations, like all groups with long histories, were crisscrossed by friendships, animosities, and alliances. Given the turbulent political history of the previous two decades, many party members had ample evidence at hand with which to implicate others. The 550 comrades seated in the hall learned a useful lesson from Bykhovskaia's behavior: the willingness to jettison a spouse, a knowledge of longstanding ties, an aggressive defense, and a record of active denunciation might together be just enough to save a person.

TAINTED RELATIVES AND SPOILT BIOGRAPHIES

Central party leaders gave local party committees little explicit guidance on how to unmask the alleged enemies in their ranks. The local organizations were instructed to uncover "active" oppositionists, even as they were also cautioned that former oppositionism was not synonymous with current enemy activity. At the February–March 1937 Central Committee plenum, Stalin and Zhdanov both warned the delegates that they needed to "know" their cadres and check them carefully. Only a detailed knowledge of members' political biographies – including their social origins, their positions in previous party debates, and the identity of their sponsors for party membership – could reveal the enemies in their midst. The lack of objective criteria by which to identify such "enemies" left the party committees groping in a poisonous mist, at once anxious to expose and exclude alleged enemies before the NKVD arrested them, and yet also perpetually uncertain about precisely who ought to be exposed. In the shifting world of "enemies" and "friends," there seemed to be only one form of incontrovertible proof: a person arrested by the NKVD was sure to be guilty of *something*.

Party members and candidates were required to complete lengthy biographical questionnaires in order to join the Party, fill leading positions, or undergo its periodic organizational purges. These forms demanded detailed information about the respondent's social origins, work history, political activities, and relatives. One of the questions asked, for example, was "Do you have any relatives who belonged to anti-party groups?" Many party members had small or large "blots" on their biographies that they either fully or partially concealed: relatives who had been kulaks or traders, friends who were former oppositionists, or personal contacts abroad. They understood even before the terror that total honesty might damage their chances of joining the Party or being appointed to coveted posts. The Party was thus filled with loyal members who were also, in a manner of speaking, "secret sinners." Once party leaders began pressuring local officials to recheck their records and identify "enemies" before the NKVD arrested them, party members faced new and difficult choices about revealing the secrets of their "spoilt biographies." The desire to hide the existence of their own tainted relatives made many members even more zealous in their persecution of others.

The case of Shtrul, a party member in Trekhgornaia Manufaktura, demonstrated how easily family ties could destroy even a committed Communist. Shtrul had been born in 1911, in Latvia, where his father was a factory worker. He had six sisters and two brothers. Six of the siblings emigrated from Latvia to the Soviet Union and joined the Party as young adults. Both of Shtrul's two brothers were active party members; one had risen to the important local post of district party secretary. Shtrul himself, eager to join the new socialist society, left Latvia with three of his sisters in 1926 to join a fourth sister who was already in Moscow. Still just fifteen years old, he began work at Trekhgornaia Manufaktura. He eventually joined the Komsomol (Communist Youth League), was elected Komsomol secretary, entered a workers' training program, joined the Party, and married a fellow party member in the factory. Around the time of young Shtrul's arrival in Moscow, one of his brothers had joined the Trotskyist opposition. The brother's political biography over the decade that followed was similar to those of thousands of other oppositionists: in 1927 he was expelled from the Party and exiled, in 1930 he rejoined the Party and returned to Moscow, and in 1935, after Kirov's murder, he was arrested. Shtrul informed Severianova, head of Trekhgornaia's party committee, of his brother's arrest, but he neglected to bring the matter up again during the review and exchange of party documents later that year. Severianova quietly ignored Shtrul's admission; like many other party committee heads in 1935 and 1936, she saw no reason to make a fuss over something that a member had willingly disclosed. The ticking time bomb of Shtrul's brother's arrest thus appeared to have been defused by Severianova's goodwill and Shtrul's own reserve.

By 1937, however, the arrest of a relative had become a serious political liability. In March, Shtrul confessed to a factory-wide party meeting that his brother was a Trotskyist and had been arrested. At least one comrade had already called for Shtrul and his wife to be expelled, claiming that he, like his brother, was a "Trotsky-ist," and she "the wife of a Trotskyist." Shtrul defended himself and, in so doing, implicated Severianova. "I informed the party committee that my brother was a Trotskyist," he explained. "I didn't mention it again when we had the exchange of party documents; that was my mistake.... I never was a Trotskyist, and I never will be." Severianova now had to justify her failure to convey Shtrul's earlier admission to the proper authorities. Already compromised by her close working relationship with the factory's director, who had also recently been arrested, she tried to minimize the accusations against Shtrul: "I am very satisfied that he criticized himself," she said. The other party members refused to accept her justification: "It's not sufficient!" one member yelled out. Severianova tried to mollify the group. "Completely true," she assented. "But what are his shortcomings? You see, he spoke to the party committee. I did relay the information to a party meeting. My mistake was that I thought of Shtrul as a known person in the factory." Severianova conceded that she had erred in trusting Shtrul and in not investigating him more thoroughly.[22] Both Shtrul and Severianova hoped that by owning up to their mistakes, they might be able to make the problem disappear. Yet their frankness would ultimately succeed only in compounding their difficulties.

Seven months later, in October 1937, Shtrul's case came up again. By then, his situation had worsened considerably. The first of his brothers was still in prison, and the other, just recently arrested, was sentenced to be executed. Suspicions against Latvian spies would soon culminate in mass arrests. In November, Ezhov would order NKVD units to eliminate the danger posed by "Latvian counterrevolutionary organizations established by the Latvian secret service and linked to the intelligence services of other nations."[23] Shtrul's

22 TsAOPIM, f. 369, o. 1, d. 171, ll. 88, 105.
23 Barry McLoughlin, "Mass Operations of the NKVD, 1937–8: A Survey," in McLoughlin and McDermott, *Stalin's Terror*, p. 122.

birthplace was now an additional black mark against him. The party committee subjected him to a grueling interrogation about his family: "Why did you never tell anyone anything about your relatives?" "When did you arrive from abroad?" "Do you help your relatives abroad?" "Why didn't you tell anyone your brother was a Trotskyist?" Falling back on the common strategies of pleading ignorance and shifting blame, Shtrul tried to defend himself: "I told Severianova," he said. "I thought if she knew, that was sufficient. But she didn't inform anyone." He claimed not to know where his brothers worked or what they did. The party committee members were unconvinced. "It's strange that he doesn't know where his own family works," declared Pavlov, a party member who worked in the factory's garage. "I think that he is not frank. He can't stay in the Party." Agreeing that Shtrul should be expelled for his "lack of frankness, concealing the arrest of his Trotskyist brother, and not knowing where his brother and sister worked," the committee voted to exclude him.[24] Shtrul, like many party members, had initially tried to downplay the political troubles of his relatives. Severianova, head of the party committee, helped him by looking the other way. Then, between March and October of 1937, the political climate shifted. The arrest of a second brother and the family's Latvian origins became damning proof of Shtrul's political unreliability.

Through 1937 and 1938, an endless procession of party members presented *zaiavleniia* about their relatives to their shop organizations and party committees. Some made a habit of reporting even the most minor contact for fear they would otherwise be accused of concealing information. Zasimov, a party member in Trekhgornaia Manufaktura, noted that his wife worked as a servant for A. I. Rykov,

24 TsAOPIM, f. 369, o. 1, d. 173, ll. 1–2.

the former head of Sovnarkom (the Soviet of People's Commissars), commissar of communications, and leader of the rightist opposition, who was arrested in 1937 and executed in 1938.[25] Shegolev, another party member, testified that his daughter had visited the daughter of G. L. Piatakov, the former deputy commissar of heavy industry, after her father was executed. The girls had gone to school together. Shegolev received a reprimand for his "lack of vigilance, delay in reporting the information, and liberal attitude." According to the party committee, it was Shegolev's duty to prevent his daughter from comforting her grief-stricken friend.[26] Piatakov's daughter was now considered an enemy by virtue of her father's fate, and as such, she must be shunned.

Even the arrest of a distant relative could become an important matter for investigation. Iarkin, a party member in Trekhgornaia Manufaktura, confessed in October 1937 that his cousin, whom he had not seen since 1921, had been arrested. He had received the news through his brother, who had been contacted by their cousin's wife. One month later, Iarkin came before the party committee again, with additional information. His cousin, he said, worked on a state farm in Bashkiria and had been charged with wrecking after the cattle died. The party committee was interested not only in Iarkin's relationship with his cousin but in his ties to his own brother as well. Committee members questioned him closely:

Question: Was your brother arrested?

Iarkin: No, my cousin.

Question: Did your brother often meet with your cousin?"

Iarkin: Not since 1930.

25 TsAOPIM, f. 369, o. 1, d. 173, l. 63.
26 TsAOPIM, f. 369, o.1, d. 173, l. 73.

Question: What does your brother do?"

Iarkin: He teaches courses to improve the skills of managers and technical personnel.

Question: Do you have any other brothers?

Iarkin: Another who works in Leningrad, in the Green Planting Trust.

Question: How did you help the party organization investigate your tie to your cousin?

Iarkin: I tried to find the address of the state farm where he worked, but I could not.

Question: Was your arrested cousin a Communist?"

Iarkin: Yes.

Question: Did you live for a long time in Bashkiria?"

Iarkin: I left Ufa in 1921.

Question: How did your arrested cousin's wife find your brother?

Iarkin: I don't know.

The party committee members carefully considered Iarkin's *zaiavlenie*. Pavlov, the worker from the factory garage who had earlier moved to exclude Shtrul, took a softer line this time. "It is very unclear what relationship Iarkin had with his cousin, and it would be hard to clarify this," he said. "I think we should accept Iarkin's *zaiavlenie* about the arrest of this cousin to whom he had no tie."[27]

A month later, Pavlov himself stepped up to present a *zaiavlenie*, after his brother-in-law, who worked as a carpenter on a collective farm south of Moscow, was arrested. Pavlov soon revealed that he had been keeping a secret of his own. By the mid-1930s, many former kulaks who had been exiled during collectivization to special settlements had either escaped or been released. Some had assumed new identities; others had settled quietly outside of regime cities,

27 TsAOPIM, f. 369, o. 1, d. 173, ll. 2, 50–51.

taking jobs in construction, transport, and industry and on collective and state farms. During the summer and fall of 1937, they were arrested en masse under order 00447 of the mass operations. Many party members who had successfully concealed their kulak relatives up to that point were exposed when these relatives were arrested. Pavlov now admitted, "My brother-in-law was a kulak who was exiled far away – where exactly, I don't know. His family returned to work on the collective farm, but I know nothing about them. During my vacation, I went to the countryside and saw my brother-in-law, but I was not friendly with him." Pavlov tried to emphasize his distance from these relatives, but the party committee did not find his story persuasive:

Question: Why did you never tell us that you had kulak relatives?

Pavlov: I somehow did not attach any importance to this.

Question: How is it that up to this time you were not interested in your dekulakized relations on the collective farm?

Pavlov's sister had married a man who was subsequently exiled as a kulak. Like many other peasants, she had managed to flee the exile settlement and return to the collective farm. Pavlov himself, like many workers, returned to see his relatives in the village during his vacations. Eventually his sister's husband, too, was able to leave his place of exile and rejoin his wife. Yet his days of freedom were numbered. He fell victim to the mass operations, and Pavlov was exposed.[28] The party committee resolved to gather more information about his case.

At the same meeting, four other party members also came forward to deliver *zaiavleniia* about their relatives, including the deputy head

28 TsAOPIM, f. 369, o. 1, d. 173, ll. 55–56. For similar stories of kulaks arrested in the mass operations, see Viola, *Unknown Gulag*, pp. 159–66; Veronique Garros, Natalia Korenevskaya, and Thomas Lahusen, eds., *Intimacy and Terror: Soviet Diaries of the 1930s* (New York: New Press, 1995), pp. 111–66.

of the party committee, whose cousin was in custody, and a woman worker who explained that her husband, an NKVD officer, party member, and German refugee, had been arrested.[29] Order 00439, part of the national operations, mandated the arrest of German immigrants allegedly engaged in spying and wrecking on behalf of the Gestapo. As one historian has noted, the Soviet Union, once considered a haven for Communists fleeing fascism, had now turned into an "execution chamber."[30] The apparently unending spectacle of frightened, penitent party members presenting their *zaiavleniia* – some of them officials in leading posts – suggested that few possessed the untainted biography the Party required. There was scarcely anyone, it seemed, who had not lost a relative to prison.[31]

DOUBT AND FEAR

The arrests of relatives forced party members to question the state's insistence on the ubiquity of the terrorist threat. On learning that a family member had been arrested, a person would usually react first of all with horrified bewilderment: Could this relative actually be a masked enemy? Vara G. Schetchikova, head of the library in Serp i Molot and a party member since 1919, came before the party committee to declare that her sister, who lived in the Russian Far East, had been excluded from the Party for her "lack of vigilance"

29 TsAOPIM, f. 369, o. 1, d. 173, ll. 55–59.
30 Barry McLoughlin, "Mass Operations of the NKVD, 1937–8," pp. 122–23, and McLoughlin and Kevin McDermott, "Rethinking Stalinist Terror," p. 12, in McLoughlin and McDermott, *Stalin's Terror*.
31 Party committees in other factories were also kept busy with discussions of *zaiavleniia* about arrests. In Dinamo, for example, the head of the union announced that his two brothers had been arrested for Trotskyism; see TsAOPIM, f. 432, o. 1, d. 179, l. 131.

after her husband was arrested. The sister was now in Moscow, hoping to plead her case with Mariia I. Ul'ianova, Lenin's sister and a longtime family friend. Schetchikova, a member of an old revolutionary family, was dumbfounded at this turn of events. Schetchikova herself had joined the Party at the front during the Civil War; her mother had joined in 1917. Under questioning by the party committee, Schetchikova testified that she had learned of her brother-in-law's arrest from her mother and presented a *zaiavlenie* about it the very next day. "It never crossed my mind that my sister was a member of a Trotskyist organization," she said. "I have great pity for her. It has been very difficult for her to survive, and she is very needy and poor. I don't think she could be an enemy of the people. She has always worked in the Party. She spent three years with a rifle in hand and was considered one of the best cadres during the Civil War."[32] Although Schetchikova conceded it was possible that her brother-in-law had once been active in the Trotskyist opposition, she could not fathom why her sister should have been targeted as well.

P. M. Larkin, a member of the party committee in Serp i Molot and instructor for the district party committee, was no less bewildered when he learned that his sixty-three-year-old father had been arrested. Given the news by an old acquaintance from his village whom he bumped into on a Moscow street, Larkin was stunned. In his announcement to the party committee the next day, he cast about desperately for some conceivable reason for the arrest, reviewing what he knew of his father's life for any hint of a crime. "I don't know why he was arrested," he told the committee. "He is a member of a collective farm; he does not belong to the Party. He did not

32 TsAOPIM, f. 429, o. 1, d. 223, ll. 87–88.

owe taxes." Offering a rambling list of potential risk factors, Larkin inadvertently revealed that he considered party membership to be on a par, in terms of risk, with the failure to pay taxes. He continued, "One collective farmer said my father had a dagger, brought from the front, which everyone in the village used to slice ham. He repaired ovens. He never drank vodka. He was never mixed up with anything, anywhere."[33] His possession of a dagger, which his fellow villagers put to their own homely use, was thus the only reason Larkin could come up with, at least publicly, for his father's arrest. Schetchikova and Larkin were both baffled by the arrests of their relatives, one of whom had a storied revolutionary past, and the other no political experience at all. The sister and the son were unable fully or easily to accept the Party's judgment that their sibling and father were enemies. Both obeyed party instructions to present *zaiavleniia*, but each seemed to harbor serious questions about how such things could happen.

As the number of arrests increased, people became less fearful of the forces allegedly threatening the state and more afraid of those allegedly defending it. Compelled to choose between personal ties and party loyalty, many instead took a middle course, publicly professing their allegiance while secretly aiding relatives who were in exile or in prison.[34] They began to wonder whether the arrested, not only their own relatives but perhaps others as well, were truly all guilty as charged. The willingness to help relatives in political trouble was a clear sign of growing doubts.

33 TsAOPIM, f. 429, o. 1, d. 223, l. 91.
34 Konstantin Simonov, the Soviet writer, later described his own failure to aid someone who asked for help during the terror: "It turned out that one of our comrades, a man that I considered even weaker and more of a coward than myself, had replied to him, and had helped as many people as he could – he had sent them parcels and money." Orlando Figes, *The Whisperers: Private Life in Stalin's Russia* (New York: Metropolitan Books, 2007), p. 628.

Isaak G. Sheinin, Dinamo's deputy director, was placed under arrest in connection with the fire in the scrap shop, but a party committee investigation then revealed that his sister, her husband, Neustroev, and Neustroev's mother had all been arrested for Trotskyism before the fire. Sheinin, himself the son of a prosperous merchant, had joined the Party in 1931. Thirty-four years old, he had been active in the Bund, a Jewish revolutionary organization that later merged with the Bolsheviks. Sheinin's sister, her husband, and her mother-in-law had all been involved with the left opposition in the 1920s. Like many former oppositionists, Neustroev was expelled from the Party in 1927, reinstated, and then arrested in June 1936 in the targeting of former Trotskyists. His mother, a party member since 1919, worked with Sheinin in Dinamo. The Neustroev family was connected to Leopold Averbakh, former head of RAPP, a proletarian writers' association.[35] Averbakh, who had visited Neustroev in Moscow, was also arrested for Trotskyism in 1936. His arrest and subsequent confession led the NKVD to Neustroev and his mother, whose arrest in turn eventually compromised Sheinin.

In the review and exchange of party documents in 1935, Sheinin had claimed to have no relationship with his sister's family, but Neustroev's mother contradicted that claim during an NKVD interrogation. Sheinin, she said, had come to family gatherings and sent his sister and her children food and money while the family was in exile and after the arrests. The party committee, tipped off by the NKVD, used this information against him, expelling him for "failing to unmask" Neustroev and his mother. He was judged to

35 Averbakh was head of RAPP (Rossiiskaia Assotsiatsiia Proletarskikh Pisatelei), or the Russian Association of Proletarian Writers. The group, founded in 1922, was known variously as the Octobrists, the Young-Guardists, or the VAPP (the All-Union Association of Proletarian Writers) until May 1928, when it changed its name to RAPP. It was dedicated to the creation of a new proletarian literature.

have been "lacking in vigilance" and was found guilty of concealing Trotskyist ties: "Refusing to unmask, he objectively aided enemies of the Party in counterrevolutionary activities," the committee ruled. By then his exclusion was a foregone conclusion, for Sheinin had already been placed under arrest for various offenses related to his work in the factory.[36] In June 1937, his name appeared on a list of Trotskyists sent by the NKVD to Stalin, Molotov, and Voroshilov, with the recommendation that he be sentenced to ten years in the camps.[37]

Sheinin made an effort to help his family, but at the same time, he did what he could to try to save himself, by preemptively denouncing his friend Tolchinskii, a highly placed official in Dinamo (see chapter 2). He hid his ties to his Trotskyist relatives and extended family even as he continued to visit with them and then later give them material assistance. In the factory, he meanwhile acted the part of the loyal party member, dutifully (if secretly) accusing a colleague of "wrecking." Sheinin's ongoing contact with his sister and her family suggests that he did not subscribe to the state's view that they were dangerous enemies. His behavior, like so many others', was deeply contradictory, a complex response to divided loyalties and to his evident wish to protect both himself and those he loved.

IMPOSSIBLE DILEMMAS

The Party demanded that its members immediately break off contact with anyone who had been excluded from its ranks, had been

---

36 TsAOPIM, f. 432, o. 1, d. 179, ll. 54–55.
37 http://stalin.memo.ru/spiski/index.htm. See APRF f. 3, o. 24, d. 409, l. 195.

declared an enemy, or was closely related to an enemy. This mandate presented many party members with a hideous choice: they could obey the Party's rules, spurning desperate relatives at the moment of their greatest need, or break those rules, secretly help their families, and risk expulsion. Women, responsible for the care of children and the elderly, found it especially difficult to sever family relations for political reasons. Children whose parents were arrested were remitted either to camps or to orphanages, depending on their age. Between August 1937 and May 1938, the NKVD sent 15,347 children of repressed parents to orphanages. At least several hundred thousand children lost their parents.[38] These children were greatly stigmatized. Relatives who were willing to care for them had first to appeal to and register with the NKVD, whereupon they would be subjected to background checks, periodic reviews, and close surveillance, conditions that might have deterred even the most loving of potential caretakers.[39] Many relatives thus feared to offer aid or shelter to children, especially teenagers, whose parents had been arrested. Yet despite these obstacles, many others, and grandmothers in particular, went to heroic lengths to locate children and bring them home from orphanages.[40]

Efimova, a party member in Trekhgornaia Manufaktura, watched helplessly as her son-in-law was arrested for Trotskyism and sent to a camp in Kolyma, her daughter was exiled, and her grandchildren were consigned to a children's home. In defiance of party rules,

38 Oleg Khlevniuk, *The History of the Gulag: From Collectivization to the Great Terror* (New Haven, Conn.: Yale University Press, 2004), p. 169; Kuhr, "Children of 'Enemies of the People' as Victims of the Great Purges," p. 210.

39 Alexopoulos, "Stalin and the Politics of Kinship," pp. 106–7.

40 See also Frierson and Vilensky, *Children of the Gulag*; Rosario Franco, "Social Order and Social Policies toward Displaced Children: The Soviet Case, 1917–53," Ph.D. diss., University of Manchester, Manchester, U.K., 2006.

she went to visit her daughter and to collect her grandchildren and bring them home. Efimova's case came before the party committee after someone reported what she had done. Her comrades showed her no mercy: "I heard that Efimova said her daughter is living quite prosperously and helping her husband," one member recounted spitefully. "I think that if Efimova has connections to these people, she should be excluded from the Party." The head of the party committee lectured her, "Comrade Efimova, you should know as a Communist that having any tie to your daughter, when she herself has ties to an enemy of the people, is impermissible." Efimova escaped with a reprimand for having a "tie to the family of a Trotskyist" and for her "lack of political vigilance." Yet the Party, in its attempt to erect an impassable barrier between loyal members and so-called enemies, placed Efimova, and many others like her, in an untenable position. Commanded to disavow a daughter in need, she had to choose between exclusion from the Party, with all its attendant consequences, and her natural human impulse to aid her suffering daughter and grandchildren. Several party members noted that after her visit to her daughter, Efimova had seemed "nervous and embittered," feelings that undoubtedly also affected her attitude toward the Party.[41]

The risks involved in helping a relative in trouble were very real. Gringauz, a party member in Krasnyi Proletarii, lived with his sister and brother-in-law, Denisov, in a single room. All three were party members. When Denisov was expelled from the Party, he also lost his job, and like many former party members, he soon found that no employer would hire him. Gringauz, in an effort to help his brother-in-law, got him a job in Krasnyi Proletarii. Some time later, Denisov was arrested, and the party committee immediately

41 TsAOPIM, f. 369, o. 1, d. 173, ll. 29–30.

accused Gringauz of bringing a spy into the factory. He attempted to wriggle out of the charge, first by pleading ignorance and then by blaming the administration in Krasnyi Proletarii for failing to check into Denisov's background before hiring him. "One evening," he said by way of explanation, "my sister introduced me to him, and then she married him. I did not suspect him of spying in the factory." The members of the party committee contemptuously dismissed this statement and began questioning Gringauz more closely:

Question: You lived with him?

Gringauz: Yes, for two years. I was with him on New Year's Eve.

Question: Did you know he had been a party member?

Gringauz: I think they [the factory administration] knew this.

Question: You arranged for Denisov to work in the factory after his exclusion, but you were not interested in his political identity. So in essence, you brought a spy into the factory.

Gringauz: Yes, I am guilty of that.

The questioning continued, with each of Gringauz's hesitant answers' providing more fodder for investigation. "Did you talk about politics with him?" "Did your sister inform her party organization about her husband's arrest?" "Who came to visit you in your apartment?" No one believed his protestations of ignorance. One member asserted, "Gringauz is just confusing things, and he doesn't speak the truth. Instead he is still trying to help the enemy, presenting himself as a philistine, saying he discussed only commonplace issues with Denisov. Gringauz was not vigilant; he did not unmask in a timely manner." The party committee agreed to investigate the matter further, to check the names Gringauz had provided, and to look into the administration's decision to hire Denisov. They demoted Gringauz to "party sympathizer," an official category of party supporters who were not full members. The party committee noted, "Gringauz never contradicted or opposed Denisov's views and did not inform anyone of them." Gringauz was charged with neglecting to report his conversations with his brother-in-law and failing "to unmask in a timely manner."[42]

Gringauz's expulsion sent a clear message that members would be punished if they were found to have helped someone who was subsequently arrested. Here again, because no one could predict who would be arrested next, giving help to anyone at all posed a considerable risk. Gringauz's case also encouraged party members to inform on their relatives and to report every suspect comment and conversation. As a result, local party organizations became snake pits of mutual informers motivated by suspicion and mistrust. Each member, poised to pounce on the potential weaknesses of every other, carefully guarded his or her own precarious position.

SPURNING RELATIVES

The local party organizations insisted that their members take a hard line with politically problematic relatives. When Kondrashevo, a party member in Trekhgornaia Manufaktura, learned that his brother had been expelled from the Party for having a "tie to an enemy of the people" and would be traveling to Moscow to appeal his exclusion, he immediately informed his party committee. Kondrashevo claimed that he had warned his brother, "'If you are not reinstated in the Party, you will become a stranger to me.'" Whether he really intended to cut off all contact with him must remain uncertain, but in any event, his *zaiavlenie* fulfilled the Party's requirements

42 TsAOPIM, f. 412, o. 1, d. 87, ll. 36–39.

and provided the necessary cover for a meeting between the two. If Kondrashevo had not written a *zaiavlenie* and made a public declaration, he would have left himself vulnerable to the charge of aiding an enemy.[43]

Some people not only professed their willingness to break off relations with family members but even went so far as deliberately to sacrifice them in an attempt to demonstrate their loyalty. Questioned by comrades in meetings, they blurted out compromising information and tried to divert blame to save themselves. A. I. Malyshev, a thirty-three-year-old foreman in the electrical shop in Serp i Molot, redirected the party committee's attention to his father in order to protect himself. Malyshev joined the Party in 1932, rose rapidly through its ranks in the factory, and became deputy secretary of the agitation and propaganda section of Serp i Molot's party organization in 1937. His problems began when a cousin of his, Sidkov, was excluded from the Party and then later arrested for Trotskyism. Sidkov's case itself provided an instructive lesson in the perils of honesty. He first got into trouble when he presented a *zaiavlenie* about himself, admitting that he had attended a Trotskyist meeting in 1927. His frankness proved ruinous: he was excluded from the Party in February 1937, fired from his job, exiled from Moscow that September, and arrested shortly thereafter. One week after Sidkov's arrest, Malyshev was called before the party committee and accused of having concealed information about him. Malyshev swore that he had informed district party officials about his cousin when he was promoted to deputy secretary. "I didn't know the facts before that," he said. "I didn't see Sidkov in 1936. . . . I hadn't seen him for several years. We had nothing in common. I didn't know he

43 TsAOPIM, f. 369, o. 1, d. 173, ll. 30–31.

had gone to a Trotskyist meeting in 1927.... The last time I was at his place was in 1921, when my aunt died."[44] Malyshev, like many party members in similar straits, was pleading ignorance.

Bubnov, secretary of the party committee, was not convinced by Malyshev's protestations. He knew that Sidkov had worked with Malyshev's father in Lacquer/Paint Factory Number 2. "I have one question," Bubnov said. "Your father was head of the factory's party committee. He should have known that Sidkov lost his job in the factory six months ago. He never told you about this? Why didn't you tell the party meeting about Sidkov when you were confirmed as deputy secretary? Your father undoubtedly told you." Malyshev again insisted, "I didn't know." But Bubnov refused to accept that: "You went to the dacha for two months with your father, and supposedly you never spoke about this?" Malyshev repeated, "I learned about Sidkov's exclusion in August. My mistake was that I didn't inform the Party about it immediately." Bubnov pressed Malyshev even harder: "I am concerned about your insincerity," he said. "You did not tell the party meeting or the district committee. Your relationship with the Party was dishonest."[45]

Cornered by Bubnov, Malyshev now tried to shift the blame to his father. He wondered aloud if perhaps his father had omitted to tell him about Sidkov because *he himself* was an enemy. "It seems that things are pointing to my father," he said. "I was never at my father's dacha. My father has been a party member since 1920. He worked for the Bauman district committee and was removed [from his post] in 1929. I have a question whose answer is not clear: Why was he removed? My political training is still not very strong.

44 TsAOPIM, f. 429, o. 1, d. 223, l. 40.
45 TsAOPIM, f. 429, o. 1, d. 223, l. 41.

Up to 1931, I was a big drinker, and only the Party turned me into a human being. I don't know anything discrediting about my father, but I have thought . . . perhaps he was tied to the rightists, who were then firmly entrenched in the Bauman district committee."

Malyshev continued to ramble on about his father, betraying him ever more deeply in his struggle to save himself. "I repeat," he babbled, "I know nothing about him, but as I grew older, I began to wonder about his past. I have told all that I know. I recognize the grave political mistake I made in not informing the party organization about Sidkov's exclusion. Perhaps my mistake was due to my loyalty to my father. But I will help the party organization investigate this question." Evidently acknowledging that he had thrown his father to the wolves in an attempt to salvage his own party standing, he added, "The Party is dearer and higher to me than anything." The party committee voted to remove Malyshev from his post as deputy secretary "for concealing that his cousin was excluded as a Trotskyist," but to allow him to remain in the Party. An investigation was meanwhile to be undertaken of his father and his ties to Sidkov.[46]

Five days later, Malyshev's case came up again in a factory-wide meeting attended by more than five hundred party members. These larger assemblies, dominated by the most aggressive speakers, often voted to mete out harsher punishments than the party committees handed down. The rank and file tended to be more rabid than their leaders, and their participation was apt to produce a worse outcome for those subjected to their judgment. On this occasion, the

---

46 TsAOPIM, f. 429, o. 1, d. 223, l. 42. Golfo Alexopoulos has found that disenfranchised citizens used similar strategies in petitions to state authorities, including denouncing others to play up their own innocence. See "Victim Talk: Defense Testimony and Denunciation under Stalin," *Law and Social Inquiry*, vol. 24, no. 3 (Summer 1999), p. 640.

factory-wide meeting heard the same facts but overturned the party committee's earlier decision, voting to exclude Malyshev from the Party. In October, this second ruling was affirmed by Malyshev's shop organization. In November, the party committee held another meeting on the case to review fresh material uncovered by its investigation. The latest information indicated that Malyshev's uncle, the director of a porcelain factory, had also been arrested. Once again, Malyshev recited his story to the group. This time he offered a new excuse for his delay in reporting his cousin's exclusion from the Party and his dismissal from the paint factory: "I wondered why my father had been removed from his job in 1929 and whether he had some tie to Sidkov. I wanted to research these things. This is why I delayed telling the Party about Sidkov." Malyshev also disavowed any connection between himself and his uncle: "I had no tie to him," he stated. "He is not my blood uncle, but the husband of the sister of my stepmother. I last saw him in 1930." Malyshev had taken a gamble in attempting to implicate his father in order to save his own skin. As it happened, the investigation had turned up a fact that saved them both: his father had been fired in 1929 for incompetence, not "right deviationism." In 1937, the former, unlike the latter, was not a crime. The party committee, perhaps influenced by Malyshev's display of "loyalty," voted to countermand his exclusion and to give him a strict reprimand and warning instead.[47]

A FAMILY TORN APART

From our vantage point, Malyshev's behavior may seem shocking, but at the time, it was not unusual. Many party members

47 TsAOPIM, f. 429, o. 1, d. 223, l. 86.

sought to disengage themselves from tainted relatives, particularly if relations between them were already strained. People's reactions to such situations varied widely, and sometimes members of the same family might fight bitterly over how to respond. One family connected to Serp i Molot was destroyed by the party "loyalty" of one of its members. Three family members worked in the factory: German Pereversev, a metal turner in the casting shop; his sister Pereverseva; and her husband, Kachurin, an instructor in the education department. Pereversev and his sister had an aunt and uncle who in the 1920s had belonged to an anarchist organization named the Black Cross. In 1925, their uncle was arrested. In 1927, Pereversev moved with his aunt to Moscow, where he found work at Serp i Molot and joined the Party. In 1928, his brother was exiled for Trotskyism, and soon after that, his sister married Kachurin. Pereversev, Pereverseva, and Kachurin were now all party members working in Serp i Molot. During a routine purge in 1933, Pereversev was excluded from the Party for concealing that his brother was a Trotskyist, but he was reinstated after proving that he had in fact disclosed this information. In the review and exchange of party documents undertaken in 1935–36, however, Pereversev neglected to mention his Trotskyist brother. Like many other party members, he assumed that he had neutralized this unpleasant biographical detail by revealing it once. After passing the review, he believed – or at least hoped – that was all behind him. Then, in February 1937, his aunt was arrested.

After the arrest, the aunt's nineteen-year-old daughter turned for help to Pereversev's kindhearted sister, Pereverseva, and Kachurin, her husband. The girl appeared on their doorstep in a panic after the NKVD took her mother away; unable to find work because of her mother's arrest, she was hungry and penniless. Pereverseva, distressed by her cousin's plight, gave her some money. After the girl left, the couple got into a heated argument over whether or not they should have aided the daughter of an "enemy."

Kachurin, eager to dissociate himself from his wife and her relations, would later testify that he had strongly objected to Pereverseva's helping her cousin: "I sharply reprimanded my wife and told her not to do this. We fought. She quoted Stalin that children should not answer for their parents. I told her straight out that I was leaving her, and in February, I did. I live alone now." After he left, the marriage ended. Kachurin then promptly wrote a *zaiavlenie* to his shop organization describing his wife's aid to her cousin, her aunt's arrest, and his own political doubts about the whole Pereversev family.

In August 1937, German Pereversev was excluded by his shop organization for his "ties to and participation in a counterrevolutionary Trotskyist organization." The charge of "participation" was far more serious than that of having a mere "tie." The party committee took up his case in September, citing the fact that he had failed to mention his Trotskyist brother in the 1935 review as well as the subsequent arrest of his aunt. There was additional evidence against him in the form of the *zaiavlenie* submitted by Kachurin, his brother-in-law, denouncing the entire family. The committee affirmed the shop organization's decision to exclude Pereversev and charged him with "concealing his tie to his counterrevolutionary aunt."[48] Later that fall, Pereversev followed his aunt into prison. Still, the family's problems were far from over.

In January 1938, Kachurin himself fell victim to his association with the Pereversev family. The party committee now charged that he had failed to inform his party organization that "his wife had helped a class enemy, and that his brother-in-law [Pereversev] had

48 TsAOPIM, f. 429, o. 1, d. 223, ll. 52–53.

been excluded from the Party." By 1938, the local party organizations had lost whatever tolerance they might once have had for members with politically suspect relatives. Kachurin defended himself vigorously, claiming that though he had been married to Pereverseva since 1930, he had had no contact with the rest of her family "for years." He had fought with her over aiding her young cousin, he said, and he had been completely honest with the party committee. "I deny giving any help to this girl," he insisted. "I have hidden nothing from the party organization. I repeated what I knew. I broke off relations with my wife and her relatives because they were an insufficiently Soviet family. I myself am the son of a worker and a peasant." Kachurin added that he had explained everything in the *zaiavlenie* that he had submitted to his party organization many months before, just after his wife's young cousin turned up at their door. He blamed Egorov, a member of the party committee, for not having brought his *zaiavlenie* to the immediate attention of the group.

Kachurin's comrades made little effort to distinguish rumor from fact, or even to acquaint themselves with the key elements of the case. Egorov, for his part, was furious at being dragged into the mess and tried to discredit Kachurin: "The masses and individual members of the Party say he was a poor teacher," Egorov declared. "The *zaiavlenie* should have been submitted earlier. Exclude him!" Another comrade accused him of boring the workers in his classes. "He's not effective," he said. "The workers sleep through his class with their heads on one another's shoulders." But more important, he argued, was that Kachurin "has not been honest." With these words, reason was flung to the wind, and the meeting became a free-for-all of unsubstantiated charges. No one was called to account for even the most foolish utterance. Another party member suggested with righteous illogic, "He had a tie to an anarchist organization, and even if he was not active in this organization, he helped it." The modest sum of ten rubles that Kachurin's wife had slipped to her hungry cousin was now recast as "aid to the class enemy." In the end, Kachurin was expelled. He made a final plea to keep his party card: "The Party brought me up," he said. "I am guilty for my connection with Pereverseva, but I am happy that I separated from her."[49]

In her memoir of expulsion, arrest, and exile to the camps, Eugenia Ginzburg wrote, "Some actors in the horror play had been cast as victims, some as persecutors, and these were the worse off. At least my conscience was clear."[50] Ginzburg was expelled and arrested relatively early on in the terror; by 1938, no one who remained could lay a similar claim to having a completely clear conscience. Everyone had participated in some form of persecution. Some did so eagerly, others reluctantly, but none had the option of not taking part. In all likelihood, the *zaiavlenie* that Kachurin wrote in February 1937, which reported the exile of Pereversev's Trotskyist brother, the arrest of his aunt, and his sister's aid to their young cousin, contributed to Pereversev's exclusion and arrest later that year. The *zaiavlenie* brought all of these family connections to the attention of Serp i Molot's party officials, who followed procedure and forwarded it to the district committee and the NKVD. By submitting the letter, Kachurin proved that he was a "loyal" member of the Party, willing to denounce his brother-in-law, turn away a cousin, abandon his wife, and blame his comrades, all in the name of politics. Yet despite his efforts, he was excluded from the Party and fired from

49 TsAOPIM, f. 429, o. 1, d. 261, ll. 6–15.
50 Eugenia Semenovna Ginzburg, *Journey into the Whirlwind* (New York: Harcourt Brace Jovanovich, 1967), pp. 40–41.

his job. Separated from his wife, loathed by her family for his role in their troubles, he was left alone to ponder his predicament as both persecutor and victim.

CONCLUSION

The state launched assaults on former leftists, rightists, clergy, aristocrats, and kulaks as well as people of particular national origins, yet the members of each one of these targeted groups were bound to others outside the group by bonds of marriage and kinship. Party leaders sought to isolate "enemies" from loyal citizens, but the terror reached well beyond the intended victims, blighting the lives of even those ordinary people and faithful party members who were not otherwise at risk of being arrested. The mass and national operations, aimed at specific populations, revealed that an unexpected number of loyal party members had hidden ties to individuals who were regarded as "enemies" by the state. The family unit linked kulaks with workers, Latvians with Russians, and oppositionists with Stalin's staunchest supporters. Viewed through the lens of the family, the terror cannot be construed solely as a series of targeted strikes against particular victim groups. Rather, it emerges as a far broader and more diffuse phenomenon affecting those with and without specific risk factors. Russia's tumultuous history of opposition, collectivization, and immigration found a reflection in every family, creating intimate ties that led the NKVD from "enemy" to friend.

The Party treated those it deemed to be "enemies" as if they were carriers of a dangerous and highly contagious disease requiring strict quarantine. Party members were warned to shun arrested relatives and their immediate families. Political victims, like people with visible marks of the plague on their bodies, were to be assiduously avoided. A party member who had contact with an enemy was to be isolated and expelled. Yet many party members had "infected" relatives. Sheinin's extended family was arrested for Trotskyism, Shtrul's brothers for their Latvian origins and Trotskyism, and Pavlov's brother-in-law for being a kulak. The list went on and on.

Were family bonds strengthened or weakened by the terror?[51] Without question, it forced family members to consider these bonds in ways that few have to do under normal conditions. Loyalty to family was generally stronger than that to friends or coworkers, but it did not always supersede fear of or loyalty to the Party, or even political or professional ambition. When forced to choose, people responded in different ways. Many tried to commingle their loyalties to Party and to family through acts of omission intended to preserve both political and social relationships. They employed modest stratagems to protect their party standing. A surprising number actually lied in the review and exchange of party documents by purging their biographies of incriminating relatives. At the same time, many maintained secret contact with family members who were in prison or in exile. They postponed submitting declarations about the arrests or expulsions of their relatives, gambling that their comrades would never connect them with the names of the victims. Like army officers who failed to report a retreat to central headquarters in expectation of recapturing lost territory, party members delayed writing *zaiavleniia* in the hope that word of the arrest would not get out, or that the relative would somehow be reinstated in the

51 Sheila Fitzpatrick, "Signals from Below: Soviet Letters of Denunciation of the 1930s," *Journal of Modern History*, vol. 68, no. 4 (December 1996), p. 849. Fitzpatrick poses this question and suggests that "family bonds in Russia were strengthened, not weakened by Soviet Terror."

Party. During World War II, Red Army officers would be harshly disciplined for the military version of this tactic, and in the years preceding, party members fared no better when they tried its political equivalent. This choice – or rather, this *refusal* to choose – seemed to be the most common strategy among party members facing such dilemmas. Through small deceptions, party members attempted to put off decisions that they found impossible to make.

Some people – not very many – refused to disavow human ties for politics. They did not try to reconcile their actions with party loyalty or justify them politically. They acted out of simple human feeling. Most of those who helped arrested or exiled family members did so in secret. Efimova flouted party rules and aided her daughter, undertaking a long, hard journey to rescue her grandchildren from an NKVD orphanage. Gringauz got his brother-in-law a job in his own factory after he was expelled from the Party and lost his job. Pereverseva gave money to her cousin. Sheinin sent food and supplies to his relatives in exile. All of these people acted quietly and concealed their activities from the authorities. They decided where their real loyalties ought to lie, but for fear of the consequences, they did not make those decisions public. When their behavior came to the attention of their comrades, they invariably got into trouble. The party organizations did not countenance its members rendering aid to "the enemy."

In a bare handful of cases, people did make their choices public by standing up for their arrested relatives. Torbeeva put politics aside and spoke out on behalf of her husband, the alleged "Trotskyist" who had encouraged her to study and fathered her children. Yet such unrepentant public avowals were unusual. Very few party members or other citizens publicly admitted to or defended giving aid to relatives who had been excluded, imprisoned, or exiled.

Party members in particular understood the Party's prohibition on helping the "enemy" and recognized the impossibility of mounting a defense based on emotional family ties. Attempting to defend aiding a politically tainted relation would be tantamount to challenging the entire logic of the terror – and in particular, questioning whether the victims were in fact dangerous enemies. No party member, and no citizen, could pose this question openly without risking arrest. Everyone, no matter what his or her level of political sophistication, knew that much.

Some people chose to jettison family. The political pressures were great enough, in such cases, to deform even the most intimate of ties. Whether out of fear, moral cowardice, or a true belief in the Party's rules, these individuals disavowed their relatives and tried to save themselves. Bykhovskaia denounced both her first and second husbands in an attempt to forestall her own expulsion. Her marital loyalties evaporated under the heat of questioning. Kachurin left his wife and renounced, then denounced, her whole family. His denunciation in all likelihood resulted in the investigation and eventual arrest of his brother-in-law. Malyshev suggested that his father was a "rightist" and blamed him for his own failure to submit a timely *zaiavlenie* about the arrest of his cousin. His testimony launched an investigation of his father's background and political history. All of these people disregarded familial ties and placed others in danger. They chose the Party over family.

People thus exhibited a wide range of behaviors toward family members. Moreover, depending on the specific circumstances and the particular relationship involved, the same person might act very differently in different situations – behaving nobly in one instance, perhaps, and despicably in another. Sheinin, for example, secretly aided his relatives in exile even as he denounced a coworker in his factory. No one's actions were either wholly selfless or entirely self-interested. People were repeatedly forced to make painful choices; sometimes they chose personal ties over political duty, and often they chose the converse. Very few were exempted from having to choose at all.

Within the factories, the party organizations that adjudicated cases did not determine their outcomes in advance. Shops organizations, party committees, and factory-wide meetings frequently arrived at differing decisions in the same case. Furthermore, the votes within any one meeting were often split, a sign that members were able to vote according to their individual inclinations. Those accused would usually prepare carefully for such meetings, indicating at least some belief that the outcome could be influenced by their presentation. Interrogations proceeded according to a basic script: party members focused on social origins, "enemy" contacts, associational ties, and previous political positions. The defense also followed set lines, with the accused inevitably downplaying or denying contact with "enemy" relatives, pleading ignorance, blaming others, and naming names. As a general rule, close-mouthed party members minimized damage to others, while nervous babblers tended to implicate larger circles of people. On occasion, however, those who aggressively named names and threatened to bring down others did succeed in saving themselves. Women were apt to receive lighter punishments than men; party committees considered them more "backward" politically, thus less responsible for their own actions. People who got into trouble early in 1937 had a better chance of escaping expulsion than those who were accused later, when the atmosphere of every meeting bore traces of complicated vendettas and previous exclusions. Yet each case was also unique. Unexpected information might spill out, counteraccusations could send the line of questioning spinning in unforeseen directions, and group dynamics were always unpredictable. The process was neither fully logical nor consistent, and similar offenses often resulted in different outcomes. Bykhovskaia, for example, merely received a reprimand despite her successive marriages to two "enemies of the people," whereas Kachurin was excluded even though he left his wife and wrote a *zaiavlenie* against her family. Shtrul was excluded for his ties to his two arrested brothers, but Malyshev was only reprimanded for his connection to his "enemy" cousin. The outcomes varied enough that no party member could ever feel entirely safe.

What role did fear play in this process? And fear of whom? Did party members genuinely believe that masked enemies lurked in their ranks? Or did they fear the NKVD and the leaders who urged them to expose such enemies? Fear and belief were intertwined throughout the great terror. The process of "unmasking" was initiated by the central authorities and enforced through heavy pressure on the party committees. Many people were originally persuaded that real enemies threatened Soviet security. A potent mixture of truth, half truth, and lies, widely disseminated by newspapers, discussion circles, and party leaders, had considerable popular support. People's fears were thus first created and then shaped by their faith in the Party and its message. They wrote numerous *zaiavleniia*, reporting rumors, nonsense, and transgressions both large and small. Even at moments when everyone might have remained silent at no cost, a voice from the floor would invariably shout, "The punishment is too lenient!" or "Exclude!"

Yet as the arrests multiplied, it became harder for many to maintain the belief that all of those arrested were enemies. The closer the terror came, the stronger their doubts grew. Each individual confronted the transition from belief to fear in his or her own time.

Some never questioned the state's claim that spies and enemies were hidden everywhere; others were assailed by uncertainty after a trusted friend or relative was expelled or arrested; and still others were privately shaken by the state's actions soon after the Kirov murder. Many party members who had devoted their lives to the revolutionary cause could not comprehend that the Party might sanction the arrests of innocent people. At the same time, they were skeptical that close relatives or friends were truly "enemies." They could not reconcile the state's judgment with their personal experience.[52] The clash between these two firmly held yet contradictory beliefs caused great mental suffering and conflicting behavior. Painfully aware that an arrest in the family would have terrible consequences for everyone involved, party members agonized over whether to reveal compromising information or remain silent. Lies of omission and other stratagems of evasion were clear indicators of doubt in the existence of a genuine enemy threat. In meetings, party members well understood that *all* were vulnerable to investigation and attack. And if no one was immune, then who in fact was "the enemy"? The line between loyal comrade and "enemy of the people," drawn in invisible ink, became apparent only when an arrest was made.

Belief and fear were thus inversely linked: so long as people believed the state's version of events, they felt little personal fear.

52 The inability to square personal knowledge with the state's proclamations was later expressed by a joke that became popular in the more lighthearted Brezhnev era. A man goes to a doctor and says, "Doctor, I need to see a specialist." "What kind of specialist do you need?" the doctor asks. "I need somebody who treats eyes and ears." "Well, we have a specialist for eyes and a specialist for ears," the doctor replies, "but no one who treats both." "No," the man insists, "I have to see someone who treats both." "Why?" the doctor asks. "Because," the man answers, "what my eyes see and what my ears hear are two very different things."

After all, they were loyal party members, not terrorists. Yet as ordinary citizens became ever more frightened for their families and their own personal security, their trust in the state wavered. Of course, no one dared to voice such doubts publicly; everyone continued to play by the iron rules of the game. Party members, fearful of exposure, sought to cover their own weaknesses by zealously revealing others' faults. And they knew their zeal would stand them in good stead. Bykhovskaia, for instance, was helped in her interrogation by her prior denunciations of others. People's outward actions, no matter what their private beliefs might be, helped to fuel and spread the terror. The accusations and counteraccusations at party meetings, the intensifying witch hunts in the workplace, the growing mistrust among comrades – all of these made it difficult to accept the Party's insistence on "real enemies." Party members lived in constant dread that some "enemy" tie, ideological mistake, or suspect relative of theirs might be discovered. Everyone was a secret sinner in a group bent on revealing sin. Many of the first perpetrators of the purge became victims of the very processes they had promulgated, and local party organizations devoured themselves. Paradoxically, the more "masked enemies" party members exposed, the less faith they had in the victims' real guilt. In this sense, the collective political atmosphere took on a profoundly schizophrenic quality: the more frenzied the outward behavior of the group, the greater the internal doubts of its individual members.

4: Love, Loyalty, and Betrayal

THE EARLY-MORNING SKY WAS AS BROWN AS THE SNOW blanketing the yards of Moscow's leading steel factory, Serp i Molot. Ash from the tall, belching smokestacks mingled with snowflakes and fell steadily over the thousands of workers who streamed through the front gates. The factory, with its sprawling array of redbrick and wooden buildings, blast furnaces, rolling mills, outlying yards, and loading docks, along with its spur railroad, covered dozens of square blocks within the southeastern section of the city. Pushing past the jostling crowd of sleepy workers, Aleksandr Somov made his way briskly through the dark yards and into the factory. He passed a group of workers from the open hearth furnace, one of the most dangerous shops. Their dirty padded jackets, pocked with burn holes, bore mute witness to the wild sparks produced by the furnace, in which steel was smelted and poured. As head of Serp i Molot's party committee in early March 1937, Somov knew hundreds of the factory's employees, from the workers of the open hearth up to the director himself.

As Somov strode into the office of the party committee, his mind was filled with the business of the day ahead. The small room was crowded with shop organizers smoking and chatting by the desks.

Young Communists were picking up stacks of the factory's daily newspaper, *Martenovka*, more than four thousand copies of which were to be distributed to the shops. For months, the paper had been denouncing shop heads, party officials, and factory administrators for a variety of abuses, under headlines such as "Not a Single Accident Should Pass Unnoticed!"[1] The head of the cold rolling mill, a party member, had recently been exposed as a "wrecker" and stood accused of having deliberately poisoned workers in a chemical accident. Somov, as leader of the large Communist contingent in a factory with some ten thousand employees, had his hands full. Abruptly, even rudely, he cleared the room, barking orders to the smokers and idlers, dispatching people to the shops.

Loyal, energetic, and unburdened by family commitments, Somov was thirty-one years old when the terror reached its fever pitch in 1937. He had impeccable working-class credentials: his father had worked in Serp i Molot for forty years, and at the age of eighteen, in 1925, Somov had followed him into the factory, where he was assigned to the open hearth furnace. Somov was proud of his family background. Born in 1906, he was not old enough to participate in the 1917 revolution, but like so many of his generation, he saw his future in the dreams and plans of the Party, and he enthusiastically joined the Komsomol, its youth organization. In 1928, he was called up into the Red Army. During his two years of service, which he spent fighting bandit groups in the Caucasus, he became a candidate member of the Party. On his return to Serp i Molot, he entered the Party, leaving behind his hot, perilous job in the open hearth furnace for a more comfortable position as a

1 "Ni Odna Avariia ne Dolzhna Proiti Nezamesennoi," *Martenovka*, February 27, 1937, p. 1.

party organizer. He had only a third-grade education, so the Party sent him to school. By early 1937, he had reached the pinnacle of the factory's party organization: as the elected head of the party committee, he oversaw a governing body of about forty people, representing Serp i Molot's seven hundred party members. He also held several other posts, simultaneously serving as party organizer in the open hearth furnace; head of the "special department," which dealt with sensitive personnel and political matters within the factory; and instructor for the district party committee. A worker and the son of a worker, he now stood at the helm of the leading political organization in a flagship iron and steel plant, in the midst of a great national drive to develop heavy industry. He was in every way a golden child of the revolution, perfectly poised to go on to further successes.

Less than a year later, however, Somov's career would lie in ruins. He had been expelled from the Party, fired from his job as head of the special department, and dismissed from his posts as district instructor and shop organizer. The accusations leveled against him centered on his relationship with a pretty comrade named Esfir Z. Krivitskaia, a dedicated Communist who had fled her native Poland to seek refuge in the Soviet Union. Denounced by Mariia F. Zhidkova, a friend and fellow party member, Krivitskaia had been arrested in the national operations launched in the summer of 1937. Imprisoned in a stinking cell and interrogated repeatedly throughout the fall, she finally confessed to having an intimate relationship with Somov. In a series of grueling meetings, Somov was subjected to endless questions about his ties to the "Polish spy." He adamantly maintained that he had no personal relationship with Krivitskaia. His fellow party members, convinced that he was concealing information, wanted to uncover "the truth." Intent on establishing total honesty, his comrades had abandoned factory organizing in favor of inquisitorial practices aimed at baring the soul.[2] The "truth," though, remained elusive, hovering somewhere in the gaps among Zhidkova's denunciation, Krivitskaia's coerced confession, and Somov's desperate desire to salvage his career. The golden child had become collateral damage in the Polish operation. Once a living symbol of the "pure proletarian" celebrated by the state, he was now little more than a degraded casualty of its attempt to police the line between its heroic workers and its alleged enemies.

MARIIA ZHIDKOVA, A TRUE BELIEVER

In early 1937, Serp i Molot, like every other workplace in the Soviet Union, was a hive of political unease, humming with rumors and denunciations. Some employees were nervously guarding family secrets, others were writing *zaiavleniia* to expose their comrades, and many more were doing both. Zhidkova, a loyal, even fanatical member of the party committee, worked in the Party's education center (*Uchebnyi Partiinyi Kabinet*, or *partkabinet*), organizing political study groups for workers and party members. Born into a revolutionary family, she had initially welcomed the search for enemies as an opportunity to rectify what she perceived to be the insufficient loyalty of others. Zhidkova prided herself on her honor, her commitment to the Party, and her family's sacrifices for the revolution.

---

2 On inquisitorial practices in the 1920s and 1930s, see Igal Halfin, *Intimate Enemies: Demonizing the Bolshevik Opposition, 1918–1928* (Pittsburgh: University of Pittsburgh Press, 2007), and *Stalinist Confessions: Messianism and Terror at the Leningrad Communist University* (Pittsburgh: University of Pittsburgh Press, 2009).

Her two older brothers had fought in the Civil War, and one had died in the struggle for Soviet power. Zhidkova, a young girl at the time, had grown up worshiping them both. She was committed to the ideals of socialism: equality, internationalism, and economic justice. Her one brother had made the ultimate sacrifice for these ideals, and she believed that all party members should be willing to do the same. Loyalty to the Party must come above all else, guiding a member's behavior toward friends, family, and loved ones. Zhidkova had no qualms about writing to the NKVD to denounce those she considered "suspicious" in thought, behavior, or attitude. The NKVD, final arbiter of truth, would sort out the information it received. A *zaiavlenie* could only help it to do its proper job.

In January 1937, Zhidkova denounced David Sagaidak, head of Serp i Molot's cold rolling mill, for an alleged theoretical "error" he had made in answering a question in a study circle. Zhidkova, who observed the lesson as part of her job in the Party's education center, carefully noted Sagaidak's response at the time. Less than two weeks later, she penned a long article in the factory newspaper about his mistake.[3] Sagaidak, like many shop heads and managers, was also the target of other denunciations, including a long, incoherent accusation by a woman worker affronted by his "rudeness" (see chapter 1). He publicly apologized for his error, but the accusations soon led to charges of "wrecking," triggering an investigation that occupied the party committee for months. In February, the factory newspaper called for Sagaidak to be "unmasked" and made reference to a series of accidents in the mill.[4] In March, party members in the

3 M. Zhidkova, "Oshibki Propagandista Sagaidaka," *Martenovka*, January 22, 1937, p. 1.
4 D. Sagaidak, "Oshibki Propagandista Sagaidaka," *Martenovka*, February 2, 1937, p. 2, "Na-ruku Vragu," *Martenovka*, February 28, 1937, p. 3.

cold rolling mill held a marathon meeting, lasting eleven hours, to hear the charges against him. By the end of that month, he had been excluded from the Party and arrested.[5]

Following the common pattern, Sagaidak's arrest led to the expulsion from the Party of others who were close to him. Dorozhin and Rovnov, coworkers in the cold rolling mill, made the grave mistake of going to see their former boss at home after he was expelled. Sagaidak, fearfully awaiting arrest, welcomed these sympathetic visitors who brought the latest news from the mill. Shortly thereafter, both men, accused of being "splinters of Sagaidakovshchina," were excluded for visiting an "enemy."[6] Fallout from the actions against Sagaidak would continue to affect the factory for months. Articles in the factory newspaper, *Martenovka*, sharply criticized P. F. Stepanov, the director; Rodzevich, the technical director; L. V. Marmorshtein, the head engineer; Tarantul, a foreman in the cold rolling mill; Kosilov, head of the factory's Ferrous Metallurgical Union; and Mikhailov, a labor inspector, for overlooking "the mess in the chemical baths" in the cold rolling mill, along with the poor ventilation system. According to *Martenovka*'s editor, workers were frequent victims of chemical accidents and inadequate ventilation, but their shop heads blithely ignored their complaints. The paper

5 On the Sagaidak case, see the following articles in *Martenovka*: "Kak Proiskhodiat Avarii v Kholodnom Prokate," February 27, 1937, p. 2; "Pod Vidom 'Opytnoi' Produktsii," March 1, 1937, p. 1; "Segodnia – Partiinoe Sobranie v Tsekhe Kholodnogo Prokata," March 3, 1937, p. 1; "Fakty i Vyvody," March 5, 1937, p. 2; "S Partiinogo Sobraniia v Tsekhe Kholodnogo Prokata," March 6, 1937, p. 1; "Glavnyi Inzhener Zavoda Tov. Marmorshtein v Neblagovidnom Roli Advokata," March 17, 1937, p. 3; "Uroki Dela Sagaidaka" and "Kak Sagaidak Orudoval v Tsekhe Kholodnogo Prokata," March 20, 1937, pp. 1, 2. Tsentral'nyi Arkhiv Obshchestvenno-Politicheskoi Istorii Moskvy (TsAOPIM), f. 429, o. 1, d. 269, ll. 1–68.

6 "Posobniki Vraga Iskliucheny iz Partii" and "O Chem Rasskazal Dokladchik," *Martenovka*, May 26 and August 10, 1937, pp. 2, 2.

accused the engineering and technical personnel of "overlooking" Sagaidak's "wrecking" through their refusal to engage in "criticism and self-criticism." Marmorshtein and Stepanov were also assailed for encouraging the shop bosses in their "vulgar cursing" and disrespectful attitudes toward the workers. Frightened by the attacks, several of the accused wrote long articles of their own, attempting to defend their reputations and shift the blame.[7] Their responses in turn implicated others and widened the scope of the case against Sagaidak. Zhidkova was not solely responsible for the latter's arrest and its repercussions within the party organization in Serp i Molot, but her assiduous public prosecution of his "theoretical error" added significantly to his troubles, and her accusations figured prominently in his expulsion.

MARIIA ZHIDKOVA AND ESFIR KRIVITSKAIA: COWORKERS AND FRIENDS

While the party organization was dealing with the Sagaidak case, many party members were secretly struggling with personal problems caused by the growing number of arrests. Krivitskaia, like many Polish Communists in the Soviet Union, had fled her native land to escape political persecution. She settled in Moscow, married a fellow Communist named Evdokimov, and took a job in Serp i Molot. In 1934, at the age of twenty-seven, she joined the party organization in the factory and soon became friendly with some of

---

7 "Glavnyi Inzhener Zavoda Tov. Marmorshtein v Neblagovidnom Roli Advokata," "Chuvstvoval, Chto v Nos Udariaet," "Naporistosti My Ne Proiavliali," and "Sredstv Net, Razorbite Menia," *Martenovka*, March 17 1937, p. 3; "Po Povodu Stat'i Tov. Rodzevicha," *Martenovka*, March 18, 1937, p. 2; "Uroki Dela Sagaidaka" and "Kak Sagaidak Orudoval v Tsekhe Kholodnogo Prokata," *Martenovka*, March 20, 1937, pp. 1, 2.

its leading members, including Zhidkova and Somov. She worked in the Party's education center as a political instructor and assistant to Zhidkova and also held several other posts in the factory. At the end of 1934, Krivitskaia and Evdokimov hosted a New Year's Eve celebration to which they invited Somov; Izotov, head of the party organization in the cutting foundry; Zhidkova and her husband; and several of Evdokimov's coworkers from the administration of the Party's Central Committee.[8] Kirov's assassination, which had occurred on December 1, cast a shadow over the merriment. Yet as the guests raised their glasses in a toast to Stalin, the Party, and the New Year, none could have imagined that this small, innocent gathering would eventually become the focus of a relentless party investigation.

Over the next two years, Krivitskaia and Somov grew closer as Krivitskaia's marriage began to crumble. Other party members noted that she seemed fond of Somov and frequently called him "Sasha," or "Sashenka," both tender Russian diminutives of his given name, Aleksandr. He presented her with a watch, a valuable gift, after she had problems getting to work on time. She often stopped by the open hearth furnace, where Somov worked as an organizer, to visit him. A member of the shop later said, "We began to joke that something made her stop by here very often." She confided her feelings for Somov to Zhidkova. The two women saw each other regularly in the education center, and Krivitskaia felt close enough to Zhidkova to speak with her about her personal life.[9]

In early 1937, Krivitskaia got into political trouble. Evdokimov, her husband, came under investigation by his party organization

8 TsAOPIM, f. 429, o. 1, d. 223, l. 101.
9 TsAOPIM, f. 429, o. 1, d. 261, ll. 35–36, 30.

after it was discovered that he had concealed information about his brothers: one had been previously arrested as a kulak, and the other had fled abroad. The party committee expelled Evdokimov, leaving Krivitskaia with a painful choice: she could stand by her husband, thus guaranteeing that she, too, would be expelled for supporting "an enemy," or she could disavow him. The marriage, already shaky, collapsed under the weight of Evdokimov's political difficulties. Krivitskaia left him. At this point, a party official in Serp i Molot suggested to her that she write a *zaiavlenie* about her husband, explaining their relationship and his expulsion. After she submitted the *zaiavlenie*, the party committee, uneasy about keeping her on in the factory, asked her to leave. She resigned in good standing and took a new job as an informer (*informator*) with the Taganskii district party committee. Among her duties in that post was gathering information on workers' attitudes, prices in shops, and other matters of political interest to the district party organization. Many informers also doubled as instructors and reported on individuals in their study circles, making particular note of the name and shop of anyone whose comments were deemed anti-Party or anti-Soviet.[10] For many months after leaving her position in Serp i Molot, Krivitskaia continued to visit the factory and even led a study circle in the sheet rolling shop.[11]

Around the same time that Krivitskaia's husband was expelled from the Party, Zhidkova learned that her beloved older brother had suffered a similar fate. Dmitri Zhidkov, second secretary of a

10 The Moscow city party committee, for example, requested reports from instructor informers on how workers were responding to the first Moscow show trial, in August 1936. The reports, which included both positive and negative comments, were signed with the title "instructor/informer" and the individuals' names. See TsAOPIM, f. 3, o. 49, d. 129.

11 TsAOPIM, f. 429, o. 1, d. 261, ll. 24, 39; f. 429, o. 1, d. 223, l. 102.

Moscow district party committee, was excluded for "double dealing" (*dvurushnichestvo*). Zhidkova was deeply shaken by this news. She had idolized Dmitri since she was a young girl. Active in early struggles against the autocracy, repeatedly imprisoned, and a hero in the Civil War, he had embodied for her the sacrificial ideals and romance of the revolution. Convinced that his expulsion was a hideous mistake that would soon be rectified through the process of appeal, she nevertheless struggled to reconcile her divided loyalties to her brother and the Party. Whereas once her family feelings had reinforced her commitment to the Party, and vice versa, she was now forced to choose one or the other. Zhidkova managed to maintain her mental equilibrium, but the strain had a powerful and peculiar effect on her behavior.[12]

In February, Zhidkova heard what had happened to Krivitskaia's husband. Whether Krivitskaia told her personally or she found out as a member of the party committee is unclear. In any case, Krivitskaia's situation clearly paralleled her own: both young women were having to cope with the expulsion of men who were close to them. Yet Zhidkova did not comfort or support her friend, nor did she share with her the news about her brother. Zhidkova kept Dmitri's expulsion a closely guarded secret, never mentioning it to anyone in the party organization. Instead, she wrote a denunciation of Krivitskaia to the NKVD. Eager to do what she perceived to be her revolutionary duty, Zhidkova marched with her *zaiavlenie* directly to the Lubianka, the menacing, yellow-brick NKVD headquarters and prison covering a full city block in the center of Moscow. She made a copy for the district NKVD. In her letter, Zhidkova did not accuse Krivitskaia of specific wrongdoing; rather, she cast vague

12 TsAOPIM, f. 429, o. 1, d. 223, ll. 138–41.

aspersions on her character, noting, for example, "She was conde-scending toward the workers; she was insincere."[13]

Amid the jumble of allegations, one stood out and commanded the attention of NKVD officials: Zhidkova claimed that Krivitskaia was romantically involved with Somov. This allegation would have had less impact if Somov were not so highly placed, but the possibil-ity that the head of Serp i Molot's party committee was having an affair with a foreigner – and a foreigner, moreover, married to a man who had recently been expelled from the Party – gave Zhidkova's *zaiavlenie* some weight. The NKVD official who reviewed it decided that Somov's ties were a matter for the Party to consider, and he forwarded it to the offices of the party committee for the Taganskii district, in which Serp i Molot was located. There the *zaiavlenie* landed on the desk of an official named Fedotov, who read it and then promptly took it upon himself to write another *zaiavlenie* to his superiors in the Moscow party committee, stating that Somov was personally involved with Krivitskaia.[14] Zhidkova's allegations had now left a slimy trail through several organizations: the district and central offices of the NKVD and the district and city party committees.

What had motivated Zhidkova to denounce Krivitskaia, her friend and comrade? Like many others who wrote *zaiavleniia* to pro-tect themselves or to preempt accusations, she may have been seek-ing to distance herself from her subject: as Krivitskaia's supervisor, she may have feared that she would be damaged by her assistant's political troubles. Yet Zhidkova, who by all accounts had a humor-less and rigid personality, was also propelled by feelings other than

13 TsAOPIM, f. 429, o. 1, d. 223, l. 140.
14 TsAOPIM, f. 429, o. 1, d. 223, l. 101.

self-interest. Her brother's expulsion did not soften Zhidkova's judgmental approach to others; on the contrary, it seemed to amplify her severity. Zhidkova felt that Krivitskaia was too frivolous in her attitude toward others and the Party. She was disturbed by the evident ease with which Krivitskaia had jettisoned her husband after he was expelled. "I don't like the insincerity of Krivitskaia," she later explained. "When they excluded her husband from the Party, she very quickly decided to move to another apartment. She hurried to leave a person with whom she had lived for several years."[15] Although party members were required to disavow spouses or close relations who were excluded or arrested, Krivitskaia's seeming readiness to drop her husband, and her lack of interest in investigating the reasons for his expulsion, bothered her supervisor.

Yet why should Zhidkova care? She herself was still hiding the secret of her brother's exclusion. Her fierce attachment to him made it difficult for her to understand how anyone could so indifferently break off contact with a loved one. Zhidkova also disapproved of Krivitskaia's flippant attitude toward the growing number of arrests. She later told the party committee, "One time I asked Krivitskaia why Zabrodskii had been removed from his job. She replied, supposedly not knowing, 'How did they remove him? Did they take him away?'" Krivitskaia then told her, by way of explanation, that the man who had recommended Zabrodskii for party membership, V. Ia. Furer, had been arrested and shot. In fact, that was incorrect: Furer, a well-known party member who had organized the national propaganda campaign around Stakhanov, had actually killed himself at the end of 1936. In his suicide note, he wrote that he could no longer reconcile himself to the arrests and executions of innocent

15 TsAOPIM, f. 429, o. 1, d. 223, l. 140.

people. In December, Stalin dismissed Furer as an "oppositionist" who had used his own suicide to deceive the Party one last time.[16] Zabrodskii was in effect a victim of his mentor's death. Yet neither Krivitskaia nor Zhidkova knew the truth about how Furer died, and Krivitskaia, in referring to his supposed execution, was merely passing on the current rumor. According to Zhidkova, she then remarked airily, "Furer was clever, but Zabrodskii was a milksop." For Zhidkova, this was the last straw: irritated by Krivitskaia's trivial disregard for her former comrades, she resolved to take action. As she later explained, "I was very suspicious of her behavior. I decided to write about everything to the NKVD."[17]

Zhidkova, a model of revolutionary rectitude, was also, in her own way, a person of principle. She truly believed that the country was being threatened by spies and enemies and deemed it her revolutionary duty to inform the NKVD of any wrongdoing she happened to witness. The crisis in her own family, however, appeared to make her less rather than more sympathetic toward others. Shaken by her brother's expulsion, anxious about his future, she just could not understand her assistant's behavior. Krivitskaia's easygoing attitude toward her marriage and the grave issues of the day struck Zhidkova as being disrespectful of sacred ideals. Why was Krivitskaia not suffering as she was? The simple answer was that Krivitskaia did not love her husband in the same way that Zhidkova loved her brother. Evdokimov's expulsion did not threaten to shatter her world, as Dmitri's did his sister's. Yet Zhidkova came up with a different explanation: her assistant seemed insufficiently serious and lacking

16 On Furer, see Vadim Zakharovich Rogovin, *Stalin's Terror of 1937–1938: Political Genocide in the USSR* (Oak Park, Mich.: Mehring Books, 2009), p. 143.

17 TsAOPIM, f. 429, o. 1, d. 223, l. 140.

in vigilance because she was covering up "suspicious" behavior. In another era, Zhidkova might have been a wonderful comrade, steadfast in her loyalties and selfless in her willingness to sacrifice for others. In 1937, though, those same qualities turned her into a small juggernaut of terror. Fueled by righteous certainty, she helped ruin the lives of at least three comrades, Sagaidak, Krivitskaia, and Somov, as well as their respective circles of coworkers and friends.

ALEKSANDR SOMOV: BRINGING DOWN THE MIGHTY

In April, party members in factories and workplaces throughout the country cast their votes to elect new party committees. The elections were mandated by the Central Committee as part of its campaign for party democracy, launched at the February–March 1937 plenum. Breaking with past organizational practice, whereby the party committees had compiled lists of candidates for rote affirmation by the rank and file, the new elections featured genuine contests among contending candidates, voting by secret ballot, and a close review of every nominee by the membership. Party officials were required to hold "accounting" meetings in which they presented summaries of their activities, solicited criticism, and analyzed their failings. The common practice of appointing officials to elected positions (*kooptatsiia*) was to be abolished.

Rank-and-file party members greeted the elections and the campaign for party democracy with enthusiasm, taking the accounting meetings as opportunities to air their grievances with the outgoing leadership. Somov, as head of Serp i Molot's party committee, took a drubbing. In March, his fellow officials, keen to clear their own names, jumped aboard the democracy bandwagon and blamed him for "violations of party democracy" and "suppression of criticism."[18] In April, in a series of tumultuous meetings organized over three days, more than seven hundred party members gathered in a large auditorium to hear Somov's report on party activities in the factory and to discuss the 104 candidates on the ballot for the upcoming election to the party committee. Each candidate presented his or her biography and was closely evaluated by the rank and file. Party members spoke out angrily against Somov and Stepanov, the factory's director, both of whom were seeking reelection. They berated the two men for failing to address problems in the shops, including accidents, stoppages, and alleged wrecking. The outgoing party committee was assailed for "suppressing criticism," the fashionable slogan of the moment. When one shop head attempted to defend himself against this latter charge, members of the audience shouted him off the podium, yelling, "Tell about how you suppressed criticism!" and "Why don't you talk about the failings of the shop party organization?" The rank and file were clearly dissatisfied with Somov and his colleagues: "The party committee rarely visits the shops," one comrade complained, adding that its members only issued directives and provided no real help to rank-and-file organizers. Another declared, "There are lickspittles among us. . . . The party committee violates principles of party democracy." Although some party members may have done little more than mouth popular slogans, many others took the new democracy and election campaign seriously. When a visiting official from the district party committee spoke up in support of Stepanov's reelection, several party members angrily accused him of attempting to impose his candidacy from above, thereby infringing on their right to select their own

18 "V Partiinom Komitete Zavoda," *Martenovka*, March 20, 1937, p. 2.

candidates.[19] The district official, accustomed to deference, quickly retreated before the anger of the rank and file.

Although all the members of the party committee were subjected to harsh criticism, Somov, as their leader, was its main target. People were offended by his rudeness, highhandedness, and abusive manner. One party member noted, "Somov only curses and abuses the party organizers, he doesn't help them."[20] Some defended him, citing his energy, loyalty, and enthusiasm, but most of the speakers opposed adding his name to the list of candidates. Numerous party members stepped forward to relate anecdotes about his unpleasant conduct. In addition to his rude and threatening behavior, his lack of political education was singled out as a fault. When an instructor in a workers' study circle had asked him if he noticed any shortcomings in the lesson, Somov had allegedly replied, "The chair squeaked." The speaker concluded, "This answer sufficiently characterizes the level of leadership of Comrade Somov."[21]

Zhidkova, included on the list of candidates, also presented her biography to the rank and file. Once again she failed to disclose that her brother had been expelled from the Party. Zhidkova knew that deliberate concealment was grounds for expulsion, but still she kept her secret. Perhaps she was hoping that Dmitri would soon be reinstated, or perhaps she feared the effect that his expulsion would be sure to have on her candidacy. In any event, her secret failed to soften her political judgment of others, and she spoke out sharply against Somov. In the end, the weight of party opinion was against

19 "S Zavodskogo Partiinogo Sobraniia," *Martenovka*, March 30, 1937, p. 2; "S Zavodskogo Partiinogo Sobraniia," *Martenovka*, April 10, 12, and 15, 1937, p. 1.
20 "S Zavodskogo Partiinogo Sobraniia," *Martenovka*, March 30, 1937, p. 2; "S Zavodskogo Partiinogo Sobraniia," *Martenovka*, April 10, 1937, p. 1.
21 "S Zavodskogo Partiinogo Sobraniia," *Martenovka*, April 15, 1937, p. 1.

him, and his name was removed from the list. Zhidkova, meanwhile, was reelected to another term on the party committee.[22]

Somov was badly rattled by the three days of meetings and the many remarks directed against him. The accusations and malicious anecdotes hurt his pride and bruised his confidence. As was the case for many rising officials from humble backgrounds, Somov's real strengths consisted not in fine manners and intellectual sophistication but in loyalty, the willingness to work, and a deep dedication to the new Soviet system. He accepted the blame for the party committee's many shortcomings. Seeing that Somov had been stung by the criticism, Krivitskaia tried to comfort him. She remarked to Zhidkova at the time, "He is such a good man. I felt so bad for him. They say that he is arrogant, but they do not understand him, and you have to understand him."[23] Krivitskaia was obviously less enamored of the democracy campaign than she was of Somov, and her main concern was its effect on him. Both she and Zhidkova were agitated by hidden emotions during the party meeting, the one brimming with sympathy for the failed candidate, the other concealing her brother's arrest in the hope of winning her own bid for reelection.

NATIONAL OPERATIONS AND COLLATERAL DAMAGE

By the late spring of 1937, Somov, Krivitskaia, and Zhidkova had each been touched by the terror, though to all outward appearances, they remained loyal party members in good standing. Krivitskaia no longer considered Zhidkova a friend and now treated her

22 *Ibid.*
23 TsAOPIM, f. 429, o. 1, d. 223, l. 139.

coolly; Zhidkova would later speculate that someone in the district party committee, where Krivitskaia had begun working, might have told her about her earlier denunciation. In June, Zhidkova finally informed the party committee that her brother had been expelled. Her colleagues, furious that she had not disclosed the information during the election meeting in April, removed her from her leadership posts in the party education center and on the committee and gave her a reprimand for having failed to submit a timely *zaiavlenie*, as well as for exhibiting "dull class vigilance, having a tie to her double-dealing brother, and covering for a Trotskyist."[24] Her case would come up again, but for now, Zhidkova, chastened and demoted, remained in the Party.

As the days lengthened and a hazy green began to wreath the trees, Krivitskaia continued to work for the district party committee as an informer and to pay regular visits to Serp i Molot in her post as a political instructor. Stalin's newly planted poplars were blooming, but time was running out for Krivitskaia. She now had three strikes against her: she was the former wife of a man who had been excluded from the Party; she was the subject of at least two *zaiavleniia*, one from her comrade and former friend Zhidkova and the other from an official in the district party committee; and she was a Polish national. Unbeknownst to her, her fate had already been decided.

That summer, the Politburo initiated the "mass and national operations," selecting suspect social and national groups for arrest and execution by the NKVD. Target arrest figures for Poles, Latvians, Germans, and other immigrant groups residing in the Soviet Union were set in Moscow and distributed to the provinces,

24 TsAOPIM, f. 429, o. 1, d. 223, ll. 138–41.

triggering mass arrests. The Politburo launched the "Polish operation" on August 9, sending order number 00485 to the NKVD with
a letter detailing Polish spying and terrorist operations, under the
heading "On Fascist-Insurgent, Espionage, Sabotage, Defeatist, and
Terrorist Activities of Polish Intelligence in the USSR." Although
the letter explicitly called for the arrest only of "Polish spies,"
it nevertheless placed the entire Polish population of the Soviet
Union under suspicion. It explained that a Polish intelligence organization had taken over leadership of the Polish Communist Party
and had sent thousands of new agents over the border disguised as
political refugees. An NKVD officer would later admit that NKVD
units interpreted the order as sanctioning the arrest not merely of
"Polish spies" but of "absolutely all Poles." Local investigating
NKVD officers determined the verdicts, sentencing the accused
either to incarceration or to death by shooting. The names of the
accused and their sentences were then compiled in long lists and
approved by a local prosecutor and an NKVD official, neither of
whom had any information about the individual cases. The approved
lists, collected in an "album" format, were then forwarded to N. I.
Ezhov, head of the NKVD, and A. Ia. Vyshinskii, the USSR Prosecutor in Moscow, for final approval. Ezhov and Vyshinskii entrusted
this work to departmental heads, who reviewed and signed off on
two to three hundred sheets, bearing thousands of death sentences,
at a time. They considered the task a "tiresome burden." Between
August 1937, when the "Polish operation" began, and August 1938,
when it ended, 143,810 Poles were interrogated, 139,835 sentenced,
and 111,091 (nearly 80 percent of those sentenced) shot. Almost
all the members of the Polish Communist Party and the Polish
Socialist Party who immigrated to the Soviet Union were extermi-
nated under this order. The overwhelming majority of victims were

either peasants from border areas or workers in factories and on the railways.[25]

The "Polish operation" sealed Krivitskaia's fate. Accused of being a spy, she was arrested by the NKVD in the summer of 1937. Sometime after her arrest, Somov wrote the obligatory *zaiavlenie* to the party committee about his relationship with her. The facts, as he presented them, were few: he had known her since 1934 and had met with her several times. After months of questioning, Krivitskaia finally confessed to spying. Yet throughout those months of interrogation, she continued to protect Somov, insisting that he had known nothing about her alleged activities. In August, around the same time that Krivitskaia disappeared into prison, Zhidkova's brother Dmitri was also arrested.[26]

In his *zaiavlenie*, Somov denied having had a relationship with Krivitskaia. Yet by the time he wrote that, Fedotov's declaration, attesting to just such a relationship, had already reached the Moscow party committee, which then contacted the party committee in Serp i Molot. The two *zaiavleniia* were obviously at odds. With Krivitskaia's arrest, the allegations took on a more serious cast. Had Somov been intimately involved with a "Polish spy"? Between November 1937 and January 1938, the party committee met three times to grill him about his alleged affair with Krivitskaia. He was no longer head of the party committee, but he still held several other

25 "Operativnyi Prikaz Narodnogo Komissara Vnutrennikh Del Soiuza SSR No. 00485," in V. N. Khaustov, V. P. Naumov, and N. S. Plotnikova, eds., *Lubianka. Stalin i glavnoe upravlenie gosbezopasnosti NKVD, 1937–8. Dokumenty* (Moscow: Izdatel'stvo 'Materik', 2004), 301–3; Nikita Petrov and Arsenii Roginskii, "The 'Polish Operation' of the NKVD, 1937–8," in Barry McLoughlin and Kevin McDermott, eds., *Stalin's Terror: High Politics and Mass Repression in the Soviet Union* (Basingstoke, Hampshire: Palgrave Macmillan, 2003), pp. 153–64.

26 TsAOPIM, f. 429, o. 1, d. 223, ll. 101, 138.

important political positions, among them that as head of Serp i Molot's special department. Fellow party members pried into every aspect of the connection between him and Krivitskaia. Aleksandr Somov, the "golden child" of the revolution, he of the impeccable working-class background, unimpeachable loyalty, and unswerving dedication, was now grossly tainted by his contact with an "enemy."

THE FIRST INTERROGATION

In November, approximately sixty party members attended an expanded meeting of the party committee to discuss Somov's tie to Krivitskaia. Somov elaborated on his earlier *zaiavlenie*, testifying that he had first met Krivitskaia in 1934, when he was invited, along with other party officials in the factory, to a small New Year's Eve celebration in her apartment. He named others, including Zhidkova, who had also been there. He said that he had seen Krivitskaia outside the factory only three times: twice at her apartment and once when he met her by accident on the stairs at district party headquarters. He had written a *zaiavlenie* immediately upon learning of her arrest, and he swore that he had "had no special personal relationship with her." Stressing his party loyalty, Somov offered a dramatic disavowal of Krivitskaia, stating, "If I had known she was a spy, I would have strangled her with my own hands." Unconvinced, his comrades began peppering him with questions: "Did you help her find work at the factory?" "Did you go out with her?" "Did you have any suspicions about her?" Somov answered all of these queries in the negative.[27]

27 TsAOPIM, f. 429, o. 1, d. 223, l. 101.

Bubnov, the new head of the party committee, suspected that Somov was withholding information. Speaking to his predecessor earnestly and not unkindly, he encouraged him to be completely honest: "You have not been open. You did go out with her. I believe that you would not consciously betray [your country], but she is such an imposter, she could use you for her own interests." Somov stuck to his story: "This is not possible," he said. "I never even went to the theater with her. We only went to the workers' club, like everyone else. She did party work here." Bubnov probed further: "We are interested only in how she might have used you. Perhaps she asked you about the factory?" Somov insisted, "I saw her only twice. We never discussed political issues."[28]

Some of Somov's comrades initially rallied to his defense, casting him as Krivitskaia's victim. Their concerns centered mainly on whether the relationship had compromised his ability to carry out his duties as head of the special department:

Roshchin: Somov is not a bad guy, but I think he should not be left in the special department.

Bogdanovich (deputy director of Serp i Molot): Women provocateurs go directly to our men for political information. We know Somov as a good Bolshevik. Krivitskaia herself said he did not know [that she was a spy]. I have no basis not to believe Somov.

Dulin: I have no doubt that Somov is one of us. But he did not understand that along with personal business, enemies attempt to use people in their interests. I think Krivitskaia was afraid to use him for her aims but wanted to exercise authority in the party organization through him.

Iakunin: He should not be in the special department. He should tell us more about his ideological relationship with her.

28 TsAOPIM, f. 429, o. 1, d. 223, ll. 101–2.

Orlov: We know Somov. He is a firm Bolshevik. He led and still leads according to the general line of the Party. But I think that it is not true that he met with her only twice. He should be removed from the special department.

Galkina (organizer in the cold rolling mill): Krivitskaia was a very able person. She was able to use Somov. Everyone noticed that she wanted him to like her. Gubyrin told me that Somov had a strong relationship with her. Inasmuch as there was talk in the factory about his relationship with her, he should not remain in the special department.[29]

Many of Somov's comrades felt certain that he was lying about his relationship with Krivitskaia, though they conceded that they could not prove it. They argued that in any case, even the rumor of close contact with a spy ought to disqualify him from holding a leading post. Somov, for his part, continued to deny everything: "I declare that I did not have a relationship with Krivitskaia," he angrily exclaimed. "When she worked here, of course we met at work every day. I was not interested in her personally. She was sent to the factory by a higher party organization. If I had known what she really was, I would have knocked her teeth out."[30] Here Somov adopted the common strategy of shifting blame. *He* had not been responsible for Krivitskaia's presence in Serp i Molot; higher party officials had placed her in the factory. Why should he suffer the consequences of a decision made by his superiors? *They* were the ones who should have checked into her background. Nor did he hesitate to vilify Krivitskaia herself. His claim that he "would have knocked her teeth out" if he had known she was a spy served as a brutal bookend to his earlier assertion that "I would have strangled her with my own hands." Whatever their relationship had once

29 TsAOPIM, f. 429, o. 1, d. 223, l. 102.
30 *Ibid.*

been, Somov showed little allegiance to her now that she had been arrested. If anything, he seemed furious that she still had the power to compromise him from prison.

Bubnov once again tried a more rational approach. "We are not interested in whether he attended parties with her, or drank tea with her, or went to meetings with her – none of this is such a big crime," he announced. "If we remove him from his post, it means that we are expressing a lack of confidence in him, and we have no factual basis for this. Somov maintained vigilance in the factory, but he is guilty of letting it lapse in his personal life. We all know Somov. Krivitskaia attempted to use him, but he did not realize it. I do not believe that he was connected to her in any ideological way." Unlike many other party members who were excluded for having close connections to politically compromised relatives, spouses, or coworkers, Somov was able categorically to deny – whether truthfully or not – that he had ever had any such tie to Krivitskaia. She was not his wife, not his relative, not even his colleague in the same department. Although members of the party committee were skeptical of his story, they had no evidence that he was lying. His harsh disavowals and eager-ness to renounce his alleged lover satisfied them that he was still "one of us." Bubnov's reasonable reminder that the party committee had "no factual basis" for stripping Somov of his post also helped his case. The party committee voted to make a notation of Somov's "lack of personal vigilance" in his party file. This punishment, milder than a reprimand or a "strict" reprimand, had no immediate con-sequences. Somov was permitted to retain his party membership and his various positions, including the top post in the special department.[31]

31 TsAOPIM, f. 429, o. 1, d. 223, l. 103.

THE SECOND INTERROGATION

While Somov aggressively parried questions from his comrades, Krivitskaia faced a far harsher interrogation in prison. By the fall of 1937, prisoners were routinely subjected to violence designed to break them in body and spirit. About three months after her arrest, Krivitskaia, whether as a result of beatings, sleep deprivation, isolation, or sheer human despair, broke down. She admitted to her interrogator that she "loved Somov as a man and respected him as a human being." She said she had known him for three years, and they had discussed political themes related to work.[32] The NKVD promptly informed the Serp i Molot party committee about her confession.

In December, the party committee revisited Somov's case in light of Krivitskaia's statement and the new information from the NKVD. Bubnov opened the meeting. Having previously defended Somov, the head of the party committee now found himself in an uncomfortable position, vulnerable to accusations that he had "ignored signals" or "overlooked an enemy." This time, he presented the case with a less sympathetic slant. "It is clear," he noted, "that Somov went out with her and lived with her. He went to her apartment. She took his watch with her to prison." Once again, the party committee speculated about the nature of his relationship with Krivitskaia, with Somov's angrily rebutting the allegations. "I never lived with her," he declared sharply. "I don't know what she wanted from me. After she left the factory, I saw her only twice." One member chided him, "Everyone says you lived with her." "This is a lie," Somov replied. "If I had lived with her, I would not hide it. Larkin and Polukarov

32 TsAOPIM, f. 429, o. 1, d. 223, l. 117.

[both party members] worked with me. Let them state that they saw her with me." Another member called out, "Was the watch a present from you?" Party members questioned him closely, but Somov held firm. Finally, Bubnov intervened. "Somov should be removed from the special department," he said flatly. "We should be careful around him." On hearing this, Somov exploded. "For what?" he demanded. "It is a tactic of enemies to discredit people. I am guilty because I overlooked an enemy, but you cannot cripple a human being for that." Bubnov responded calmly, "We have no data with which to exclude you from the Party, but everyone must be careful around you. My suggestion is to remove Somov and give him a reprimand for overlooking an enemy." "I am not guilty of anything," Somov insisted. "In fact, she was a party official and was recommended by Central Committee officials." Once again, he tried to shift the responsibility for Krivitskaia's presence in the factory to higher party officials. Yet this time, there was less support for his position. Bubnov's suggestion prevailed. The party committee now voted to give Somov a reprimand, a harsher punishment than the previous notation in his file, and to recommend that the factory director remove him from his post as head of the special department.[33]

Zhidkova, who had written the original *zaiavlenie* that brought Somov's relationship with Krivitskaia to the attention of NKVD and party officials, listened to these proceedings in silence. Dismissed from the party committee and the education center the previous June for her failure to report her brother's expulsion, she now waited nervously for the discussion of Somov's case to be concluded. Her case was next on the party committee's agenda. Zhidkova, once so zealous in denouncing others, now faced her own political

33 TsAOPIM, f. 429, o. 1, d. 223, ll. 117–18.

tribulations. Her brother Dmitri, excluded from the Party in February, had been arrested in August. Somehow, Zhidkova and her sisters had managed to arrange a meeting with their brother in prison. In the desperate hope that his sisters might be able to help get him released, he gave them his version of the events that had landed him there.[34] From that point on, Zhidkova worked frantically on his appeal: she wrote a *zaiavlenie* to Stalin himself, met with a highly placed party leader in the Commission of Party Control (KPK), and extracted a promise from E. Iaroslavskii, a prominent party leader and KPK member, that he would personally investigate the charges against her brother. Convinced of his innocence, Zhidkova devoted months to standing in lines for the chance to speak with prison officials, wangling interviews with party leaders, and writing letters on Dmitri's behalf.

Now the party committee had agreed to take up Zhidkova's case again and consider the new information she had obtained during her prison interview with her brother. Standing before the committee, Zhidkova breathlessly related a long, convoluted tale. Her brother, then the second secretary of a Moscow district party committee, had allegedly fallen afoul of his boss, the first secretary, in an effort to unmask a certain Trotskyist who had been close to both of them. After the alleged Trotskyist was arrested, each man then denounced the other to the Moscow party committee. Zhidkova explained that her brother had been arrested on the basis of a confession by a "lying kulak" named Abramov who had slandered him to the head of the district NKVD, who in turn had failed to investigate the accusation. Dmitri Zhidkov's case, like most others of the day, was a tangled knot of reciprocal denunciations and mudslinging by a series of

34 TsAOPIM, f. 429, o. 1, d. 223, l. 138.

frightened people all equally anxious to save themselves. Zhidkova, steadfast in her sisterly faith, told the party committee, "My brother cannot be a betrayer. He was in and out of tsarist prisons from the time he was fifteen years old. My other brother was tortured by the Whites. We have written to Stalin, to Ezhov, and to Vyshinskii to request an investigation." A committee member interrupted her rush of words to inquire, "Why are you hammering away on behalf of your brother and not speaking for yourself?" "This business is not just about Dmitri," Zhidkova replied. "It is about the whole revolutionary family of the Zhidkovs. Our brother Aleksandr gave his life for Soviet power, and no one can ever sully the honor of our family." Another party member retorted, "She wants us to think that the NKVD made some kind of mistake, but she is not sincere. She never told us that her brother had been removed from his post due to his tie to a Trotskyist. Exclude her." Another added, "Zhidkova is protecting her brother based on the revolutionary spirit of her family. According to her, the Moscow committee, the NKVD, and the Commission of Party Control all acted incorrectly. This is a struggle not to root out enemies but to protect them." The director of the factory, Stepanov, bluntly asked her, "Do you want to declare here that you are the same as your brother?" "Yes!" Zhidkova cried. "I will never be a formalist. My own skin will never be so dear to me." In righteous anger, she then turned to denounce Stepanov. "I was not and cannot be a liar," she exclaimed. "Why don't you comrades ask Stepanov why he was once a Menshevik instead of asking questions about me? You don't act in a party spirit. You are rushing to judgment. This is a crime. No one will succeed in excluding me from the Party."[35]

35 TsAOPIM, f. 429, o. 1, d. 223, ll. 138–41.

In her fraught and frantic emotional state, Zhidkova could not even imagine that her brother might fail to be vindicated. She was willing to stake her party membership on his innocence. She had no such commitment, however, to Somov or Krivitskaia. Questioned about her relationship with the latter, she spoke proudly about the *zaiavlenie* she had sent to the NKVD. She then offered additional information attesting to the intimate tie between Krivitskaia and Somov, thus refuting Somov's denials. Zhidkova had no compunction about repeating the confidences Krivitskaia had imparted to her.[36] Her brother's plight (and by extension her own) made her no more sympathetic to the political difficulties of her comrades. Stubbornly convinced that her brother's arrest had been a mistake – to be laid at the doorstep of an inept NKVD officer and a politically suspect, vindictive boss – she nonetheless seemed equally certain that others' dark fates were justified. She evidently felt no regret about the part she had played, by writing her *zaiavlenie*, in Krivitskaia's and Somov's troubles. Her behavior toward others would remain unchanged by her own brush with the terror. She publicly maintained the belief that real enemies existed everywhere, and she continued on a personal crusade to "root them out." Her own experience had little effect on her willingness to denounce others.

The party committee reacted angrily to Zhidkova's self-righteous proclamations. One member noted that Zhidkova had "had a close relationship with Krivitskaia," which had been forgotten in the furor over Somov. Zhidkova, astonished at this characterization, indignantly replied, "I sent a *zaiavlenie* to the NKVD about her, and now they are saying I had some kind of tie to her." The party committee was unmoved by her protests. Its members voted to expel

36 TsAOPIM, f. 429, o. 1, d. 223, l. 140.

her for deceiving the Party, concealing her brother's expulsion, "covering for her brother, a Trotskyist and enemy of the people," and having a tie to the "enemy" Krivitskaia.[37]

Zhidkova's expulsion contained a measure of ironical justice at a time when justice in any form was in short supply. She had helped to brand Krivitskaia as an enemy and brought her to the attention of the NKVD. Now her own tie to this "enemy" contributed to her exclusion. Yet justice, not surprisingly, played only a fitful role in this drama. Within the month, Zhidkova's exclusion would be reversed. By January, she was back in the Party's ranks, once again present at and participating in meetings, denouncing others for consorting with the "enemy."[38] Whether her brother was released from prison and reinstated is unknown, though it seems unlikely that anything short of a reversal in his case at the highest level could have prompted Zhidkova's rehabilitation and allowed her to reconcile once again her twin loyalties to her family and the Party. Whatever personal torments she may have suffered in the weeks between her expulsion and reinstatement remained hidden, and her vindication only bolstered her willingness to attack others.

THE THIRD INTERROGATION

The Party's democracy campaign, announced during the Central Committee plenum in February–March 1937, encouraged party members to demand increased participation in the rulings of the party committee. Decisions concerning the personal and political behavior of party members, once the prerogative of shop and party

37 TsAOPIM, f. 429, o. 1, d. 223, ll. 140–41.
38 TsAOPIM, f. 429, o.1, d. 261, ll. 31–32.

committees, were now placed on the agendas of factory-wide party meetings. In some of the bigger factories and institutions, hundreds attended these mass meetings. The dynamics differed from those of shop or party committee meetings, in which small groups met regularly and worked together over an extended period of time. Ungoverned by set routines or relationships, the larger meetings were volatile, boisterous, and unpredictable. The floor was open to anyone who wished to speak, discussions veered from one topic to another, and the most self-righteous voices tended to prevail. A focused, reasoned debate among five hundred or so people was all but impossible. Bubnov, head of the party committee in Serp i Molot, was able to exert some influence over his smaller group, but he had little control over the outcome of these general meetings.

In January 1938, hundreds of party members, tense with anticipation, filed into the factory's auditorium to hear and discuss the expulsion cases under consideration by the party committee. Somov's case was one of several on the agenda. As Somov took his place before the rostrum at the head of the hall, Bogomolov, deputy head of the party committee, summed up the "facts" once again: Somov had first met Krivitskaia in 1934, when he was head of the party organization in the open hearth furnace and she was working in the factory. According to a *zaiavlenie* written by Fedotov, a district party official, Somov had had a close relationship with her for three years and often stayed in her apartment. Somov's own *zaiavlenie*, however, written after Krivitskaia's arrest, stated that he had visited her only twice, once at a New Year's Eve party in 1934. The few remaining facts were not in dispute: Somov gave Krivitskaia his watch. Krivitskaia worked in the education center as an assistant to Zhidkova. Krivitskaia left the factory, took a job as an informer with the Taganskii district party committee, and was then arrested as a

Polish spy. The party committee had placed a reprimand in Somov's file.[39]

The audience stirred angrily on hearing of the committee's ruling. Someone yelled, "Too little, too light a punishment!" Bogomolov announced, "The question now stands before the meeting, and the meeting will decide." Somov was then invited to address the assembly. Once again, he stuck to his version of the truth: "In 1934, on New Year's Eve, Izotov, Zhidkova and her husband, and I went to Krivitskaia's apartment." Somov deliberately named names: Izotov was the head of the party organization in the cutting foundry, a party member in good standing, and Zhidkova had by this time apparently appealed her expulsion and succeeded in having it reversed. In fact, as Somov spoke, Zhidkova was sitting in the crowd, watching him warily. Her friendship with Krivitskaia had figured prominently in her earlier exclusion, and what Somov said now could have a significant effect on her future. In his defense, Somov employed a common tactic: by naming others in good standing who also had been present during that compromising evening at Krivitskaia's, he sought to defuse the accusations against him. In essence, he asked the audience: Why punish me alone? Somov was also careful to admit to meeting with Krivitskaia only in public, in places where others might have seen them together. He continued to deny that he had ever had any personal relationship with her. When he had finished speaking, members of the audience fired a barrage of hostile questions at him:

Question: Were you there as guests?
Somov: I drank a little wine. I did not get drunk. I borrowed some books. After she went to work for the Taganskii district, I did not see her again

39 TsAOPIM, f. 429, o. 1, d. 261, l. 24.

except on the staircase at the district party committee, and we sat together at the Moscow party committee meeting in 1936. When I learned that she had been arrested, I immediately wrote a *zaiavlenie*. I gave her a watch after she overslept. I saw her only twice in 1934, when she was a party member. Her husband worked as an instructor in the party organization of the Central Committee. I had no idea she was an enemy of the people. If I had known, I would have unmasked her. My mistake was that I overlooked an inveterate enemy of the people.

Question: Couldn't those books that you borrowed from her be found in a Soviet library?

Somov: No.

Someone in the hall yelled out, "Yes, they could!" Zhidkova now spoke up, attempting to bring the discussion back to the main point. "Was there something deeper here?" she asked. "Did he have a closer tie?" Somov responded, "None except an acquaintance." Bogomolov interrupted to note, "Krivitskaia said under interrogation that you had a sexual tie for three years." Other party members asked, "Was the watch engraved?" "How did you learn of her arrest?" Somov again took pains to drop a name: "I learned from Gubyrin. She was arrested in July or August. I wrote the *zaiavlenie* in September."[40]

Somov built his defense around several points: Krivitskaia had been a party member in good standing before her arrest; higher-ups in the Party had secured a place for her in the factory; she had been Zhidkova's assistant, not his; and many other people had also worked with her. His relationship with her was no different from that between any other two comrades or coworkers. A party member now asked another, more difficult question: "A lot of people knew her; why didn't any of *them* write *zaiavleniia*?" This got directly to the nature of the relationship: if Somov had not had a personal tie

40 TsAOPIM, f. 429, o. 1, d. 261, ll. 26–27.

to Krivitskaia, why had he bothered to write a *zaiavlenie* after her arrest? Somov answered carefully: "Because I went to her apartment and because she had my watch, I spoke with Bubnov, and then I wrote a *zaiavlenie*."[41]

Many party members did not believe Somov's account. Several related gossip they had heard in the shops about the relationship. More questions followed: "Did you discuss political themes on New Year's Eve?" "Did you know that she had only recently arrived from Poland?" "How was Krivitskaia appointed to her position?" "What kind of conversations did you have with this enemy of the people, and what kind of details about our factory did you give her?" The questions, mostly challenging and hostile, covered a variety of issues, but Somov's story allowed him to dodge them nimbly: he had not known the details of her biography, and he had not provided her with any information, because he had never had a personal relationship with her.[42]

Like a dangerous whirlpool, the interrogation soon began to pull others into its depths. One party member asked, "Why didn't Izotov provide a *zaiavlenie*?" Izotov, who had been a guest at Krivitskaia's New Year's Eve celebration; Zhidkova, who had been her supervisor; and Gubyrin, who had told Somov of her arrest, would all now have to explain their relationships with her. Gubyrin spoke first and immediately tried to clear himself. He stated that he had known Krivitskaia through her work with the party committee. On hearing rumors of her arrest, he had notified Somov. Even this seemingly minor detail was open to interpretation: was Gubyrin's notification

41 TsAOPIM, f. 429, o. 1, d. 261, ll. 27–28.
42 TsAOPIM, f. 429, o. 1, d. 261, ll. 24–30.

of Somov a sign that he considered him an interested party, or had it just been one more whisper in the factory's unceasing subterranean hum about arrests? The rumors that were carried from shop to shop by frightened comrades and coworkers constituted an unofficial yet crucial network of communication within the factory. Each new bit of news inspired a rapid mental calculation as the listener silently tallied the damage the latest victim might do to his or her future. Gubyrin chose his words with care, neither undermining nor supporting Somov's version of events. He admitted that Krivitskaia had often stopped by the open hearth furnace to see Somov, but then he added, "What kind of tie they had outside of work, I don't know. I don't think that Somov would give any information to Krivitskaia."[43] Another party member now broke in, taking a harsher line: "Somov allowed this, he opened all the gates of production in the factory to an enemy of the people. Even if he did nothing more than this, like Petrushka among the enemies of the people, he gave her access. This no one can deny." (Petrushka, a stock puppet in Russian folk plays, was also an unrequited lover in a well-known ballet.) Somov once again tried to explain that he had not been responsible for Krivitskaia's presence in the factory. "She didn't work under me," he reiterated. But his critic responded, "I think the decision of the party committee was too soft. We should exclude him."[44]

The issue of Krivitskaia's position within Serp i Molot was a particularly dangerous one for Zhidkova, who had been her supervisor. Somov's last remark had been a direct slur against her, and now

43 TsAOPIM, f. 429, o. 1, d. 261, ll. 30–31.
44 *Ibid.*

she felt the need to defend herself. Just a month before, she had been excluded for having a tie to Krivitskaia, among other things, and she well understood that if things went badly for her now, she might again be found guilty by association. Eager to extricate herself from this mess, Zhidkova sought to make a distinction between her situation and Somov's. "What is important when we judge a member of the Party," she primly noted, "is, first, his unselfish sincerity." Zhidkova prided herself on this quality and had demonstrated it in defense of her brother. Now she needed to protect herself against the possible charge that she had failed to write a *zaiavlenie* after Krivitskaia's arrest. She had already been punished for not writing after her brother's exclusion, and she was anxious to avoid a repeat of that earlier misfortune. She continued, "It is not necessary to write a *zaiavlenie* if you occasionally met [Krivitskaia] somewhere or met her once on New Year's Eve, no, but if you were closer, if you had the chance to discern what sort of person she was and at the time did nothing, then you should carry party responsibility for this." In this way, Zhidkova exempted and excused her own relationship with Krivitskaia. "[Somov] has deceived the meeting that he had only innocent relations based solely on work, only relations like those between fellow party officials," she asserted. "This is a lie. Somov and Krivitskaia had close, intimate relations. She confided in me. The point is not that he gave her a watch, but that he has not been sufficiently sincere before the party meeting." Standing by her vaunted principles, insisting on total honesty before the Party, Zhidkova maintained that Somov's fault lay in his insincerity, his refusal to acknowledge the real nature of the relationship. She thus located his guilt not in his official or professional association with Krivitskaia, which was similar to her own, but rather in his deception. Zhidkova proudly reminded the audience of her own denunciation of Sagaidak, former head of the cold rolling mill, who was later arrested, and of Somov's failure to act on her warning: "When Sagaidak was pushing his counterrevolutionary theories, he received support from the party committee. After this, I said he needed to be removed, but Somov replied, 'This is not your business.' I had to go to the district and party committees at the same time because of Somov's liberalism." Yet in her final remarks, Zhidkova relented somewhat, recommending to party members that they not exclude Somov. She explained, "I think that if Somov consciously entered into a relationship with an enemy of the people, then he should not have a place in the Party's ranks, but if it is a question of [a lack of] political vigilance and a lack of sincerity, then I think a strict reprimand is sufficient." Zhidkova thus called Somov a liar, provided evidence of his affair with Krivitskaia, but argued against his expulsion. In so doing, she abided by her own principles while showing some mercy to the offender. In her smug and rigid self-assurance, she simply could not understand the larger damage that those principles of hers might do to others.[45]

Many people in the audience had had personal dealings with Somov. As a former head of the party committee, he had presided over many airings of allegations, expulsions, and arrests. It was not surprising, then, that personal resentments, too, should find a place in the discussion. One woman, clearly nursing a grudge, delivered a garbled statement against him: "Why do I dwell on the slanders against me that Somov permitted? I am a nervous person, seventy-five percent of people consider me not normal, ill, but I would not permit such slanders as Somov permitted. There were mean and base subterfuges against me." She then managed to translate her personal

45 TsAOPIM, f. 429, o. 1, d. 261, ll. 31–33.

anger over Somov's failure to protect her into more acceptable, if still nonsensical, political language: "He was insufficiently vigilant," she said. "I can illustrate how he regarded party studies when I was a propagandist. He made not only the one mistake, but look at his relations with people in general. His pledge to discover enemies, his feeling of correct relations with people – this simply did not exist on his part. One mistake is a mistake, so are two, but three is already a system." Another speaker tried to direct the debate back to Somov. "Comrades," he said, "it is not important whether Somov had a tie to Krivitskaia as a woman. The question is what political issues they discussed. We must remember, as we discuss Comrade Somov, that he was a worker, and his father was a worker. But it was precisely then, when he was head of the party committee, that enemies rallied around him. They go to the head, they find who sits in the leadership, and they get close to that person. Krivitskaia shows us this. Always elegant, sincere, in smart clothing, she aimed to get close to find out what she needed. As an enemy of the people, Krivitskaia did not go to a worker and ask him about his business; she went to the secretary of the party committee and invited him over for New Year's Eve. What kind of questions did she ask him about production in the shops? And the plan of the factory? It would be stupid to think that Krivitskaia would tell the head of the party committee, 'I am an enemy of the people. I am a spy.' I think this is all very serious, and Somov has no place in the Party."[46]

Party members repeatedly returned to several issues. Had Somov lied? Had he known that Krivitskaia was a spy? Had he revealed important information to her? Almost all of those who spoke believed that he was concealing something. One woman said,

46 TsAOPIM, f. 429, o. 1, d. 261, ll. 34–35.

"At first I was surprised at the decision of the party committee because I think that Somov did not consciously enter into a relationship with an enemy of the people, with a spy, but false notes sounded in his speech that made me doubt him. I saw how tender Krivitskaia was toward Somov, calling him Sasha, Sashenka, but I don't want to talk about this. Did Somov know that she had recently come from abroad, from Poland? Why is it that other people knew this, but he, who had a close personal tie to Krivitskaia, did not know? . . . I think that not only should he get a strict reprimand, but it is also necessary thoroughly to check the information we have, because in his speech, Somov was clearly playing false notes."[47] Another made a strong case for exclusion: "Comrade Somov bears a heavy accusation – that he had a relationship with a spy. Somov does not admit to this relationship. It has been said that they were drunk. But in drunkenness everything is blabbed. And this was not the only time. Pandul, head of the party organization in the open hearth furnace, worked with Somov. He [Pandul] was an enemy of the people, and he has already been sitting in prison for a year. An entire nest of spies was uncovered during Somov's tenure. After the change in leadership of the factory, ten spies were uncovered. I think the Party's decision in Somov's case is too liberal. If Rovnov went to visit Sagaidak and said the devil knows what, in that case, it might be possible to believe that a person was not conscious. Personally, I would have known not to drop by [Sagaidak's apartment]. But in this case? Three years, a close tie to a spy, and still the head of the party organization. I think that after this, Somov has no place in the Party."[48]

47 TsAOPIM, f. 429, o. 1, d. 261, ll. 35–36.
48 TsAOPIM, f. 429, o. 1, d. 261, ll. 36–37.

More people clamored to speak, but Bubnov tried to bring the discussion to a close. Other cases still had to be considered. "Let's end it," he said. "Let Izotov speak. He was with [Somov] on New Year's Eve." Izotov, head of the party organization in the cutting foundry, was keen to minimize his own connection to Krivitskaia. "I did not have a tie to an enemy of the people," he declared. "After I entered the leadership of the party organization, I became involved with the party education center. . . . After the lesson, they spoke about where to meet for New Year's Eve. I had no family; I was a bachelor then. Somov said, 'Let's go there.' So we went to Krivitskaia's. We went at ten o'clock and found there Zhidkova and her husband, [Krivitskaia's husband] Evdokimov, and a Central Committee instructor whose last name I don't know. We stayed for an hour or so and then left. After this, my connection to Krivitskaia ended. I was not in close contact with her, I never saw her anywhere, and in general, it was understood that where there are two, a third is superfluous. I knew this much from working in the party organization." With these last remarks, Izotov turned against Somov, making it clear that he had in fact had an intimate relationship with Krivitskaia. In Izotov's opinion, Somov was not being honest with his comrades: "I should say that Somov did not state everything. Everyone in the party organization knew that the relationship between Somov and Krivitskaia was more than casual. In regard to Pandul, he was the complete master of the open hearth furnace and its party organization. All business was done, all decisions were made, by Pandul. I think that Somov should have unmasked Krivitskaia and been sincere, but because he was not sincere, I think he should be excluded from the Party." One party member now addressed Izotov: "According to Somov's *zaiavlenie*, he visited Krivitskaia's apartment twice. Did you go there twice as well?" "No, only once," he replied.

Of greater and more immediate concern to Izotov were the alleged enemies who had been arrested in his shop. On that score, he told the audience, "I can say that about twenty people from the cutting foundry have been arrested, but the party committee knows about this – and people have been arrested everywhere, not only in the cutting foundry."[49] A few more members asked questions, but none related directly to Izotov. "Where is her [Krivitskaia's] apartment?" one wondered. Another essayed a more dangerous query: "What happened when they removed Krivitskaia from the party education center?" This question had the power to do damage to the party committee, which had made the decision about Krivitskaia's dismissal. Bogomolov quickly explained that after her husband was excluded, the committee had asked her to leave the factory, adding that she had not been hindered from finding another post.[50] Luckily for the party committee members, no one inquired as to why the district committee had seen fit to hire her, given the political liability posed by her husband's expulsion.

Now Somov was asked to make a final statement. Like many others who found themselves under attack during those years, he offered a list of all the "enemies" he had denounced as proof of his loyalty. He claimed to have been at least partly responsible for unmasking both Pandul and Sagaidak: "I have been portrayed as guilty because I worked with Pandul, who was unmasked by the party organization of the open hearth furnace. If I had lacked vigilance, this case never would have been exposed. Zhidkova spoke about Sagaidak. *We* unmasked Sagaidak. Everyone participated. As a Bolshevik, I am guilty only of not unmasking a class enemy, but I

49 TsAOPIM, f. 429, o. 1, d. 261, ll. 37–38.
50 TsAOPIM, f. 429, o. 1, d. 261, ll. 37–39.

knew her [Krivitskaia] only as a party official. I did not seek her out."
Once again he declared his loyalty: "I knew Krivitskaia as a party
official," he repeated, "but if I had known she was a spy, I would
have done what every other Bolshevik would do." Somov swore he
had learned his lesson and begged his fellow party members not to
exclude him: "For me, this lesson will be a great education, because
I feel deeply that every person whom you meet, you must know, you
must crawl into his or her soul, and only then can you work together
and [truly] meet." Somov insisted on his innocence until the very
end: "I am not in any measure guilty of those accusations which
have been leveled against me. Over all my years in the factory,
serving in the Red Army and protecting our borders, working in the
open hearth furnace, fourteen years in the Party, I called all workers
to Bolshevik vigilance, to the elimination of class enemies. This
mistake serves as a great lesson to me. I ask you, comrades, to permit
me to stay in the Party."[51]

A party member noted that speakers from the audience had suggested three possible punishments: to affirm the party committee's
decision to place a reprimand in Somov's file; to increase the punishment to a "strict reprimand"; or to exclude him from the Party. After
hearing the options, however, the audience was restive; many comrades still seemed undecided about how to vote. A voice called out
from the floor, "It isn't clear whether Somov had a tie to Krivitskaia.
Did he deceive the meeting or not?" Someone replied from the rostrum that Bubnov had already read aloud Krivitskaia's confession.
The voice responded, "Krivitskaia said so, but we have all heard of
cases in which spies slandered party members, and we need to take
this into account. We must investigate this openly." Bubnov, who

51 TsAOPIM, f. 429, o. 1, d. 261, l. 39.

on a previous occasion had urged leniency due to the lack of evidence against Somov, now tried to bring the matter to a vote. Once again, he stressed the lack of evidence as a deciding factor in the party committee's earlier decision to allow Somov to remain in the Party. "I have been accused here of liberalism in regard to Somov," he noted. "We have approached this issue with great seriousness. We have his *zaiavlenie*, but we have no other documents except Krivitskaia's confession that she was close to him, that she knew him as a man, and that she loved him. The party committee never established a political connection between the two of them, only that Somov was acquainted with her as a woman, and as a result, we made our decision."[52] Bubnov spoke quietly and without bombast about Krivitskaia. He said nothing about enemies or spies; he merely repeated Krivitskaia's own poignant words. Her confession, that she "knew Somov as a man, and loved him," was heartbreakingly brief and simple. And courageously, he once again reminded the meeting that there was no evidence that Somov had ever passed Krivitskaia any political information or technical secrets about the factory.

The worst and best possibilities for behavior in this terrible time were on display at this meeting, but the differential between them, unfortunately, was not great. No one risked his or her own life to protest the underlying assumptions of the terror. No one defended Krivitskaia or suggested that she might have been unjustly arrested. No one took Somov's side and insisted that the charges against him were absurd. No one spoke out against the principle of guilt by association. And no one asked whether the very notion of "complete loyalty" to the Party might not be unworkable, unfair, and unrealistic. On the contrary, people were quick to blame others, to name

52 TsAOPIM, f. 429, o. 1, d. 261, l. 41.

names, and to shift responsibility, and proud to count the number of "enemies" they denounced or exposed. In this respect, Somov, a victim, was no different from his accusers.

Yet within the permissible limits of discussion, understood and accepted by all, several comrades did attempt to help Somov. Bubnov emphasized the need for evidence and, despite his position as head of the party committee, did little political posturing for the sake of the crowd. Zhidkova, notwithstanding her dogged defense of the "rules" and her insistence on "absolute honesty," tried to save Somov from expulsion by recommending a lighter punishment. Gubyrin and others downplayed their knowledge of Somov's affair with Krivitskaia and, in so doing, minimized his guilt. Others testified to the existence of the relationship but either did not believe or could not prove that Somov had passed political or technical information to Krivitskaia. Several party members made a genuine effort to uncover the facts of the case, hoping to determine whether Somov was lying and what sort of relationship he had really had with Krivitskaia. And some felt that even a tie between them should not in itself be grounds for his expulsion. In the end, though many in the audience were still troubled by the lack of conclusive evidence, the meeting voted to overturn the party committee's decision. The majority went against Somov, by a margin of nearly two to one: 276 members voted to exclude him from the Party, 126 voted for a reprimand, and 37 voted for a strict reprimand. The pattern of voting revealed little middle ground: those who opposed Somov did so strongly, while those who supported him tended to favor the lesser reprimand. Very few chose the option of increasing the party committee's recommended punishment to a "strict reprimand" and allowing a humbled Somov to remain in their ranks.[53]

53 TsAOPIM, f. 429, o. 1, d. 261, l. 42.

Bubnov announced the results of the vote. His voice rang out in the hall as he said, "Comrade Somov, permit me to take your party card." Somov walked to the long table on the dais in front of the auditorium and handed over his card to the committee head. He then apparently lingered long enough, in stunned silence, that Bubnov had to prompt him, "Comrade Somov, leave the meeting." Bubnov's use of the term "comrade," a common address among party members, may have been a slip, a kindness, or a veiled critique of the vote, for Somov, cast out of the Party, was "comrade" no longer to its remaining members. At last he walked down the aisle, opened the door, and passed out of the vast hall. The next case was already being called: Mironov, head of the department of technical control, was accused of being friendly with an "enemy."[54]

FAITHFUL TO THE END

Did Somov have an intimate relationship with Krivitskaia? And if he did, why did he so adamantly deny it? Bubnov broadly hinted, more than once, that the real issue was not the relationship itself so much as Somov's refusal to admit to it. Bubnov gave his predecessor ample opportunity to confess and put the problem behind him. Yet Somov kept insisting on his version of the story. Perhaps he was telling the truth, and he never did have a relationship with Krivitskaia. Perhaps her confession that she "loved him as a man" was made under duress, even torture, and the two of them were never more than casual acquaintances. This was Somov's explanation, and it is possible that it was true, but much evidence indicates otherwise. First, other party members knew that Somov and Krivitskaia were close; she often went to visit him at the open hearth furnace, and they were

54 TsAOPIM, f. 429, o. 1, d. 261, ll. 42–43.

the subject of joking gossip in the shop. Second, Krivitskaia confided her feelings to Zhidkova. Third, Somov gave her a watch. And fourth, Krivitskaia's pitiful confession in prison suggested that she genuinely loved Somov. She shielded him from any association with her for as long as she could and defended him to the last against the more serious accusation that he had provided her with information. Krivitskaia never acknowledged having any political tie to Somov, an admission that would undoubtedly have led to his arrest. After months of interrogation, and possibly torture, the NKVD could obtain from her only the grudging concession that she loved Somov as a man and respected him as person – a statement so poignant and so noble, under the circumstances, that we can only marvel at the depth of her feeling. This lighthearted, pretty young woman, once so cavalier about the arrests of others, appears to have found the strength in prison to withstand her interrogators and protect another human being until the end. Where she came by this strength, we can never know. But human motivation is mysterious. The outwardly strong may crumble under pressure, and the seemingly weak be capable of great tenacity.

Is it possible that Somov, in his own way, was trying to protect Krivitskaia by denying that they had had a sexual relationship? Can this have been some sort of chivalry on his part, a refusal to expose an intimate tie to the lurid scrutiny of a group eager for lascivious gossip? He knew he could not contest the NKVD's designation of her as a spy, yet still he spoke of that aspect of her always in the conditional mood: "If I had known she was a spy, I would have strangled her with my own hands," "I would have knocked her teeth out." Clearly he did not know she was a spy, and he may never have believed that she was. If he knew her as a woman, he refused to discuss it, even though his confession might have saved his party membership. Perhaps Somov, too, succeeded in preserving something dear to him.

Or perhaps Kriviskaia's feelings for him were never reciprocated. He may have casually flirted with her, encouraged her, even slept with her. The relationship may have been imbalanced, with Kritvitskaia's deep attachment on one side and Somov's emotional indifference on the other. Such a sad but common kind of mismatch would account for his anger at being dragged down by her political troubles. Or perhaps he was simply trapped by his own lies. Initially fearful of revealing his tie to her, he may subsequently have found himself unable, out of some sense of stubborn pride, to reverse himself. He may have become increasingly committed to his own version of events, even in the face of contrary evidence. In the end, we cannot know why he insisted on that version, or whether it was true or false. Somov's motivation is unknowable. Who can read what is hidden in the human heart at any given moment? Often people themselves are blind to their own motives.

What is perhaps more instructive in this small tale is the issue of behavior, for it was outward actions, not unvoiced thoughts, that ultimately affected others. In this sense, Somov's refusal to confess to a Party that commanded his deepest loyalty reveals something about what that Party, and its membership, had become in this time of terror – namely, a fanatical, quasi-religious organization intent on, to use Somov's own phrase, "crawling into the souls" of its members. This quest, with its attendant *zaiavleniia*, investigations, and interrogations, was ultimately destructive of all loyalties to the cause. As an ideal, it presupposed the existence of a "perfect," "pure," or "perfectible" member who in fact did not, and could not, exist anywhere. As a set of practices, it turned loyal activists into liars and transformed an outwardly focused program of social transformation into an inward hunt for hidden "sinners." Such a program could achieve little beyond the continuous purging of its own ranks.

CONCLUSION

The drama of Somov and Krivitskaia was but one of millions, yet its homely details challenge some popular notions about the "Great Terror." First, the behavior of Zhidkova and others illustrates the role of the rank and file. The terror was part of a political culture based on widespread participation. This particular drama began with the expulsion of Krivitskaia's husband, who was "tainted" by his kulak brother, and continued with Zhidkova's denunciation of Krivitskaia. The investigation soon engulfed Somov, then Zhidkova herself. Fedotov, an instructor in the district committee who read Zhidkova's denunciation, made a personal decision to inform on Somov. Neither Zhidkova nor Fedotov was forced to pursue Somov or Krivitskaia, but through their efforts, they succeeded in bringing the pair to the attention of the NKVD and the Party. Krivitskaia would ultimately be arrested as a Polish spy, but it was her husband's expulsion and Zhidkova's subsequent denunciation that first alerted Moscow's NKVD to her presence in Serp i Molot and her alleged relationship with Somov. In compiling arrest lists for the mass and national operations, local NKVD organizations relied on a variety of sources, including denunciations from responsible citizens.[55] People on whom dossiers already existed undoubtedly found their way onto these lists sooner than those who were unknown to the authorities. Krivitskaia was arrested in the Polish operation, yes,

55 David Shearer, *Policing Stalin's Socialism: Repression and Social Order in the Soviet Union, 1924–1953* (New Haven, Conn.: Yale University Press, 2009), p. 196.

but Zhidkova and Fedotov, two comrades, played a role in her arrest.

Second, rank-and-file party members in the factories were more rabid in their responses than their leaders. Somov's fate was decided not by an order from above but through the collective deliberation of his comrades. They took up his case three times, acting more decisively (but with no greater proof) on each occasion. Although Bubnov repeatedly stated that there was no proof that Somov had passed factory secrets to Krivitskaia, he was convicted anyway, largely on the strength of Krivitskaia's admission that she loved him. Party members in the audience during the mass meeting protested that a mere reprimand was too trivial a punishment for Somov's transgression. The membership could have remained silent, or voted to uphold the party committee's lesser sentence, but instead a strong majority voted him out of the Party. In this case as in many others, the rank and file proved harsher than the party committee when it came to judging a comrade.

Third, an intimate familiarity with the terror did not necessarily foster sympathy for other victims. Zhidkova also took an active role in the drama. Her firsthand experience of the terror's consequences made her not more but paradoxically *less* sympathetic to the political troubles of others. Initially, the experiences of Krivitskaia and Zhidkova ran parallel to each other. Both women were coping with the aftershocks of the expulsion of a man who was close to them. Upon her brother's exclusion, Zhidkova was confronted by an impossible choice between her loyalties to her family and to the Party. Krivitskaia, in contrast, found in her husband's expulsion an opportunity to escape a loveless marriage. Zhidkova could not understand Krivitskaia's behavior. Herself presented with a choice she could not make, she viewed her friend and coworker as heartless.

Her decision to denounce Krivitskaia was driven by both the urge for self-protection and her considerable anxiety over her brother's fate. Her actions raise questions about the effect of secrets on outward behavior, and about whether some people, when victimized in one area of life, may not more readily became victimizers themselves in another. The terror did not unify people in common suffering. People hid their troubles from others and lashed out politically against those around them. Zhidkova was reinstated in the Party and presumably outlived the terror, a woman of principle and deep feeling who nonetheless destroyed the lives of others.

And what of Krivitskaia? The overwhelming majority of those arrested in the "Polish operation" were shot. They underwent brief interrogations, were sentenced to the camps or to be executed, and had their names placed on lists, among hundreds of others, to be forwarded to Ezhov and Vyshinskii for their approval. Local NKVD authorities then waited for permission to carry out the sentences. Officials in Moscow, inundated by lists from all over the country, could not keep up with the deadly paperwork. Provincial jails were crammed with prisoners who had been sentenced to death and were awaiting final approval for execution. Krivitskaia languished in prison for months, but her case took longer for her interrogators to resolve. She appears to have been questioned at least twice, to judge from the reports the party committee received from the NKVD. Because she was charged with spying, her captors would have endeavored to discover her contacts. Once Somov's name surfaced, Krivitskaia's interrogators focused their attentions on the relationship between them and his position in Serp i Molot. In fact, Krivitskaia's stubborn refusal to betray Somov may have prolonged her life by several months. When she finally broke and admitted she loved him, it marked the beginning of Somov's troubles and perhaps the end of her own. Having outlived her usefulness to her interrogators, she was now disposable. In all likelihood, she was either shot, along with 80 percent of those arrested in the "Polish operation," or sent to the camps. Yet these are but probabilities and speculations. What happened to Krivitskaia after her confession is unknown.[56]

Somov proved to be a survivor. Not only did he live through the terror, but he eventually found his way back into the Party. He was reinstated sometime before the German invasion in June 1941. Records show that he died at the front that same year, his occupation listed as "political instructor" (*politruk*). His last moments were described by witnesses: leading his company forward in a driving counterattack, waving his rifle aloft and urging his men on, he was mowed down by a German machine gunner. Whatever his inner motivations may have been, in the end he proved his loyalty through his actions. A book published about Serp i Molot in 1959 noted that Somov had been a "modest, principled Communist."[57]

The record does not yield the "truth" that Somov's comrades sought concerning his relationship with Krivitskaia. Yet this truth, in the final analysis, is not the same truth the historian seeks. In examining the behavior of these three people, Somov, Krivitskaia, and Zhidkova, we may be able to find a larger truth. The "Great Terror" emerges as the sum of millions of actions, from a friend's

56 Krivitskaia's name can be found in Memorial's list of victims http://lists.memo
.ru/index11.htm. Her name first appeared on a list published by *Moskovskaia
Pravda*. The paper provided only two sentences about her: "Krivitskaia Esfir'
Zakharovna, born 1907, head Komvuz [Communist Educational Center of Factory], Taganskii district party committee. Lived at 3 Sverdlov Square, apt. 33."

57 *Svet nad zastavoi. Sbornik* (Moscow: Moskovskii Rabochii, 1959), pp. 248, 257.
This book about Serp i Molot was part of a series endorsed by Maxim Gorky in
the early 1930s, "Istoriia fabrik i zavodov."

denunciation to the Politburo's order for the national operations. As this story reveals, orders from above to "root out enemies," to "arrest Polish spies," and to "heighten vigilance" intersected with deeply personal motivations and relationships to create a political culture that supported mass repression and purge. The records do not disclose whether Somov loved Krivitskaia, but they do show how three people responded to the "Great Terror" and in turn created the terror that they knew.

5 : The Final Paroxysm

B Y 1938, THE DEFINITION OF THE "ENEMY" HAD BECOME sufficiently elastic to accommodate almost everyone and anyone. Beginning with the dekulakization campaign in 1929 and continuing through the urban sweeps of "socially harmful elements" in the early 1930s, the attack on former oppositionists after the Kirov murder in 1934, and the mass arrests of suspect groups in 1937–38, the meaning of the term had steadily expanded to cover social, political, associational, and national categories. The ever-lengthening list included former left and right oppositionists; industrial "wreckers"; former kulaks, priests, nobles, and White Guards; criminal recidivists; wives of "enemies"; foreign Communists living in the Soviet Union; and immigrants from hostile border states. Nor were these groups discretely demarcated. The definition of "enemy" also stretched to encompass relatives, friends, coworkers, and associates of the victims. People targeted by the mass and national operations also turned out to be parents, siblings, and partners of loyal party members. However much the Soviet government sought to sort the population into neat categories of "enemy" and "friend," identity proved far too complex to contain: individuals had multiple identities, and associational and family ties bound disparate groups. No one, in the end, was unsuited for the magically capacious category of "enemy," which grew over time to embrace even the "purest" and most faithful of party members. Local party organizations in effect devoured themselves.

The February–March 1937 Central Committee plenum, which encouraged the "little people" in the Party, the unions, and other institutions to criticize and unmask their leaders, fueled the internal hunt for enemies. The factory newspapers urged the hunt forward, setting the baying hounds on the scent first of one "enemy" and then of another. The hunters found a seemingly inexhaustible supply of victims among those party members who presented *zaiavleniia* announcing the arrests of relatives, friends, and spouses. Leadership circles were weakened and then destroyed by arrests, malice, and reciprocal denunciations. By 1938, the party organizations in the factories were occupied almost exclusively with uncovering "enemies and their supporters." Factory directors disappeared into prison, and no sooner were their successors able to master their new responsibilities than they, too, disappeared. Three different men served as director of Dinamo over the course of six months. The director of Trekhgornaia Manufaktura was arrested. And the director of Serp i Molot spent the summer of 1937 parrying hostile questions in party meetings about his biography, politics, and drinking habits.[1] Shop heads, engineers, and managers were afraid to make decisions, assume responsibility, or issue orders. Work discipline collapsed in the shops.

---

1 On the interrogation of Stepanov, director of Serp i Molot, see Wendy Z. Goldman, *Terror and Democracy in the Age of Stalin: The Social Dynamics of Repression* (New York: Cambridge University Press, 2007), pp. 235–36. See also Tsentral'nyi Arkhiv Obshchestvenno-Politicheskoi Istorii Moskvy (TsAOPIM), f. 429, o. 1, d. 261, ll. 69–109.

In mid-January 1938, the Central Committee attempted to call a halt to the frenzy of enemy-hunting. It instructed the party committees to identify and punish the "slanderers" who had been responsible for the earlier expulsions of thousands of party members as "enemies." The party committees were to review carefully the appeals of party members who had been excluded, reinstate those found not guilty of the charges against them, and expel members who had written baseless denunciations. In one last organizational convulsion, party members now tried to identify the "slanderers" and rehabilitate the "innocent." In an abrupt inversion, the Central Committee turned the world of the terror upside down. The most aggressive denouncers were transformed into potential "enemies," and former "enemies" into potentially "innocent" victims. The hazy criteria that party members had once used to identify and cast out the "enemy" were now subject to reevaluation. Not surprisingly, these latest instructions only intensified the mass confusion and chaos created by the terror.

THE RAVAGES OF TERROR

The new year of 1938 dawned with no end to the terror in sight. In Dinamo, a two-day general party meeting drew five hundred attendees in early January. Starichkov, head of the factory party committee, delivered a summary report of the committee's activities over the previous year. Since April 1937, he announced, Dinamo's party organization had "cleaned out enemies of the people and their supporters" and successfully "unmasked the nest of a vile band of Trotskyist Bukharinite reptiles." Starichkov's rhetoric about a "vile band of . . . reptiles" "unmasked" in their "nest" was striking for its mixed metaphors. But this sort of language had long since ceased to strike anyone as unusual, and the mixed metaphors were themselves a sign of how thoroughly the phrases had been incorporated into popular speech. The Party, Starichkov declared proudly to a storm of applause, had "cleaned its ranks." Yet he cautioned his listeners that there was still work to be done "in rooting out the deeply masked, cowardly remnants of the enemies of the people and their supporters." In the discussion that followed, party members apologized for the enemies they had failed to unmask, listed those they had successfully uncovered, and called for the exposure of still others, naming names. Several members pointed out that the NKVD had arrested certain enemies whom the factory's party organizations had omitted to identify. To the shame of the party organizations, M. V. Iasvoin, the former director, and A. G. Koliad, a deputy secretary of the party committee, had both been arrested before being expelled. One party member conceded, "We made a big political mistake, and this mistake was corrected by the NKVD."[2]

Although Starichkov presented the purge as a great achievement, the changes in leadership had seriously disrupted production. P. P. Khorikov, the current director, noted that almost the entire leadership of the factory had been removed. Starichkov himself had recently been promoted to head a Moscow district committee, necessitating a by-election for his Dinamo post.[3] Nearly

2 "Raboty Partorganizatsii na Uroven' Sovremennykh Zadach," "Otchet Partkoma," and "Izmeneniia v Sostave Partiinogo Komiteta," *Kirovets*, January 6, 10, and 12, 1938, pp. 1, 2, 1. Of the forty-four party members arrested by the NKVD between April 1937 and April 1938, about 40 percent were arrested before they were excluded – a black mark on the record of the party organizations inasmuch as it suggested a lack of necessary vigilance, on their part, in purging the alleged enemies in their midst. The remaining 60 percent were first excluded and then arrested. See TsAOPIM, f. 432, o. 1, d. 188, l. 9.

3 "Izmeneniia v Sostave Partiinogo Komiteta," *Kirovets*, January 12, 1938, p. 1; TsAOPIM, f. 432, o. 1, d. 188, ll. 14, 41.

all the staff of the factory administration, as well as most of the shop and department heads, had been transferred, fired, or arrested. Their replacements had been promoted mainly from the ranks of "best Stakhanovites," workers with norm-busting production records. With little education or managerial experience, they were now attempting to master new jobs as shop heads and administrative personnel.[4] The head of the union's factory committee would later observe, "Labor discipline in the factory is shattered, and turnover among the labor force has reached unusually high levels."[5] Several shops, including the foundry and the hard insulation shop, had 100 percent turnover, meaning that the entire workforce left and was replaced.[6] The foundry, which had lost many employees to arrest, fell far behind schedule, affecting production in other shops dependent on its castings. A report later noted, "The foundry is messing up the entire factory." Dinamo as a whole failed to meet its annual plan for 1937. Spending on wages exceeded allocated funds, and production costs rose above budgeted figures. The shops struggled to adjust to wildly erratic production flows, with long stoppages being followed by "storming" to make up the work.[7] Although labor turnover, cost overruns, and stoppages were endemic to industrial enterprises throughout the country, arrests further destabilized production and administration. The factory newspaper, once used by management to rally support among workers and correct problems in the shops, was now, in the words of S. Mironov, a forty-one-year-old party member who had worked in

4 TsAOPIM, f. 432, o. 1, d. 188, l. 42.
5 TsAOPIM, f. 432, o. 1, d. 193, l. 30.
6 "Po Bol'shevistski Borot'sia za Likvidatsiiu Posledstvii Vreditel'stva," *Kirovets*, August 21, 1937, p. 2.
7 TsAOPIM, f. 432, o. 1, d. 188, ll. 42–43.

Dinamo since 1910, "occupied with nothing but the defamation of Communists."[8]

The purges in Dinamo were replicated in many other factories and institutions, as well as at every level of the Party's organizational hierarchy from the district to the city to the provincial to the republic committees. Party organizations at all levels were eviscerated by reciprocal denunciations and arrests. Party members, driven by a mixture of zeal and fear, kept up a steady drum of accusations. They wrote *zaiavleniia* against one another and took the notion of "unmasking" enemies to absurd lengths. In the Red Guard district of Moscow, for instance, one person wrote a *zaiavlenie* about every member of the district committee. In Kiev, the former head of the provincial committee habitually accosted any party member who spoke at a meeting with the question, "And at least you wrote a *zaiavlenie* to someone about this matter?" As a result, about half of the members of the Kiev party committee were targets of politically compromising *zaiavleniia*, most of which were later found to be false. In Rostov, ardent denouncers excluded party members "in batches." Most party organizations did not bother to review the political records or activities of targeted individuals, focusing instead on their associational ties.[9] Great chains of guilt by association crisscrossed party organizations, linking their members together and dragging them, one after another, into prison. Higher party organizations mechanically ratified exclusions. In some areas, exclusions were affirmed in lists that included more than 250 names at a time. Exclusion from the Party usually resulted in the loss of both employment and housing, and those who were expelled found

8 TsAOPIM, f. 432, o. 1, d. 194, l. 20.
9 TsAOPIM, f. 432, o. 1, d. 193, ll. 4–5.

it almost impossible to get other work. Some former party members, desperate, hungry, and homeless, begged their local party organizations either to provide them with letters removing the ruinous imputation that they were "enemies" or, failing that, to have them charged and arrested.[10] Naturally, no local official would risk his own life and career by writing such a letter.

Guilt by association also damaged those who did not belong to the Party. Many people lost jobs because they neglected to inform their supervisors or union committees that relatives of theirs had been arrested. Some rural teachers, for example, were fired en masse, forcing village schools to close. A mere rumor of disloyalty might be enough to cost an entire family its livelihood. In one instance, a local paper published a rumor that a teacher's brother was a "bourgeois nationalist." The teacher was fired, as was her husband. It was later discovered that the rumor had been based on a false accusation.[11]

Party organizations at every level were flooded with frantic appeals. The Party's charter, adopted in 1934, gave excluded members the right to appeal their expulsion, but only to their party and district committees. During the terror years of 1937 and 1938, however, these rules were widely ignored, as members wrote desperate letters of appeal to anyone who they thought might be able to help, at every level of the party hierarchy, all the way up to Stalin himself. In many instances, appeals to N. I. Ezhov and other high-profile party leaders backfired, resulting in the letter writers' immediate arrest, though in other cases, highly placed officials did help excluded members to be reinstated. Yet the welter of accusations and counteraccusations, the pervasive fear of being responsible for

10 "Informatsionnoe Soobshchenie ob Ocherednom Plenume TsK VKP (b)," *Kirovets*, January 20, 1938, pp. 1–2.
11 *Ibid.*

reinstating someone who might later prove to be an enemy, and the impossibility of second-guessing the NKVD all made party officials reluctant to overturn expulsions. It was easier, and safer, to either affirm an earlier decision or just allow an appeal to "marinate."

Moreover, the district, town, and provincial committees were themselves often severely compromised by arrests. Investigations were interrupted, resumed, and halted as officials disappeared into prison. Not only did arrests disrupt organizational continuity, they also cast doubt on earlier decisions. If a party member, for example, was either excluded or reinstated by an official who was later imprisoned, was the decision to be reversed? Did an "enemy" automatically revert to being a "loyal Communist" if his or her "unmasker" was arrested? Given the climate of uncertainty and fear, it was not surprising that tens of thousands of appeals went unanswered.

The political atmosphere was so volatile that party officials were usually reluctant to give assignments to members who had been reinstated. The possibilities for disaster were just too many and too great: a reinstated member might still be arrested, or might have his or her reinstatement reversed for any of a myriad of reasons. For many officials, if not most, it was simply not worth the risk. Although party organizations were in dire need of cadres, reinstated party members remained in organizational limbo. Managers likewise refused to hire former party members. Their fears were neither false nor exaggerated: every official had heard grim stories of expulsion, reinstatement, reversal, and subsequent arrest. No one could predict the vicissitudes of fate or, more concretely, the agenda of the NKVD. In the view of most local officials, the wisest and safest course of action was to take no action at all.

Pervasive fear also disrupted the recruitment of new members. The Party had stopped admitting candidates during the review of party documents that began in May 1935, but enrollment resumed in November 1936. By then, however, party members were terrified to sponsor candidates, aware that if one of their protégés was later arrested, they would be held responsible for having recommended an "enemy." To protect themselves, party members thus refused to give recommendations. When prospective recruits applied to become candidate members, the first step toward full membership, their applications moldered in dusty stacks because they were unable to find sponsors. Party rules required that each candidate provide recommendations from three members with whom he or she had worked for a minimum of three years, but abrupt changes in leadership, transfers, and the decimation of party ranks had deeply eroded the stability of work relationships. Employees no sooner became acquainted with their bosses and supervisors than the latter were lost to exclusion, arrest, promotion, or reassignment. And now, even in those cases where aspiring candidates had worked with potential recommenders for three years or more, the recommenders were afraid to write.[12] Party enrollment statistics reflected these fears. In Dinamo, between November 1936 and July 1937, only five new members entered the Party. In June 1937, the Central Committee, concerned about the Party's dwindling ranks, urged the local organizations to accept new members.[13] The Central Committee's instructions had some effect: after July, more members and candidates were accepted. Yet in many departments and shops in

12 "Rost Partiinykh Riadov," *Kirovets*, July 21, 1938, p. 2. "Perestrakhovshchiki," *Kirovets*, February 13, 1938, p. 2.

13 On the Central Committee's decree, see "Postanovlenie TsK VKP (b): Ob Oshibkakh pri Rassmotrenie Apelliatsii Iskliuchennykh iz Partii vo Vremia Proverki i Obmena Partiinykh Dokumentov," in "Informatsionnoe Soobshchenie ob Ocherednom Plenume TsK VKP (b)," *Kirovets*, January 20, 1938, pp. 1–2.

Dinamo, especially those hobbled by arrests, enrollment was frozen. In the factory administration, for example, a department heavily hit, only three new members and five candidates were added to the rolls between November 1936 and July 1938.

By early 1938, the Central Committee understood that the terror was destroying the Party. Local organizations were ruining themselves in a frenzy of mutual denunciations and accusations. Party officials were immobilized by fear. The party organizations, reduced to anticipating the actions of the NKVD, had begun expelling people who *might* be arrested in order to forestall the charge of "overlooking an enemy."[14] There were few new members coming in, and the appeals process was barely functional. Thousands of embittered former party members were jobless and homeless, and countless more were dead or in prison. No one could tell enemy from friend, or trust that an official's decision would not be overturned by arrest. The flood of appeals, the absurdity of allegations, the destructive practice of mutual denunciation – all of these finally made an impression at the highest level of leadership.

CHANGING COURSE

In January 1938, the Party changed course in an effort to contain the spread of the terror through associational ties. The Politburo announced that relatives of those arrested for counterrevolutionary activity were not to be fired from their jobs solely for kinship ties, and the children of "enemies" were no longer subject to special punitive treatment.[15] The Central Committee issued a resolution

14 See Kosior's comments at the January 1938 Central Committee plenum, cited in Vadim Zakharovich Rogovin, *Stalin's Terror of 1937–1938: Political Genocide in the USSR* (Oak Park, Mich.: Mehring Books, 2009), p. 14.

15 Corinna Kuhr, "Children of 'Enemies of the People' as Victims of the Great Purges," *Cahiers du Monde Russe*, vol. 39, nos. 1–2 (1998), p. 213; Golfo

regarding "mistakes in excluding Communists from the Party" and "false bureaucratic attitudes toward appeals." Reprinted in the national and factory newspapers, its text condemned the expulsions of "honest" Communists and ascribed "serious mistakes and distortions" to the party organizations. The Central Committee absolved itself of all blame, noting that its "instructions and repeated warnings" had gone unheeded as the local party organizations excluded tens of thousands of party members who were innocent of any wrongdoing. They had furthermore failed to investigate cases, provide proper explanations for verdicts, and process appeals in a timely manner. They had expelled as "enemies" members whose only "crime" was passivity or associational ties. They were guilty, the resolution held, of "criminal frivolity" and a "soulless-bureaucratic" attitude toward individual party members.[16]

While the Central Committee pronounced itself eager to rectify these mistakes, it did not go so far as to renounce the repression of the preceding years. In effect, it simply added one more group to the list of those whose members were to be "unmasked." The resolution explained that "careerist Communists" were the ones responsible for the destruction of innocent comrades: "All these facts occurred because concealed and masked individual careerist Communists, who seek to distinguish and promote themselves into the positions of those excluded from the Party, exist within the party organizations." The Central Committee had coined a new epithet for these promiscuous denouncers of others: "bawling careerists" (*krikuny-kar'eristi*). Conceding that strategies of protection had constituted a driving

Alexopoulos, "Stalin and the Politics of Kinship: Practices of Collective Punishment, 1920s–1940s," *Comparative Studies in Society and History*, vol. 50, no. 1 (2008), p. 109. Alexopoulos notes, "[The] regime's policy regarding the collective punishment of kin first signaled the reduction of terror."

16 "Informatsionnoe Soobshchenie ob Ocherednom Plenume TsK VKP (b)," *Kirovets*, January 20, 1938, pp. 1–2.

motor of the purge, it blamed those who "aim to protect themselves from the possibility of an accusation of insufficient vigilance by applying indiscriminate repression against other party members." It also acknowledged that party members had falsely accused, shunned, and refused to defend comrades but again transferred blame for this widespread behavior to a small group of scapegoats: "Such careerist Communists think that once a party member has a *zaiavlenie* against him, even if it is incorrect or even if it is a provocation, then this party member is dangerous for the organization, and they need to run away from him in order that they will continue to appear vigilant." The resolution went so far as to suggest, moreover, that many of these "bawlers" were themselves "hidden enemies," wont to slander honest Communists in their attempts to protect their own leadership circles, divert attention from their enemy activities, and destroy the Party. It urged the party organizations to "discover and expose these skillfully masked enemies who bawl about vigilance in order to mask their enemy nature."[17] In fact, the Central Committee provided a strikingly apt description of the self-protective strategies and false accusations that were destroying the party organizations, though it neatly absolved itself of blame. As one historian would later point out, the plenum's highly accurate portrayal of party meetings was an indictment less of individual "enemy bawlers" than of the "monstrous atmosphere that had developed in 1937."[18]

The Central Committee's resolution provided explicit instructions as to how the party organizations were to go about rectifying past mistakes. They were to take an "individual approach" with

17 *Ibid.*
18 Rogovin, *Stalin's Terror*, p. 16.

each party member, stop "indiscriminate" expulsions, and review all appeals within three months. Officials who failed to verify accusations through a close investigation of supporting documentation were to be removed. Party members who were reinstated were immediately to be entrusted with party assignments. Former party members who were unemployed were to be rehired within one month. No one was to be deprived of a job as a consequence of expulsion. Finally, party organizations were to charge those responsible for unsupported accusations with slander and ensure that public retractions of all false accusations were printed in the papers. "It is time," the Central Committee announced, "to unmask as careerists those who slander Communists, who aim to advance themselves at the expense of the excluded, and who safeguard themselves through repression of party members." The Central Committee took a hard line on "incorrect" exclusions, declaring that every such case "played into the hands of the enemies of the Party."[19]

Implicitly recognizing that writers of aggressive *zaiavleniia* were destroying the Party, the Central Committee also stressed that denouncers must have substantive grounds, if not actual proof, before writing against fellow party members. By demanding that members take responsibility for their allegations, the resolution sought to discourage the fearful preemptive charges and baseless mudslinging that had come to characterize relations within the Party. It proposed that party members should no longer be excluded for having vague associational ties to "enemies" or for failing to submit timely *zaiavleniia* about arrested or excluded relatives – two charges that had resulted in many expulsions. Finally, it provided

19 "Informatsionnoe Soobshchenie ob Ocherednom Plenume TsK VKP (b)," *Kirovets*, January 20, 1938, pp. 1–2.

excluded party members with new grounds for appeal – namely, that they had been the victims of "bawling careerists" or unsubstantiated accusations.

These new policies, however, did not stop the terror or the repressions that had become endemic within the Party. The Central Committee's resolution merely added one more category – "bawlers, signalers, careerists, and slanderers" – to an already long list of "enemies of the people." It did not entail an admission that the earlier repression had been wrong, nor did it signal a shift in the prevailing political orientation. The Central Committee refused responsibility for previous exclusions of "innocent" people, instead blaming all "mistakes" on the local party organizations. Moreover, these "mistakes" pertained to only a fraction of excluded party members and did not extend to those outside the Party who had been repressed. The resolution did not criticize the NKVD, result in an amnesty of political prisoners, or establish an automatic review of all cases of repression. People who had already been shot or sentenced to the camps remained "guilty," no matter how specious the evidence against them might have been. Thus the timing of a party member's exclusion was critical, as was whether or not it had been followed by arrest and sentencing. In this sense, the resolution, which attempted to right a number of wrongs of the past year, also enshrined the NKVD as the sole, unassailable arbiter of guilt and innocence.

THE IMPACT OF THE RESOLUTION

In the realm of national politics, the resolution slowed but did not halt the repressions. Arrests continued, especially among various national groups. The NKVD arrested 936,750 people in 1937, and

683,509 in 1938.[20] As the newspapers explained, the resolution was not to be understood as putting an end to the "unmasking" of enemies; rather, its intention was that party members and officials "must unmask enemies even more sharply than before, but real enemies, and not false ones."[21] In March 1938, the show trial of Bukharin and other prominent leaders opened in Moscow amid the same sort of propaganda campaign that had accompanied its predecessors, in August 1936 and January 1937.[22] The defendants were charged with crimes similar to those considered in the earlier trials: spying for Fascist countries, conspiring to murder Kirov, plotting to assassinate party leaders, and planning to restore capitalism. The rhetoric describing them was likewise recycled: they were "Fascist hirelings," a "criminal band of vile murderers" who were "united in their hatred of socialism." With Hitler on the march, the prosecution placed somewhat greater emphasis on the defendants as "fifth columnists" bent on betraying the country in a time of war, but the trial itself, which once again relied solely on confessions and mutual denunciations, followed a by now familiar script.[23]

Once again, mass meetings attended by thousands of people were held in the factories and the streets, party orators delivered fiery

20 V. N. Khaustov, V. P. Naumov, and N. S. Plotnikova, eds., *Lubianka. Stalin i glavnoe upravlenie gosbezopasnosti NKVD, 1937–8: Dokumenty* (Moscow: Izdatel'stvo 'Materik', 2004), pp. 659–60.
21 "Resheniia Plenuma TsK VKP (b) Sdelat' Dostianiem Kazhdogo Kommunista," *Kirovets*, January 25, 1938, p. 2, reprinted from *Pravda*, January 22, 1938.
22 The defendants were N. I. Bukharin, A. I. Rykov, G. G. Iagoda, N. N. Krestinskii, Kh. G. Rakovskii, A. P. Rozengol'ts, V. I. Ivanov, M. A. Chernov, G. F. Grinko, I. A. Zelenskii, S. A. Bessonov, A. Ikramov, Faizulla Khodzhaev, P. P. Bulanov, L. G. Levin, D. D. Pletnev, I. N. Kazakov, V. A. Maksimov, P. P. Kriuchkov, V. Sharangovich, and P. Zubarev.
23 "'Pravo-Trotskistskii Blok' Ubiitsov, Shpionov, Predatelei," *Kirovets*, March 1, 1938, p. 1; reprinted from *Pravda*, February 28, 1938; "Trotskistsko-Bukhariniskim Banditam Net Poshchady!" *Kirovets*, March 3, 1938, p. 1.

speeches decrying the crimes of the defendants, and workers publicly demanded the death penalty: "Shoot them like mad dogs!" "Wipe them from the face of the earth!" "The reptiles will not escape punishment!" Workers throughout the country vowed to continue unmasking enemies. At meetings in Dinamo, more than five thousand of them voted a resolution declaring their hatred for the "evil, vile degenerates": "We will raise our revolutionary vigilance and root out and annihilate to the end all enemies of the people."[24] As before, the national and factory newspapers covered the trial in detail, printing long excerpts of the proceedings, responses from workers, and the closing speech by Vyshinskii, the prosecutor. Eighteen of the twenty-one defendants, including Bukharin and Rykov, were condemned to death by shooting, and the remaining three were sentenced to fifteen to twenty years in the camps. The trial, which was staged less than two months after the publication of the Central Committee's resolution, ensured that the national hysteria about "hidden enemies" remained at a fever pitch. Neither did the Central Committee's resolution halt arrests, which continued both within the Party and outside it, or end the mass and national operations, which persisted through the fall of 1938. In fact, shortly after the Central Committee plenum, the Politburo approved an extension of the operations, raising the arrest quotas in various areas and then later raising them again.

The resolution did, however, reduce the number of expulsions from the Party. Between January and August of 1938, some 37,000 members were expelled, down from 97,000 between July and December of the previous year, and the downward trend continued for the

24 "Izmenniki Ponesut Zasluzhennuiu Karu," *Kirovets*, March 1, 1938, p. 1; "Nikakoi Poshchadi Podlym Izmennikam Rodiny," *Kirovets*, February 28, 1938, p. 1; TsAOPIM, f. 432, o. 1, d. 194, ll. 37–39.

remainder of 1938.[25] The resolution also encouraged party members who had been excluded to appeal their cases. Up until the January Central Committee plenum, only 53,700 excluded party members had appealed. Between January and June alone, that number almost doubled, reaching 101,233. Local party organizations reviewed 85,273 of these cases and reinstated 54 percent of the appellants.[26] The reinstatements opened new fissures within the party organizations. Recently vindicated members returned to the ranks nursing grudges against their denouncers, eager to carry out the Central Committee's instructions to expel the "bawling careerists." Party members who had been quietly suffering the sting of accusations were now emboldened to strike back against their attackers and accuse them of slander. Efforts to comply with the decree and unmask "enemy bawlers" led to fresh witch hunts as party members, armed with the new epithets provided by the Central Committee, turned on the most zealous denouncers.

LOCAL PANDEMONIUM

The Central Committee's resolution sent the local organizations spinning into a new phase of chaos. Few party members who had survived 1937 had abstained from participating in the exclusion of others or making preemptive accusations to protect themselves. Those who remained survived precisely because they had been able

25 Oleg Khlevniuk, "Party and NKVD: Power Relationships in the Years of the Great Terror," in Barry McLoughlin and Kevin McDermott, eds., *Stalin's Terror: High Politics and Mass Repression in the Soviet Union* (Basingstoke, Hampshire: Palgrave Macmillan, 2003), p. 27.

26 "Po Bol'shevistski Vypolnit' Postanovlenie Ianvarskogo Plenuma TsK VKP (b)," *Kirovets*, August 8, 1938, p. 2. Khlevniuk, "Party and NKVD," p. 27, notes that some 77,000 Communists were reinstated in 1938.

to use the iron rules of the game to their own advantage. They were keenly aware that they and their comrades neatly fit the Central Committee's new description of the "enemy." Among these survivors, almost every one had been either a victim or a perpetrator at some time, and no small number had been both. As a group, they shared a bitter collective history: they all feared, mistrusted, and resented one another. The Central Committee's resolution now presented fresh opportunities, phrases, and justifications for the expression of long-simmering grievances.

In Dinamo, A. I. Efanov, Starichkov's replacement as head of the party committee, spoke to hundreds of party members about the resolution in a factory-wide meeting. He chose his words carefully, anxious that no one should misinterpret the resolution as a repudiation of the earlier and ongoing repressions. He began by explaining that enemies still existed and were supported by foreign powers. They had been "routed, beaten, but still not completely smashed." He reminded everyone that the "flushing out" of such enemies had played a "colossal role in strengthening socialism." Party members had needed real Bolshevik vigilance "to uncover and annihilate current enemies of the people." This had been the war cry of 1937, and Efanov made it clear that the battle was not over. He offered, however, one small amendment: there were some cases in which comrades had been "approached incorrectly," he said. Just as party organizations had made mistakes in not excluding certain members who were subsequently arrested by the NKVD, they had likewise erred in excluding some who were never arrested. Referring to local party officials, he noted, "Sometimes in making a decision about exclusion, they paste the label 'enemy of the people' on someone, but he walks about freely, the NKVD does not take him, he is unfairly fired from his job, he goes about without work and with the label 'enemy' affixed to him, and he is embittered."[27] Efanov thus tacitly advised local party officials how to interpret and implement the Central Committee's resolution: they should rectify their "mistakes," he implied, by reviewing the expulsions of those former party members who had been excluded but not arrested.

In his speech, Efanov also unwittingly revealed a great deal about the expanded role of the NKVD in the Party's affairs. He so much as admitted that local party organizations had ceded control and authority over their members to the NKVD, insofar as he suggested that a member who was arrested before being excluded exposed the Party's lack of vigilance, while one who was excluded but not arrested could in all likelihood be considered the victim of a "mistake." Efanov thus acknowledged that the party organizations, in their fear and disorientation, had become little more than a rubber stamp. Ezhov, head of the NKVD, had advanced a similar view of NKVD supremacy in 1937, when he labeled his agency the "armed vanguard of our Party."[28]

Efanov's implication about the expanded role of the NKVD in party affairs, albeit an observed truth, was not what the Central Committee intended to convey. Rather, its resolution urged the local organizations to differentiate between real and false vigilance, drawing an admittedly slippery distinction that Efanov now attempted to explain. "Those who screamed about vigilance and demanded that party members write *zaiavleniia* about other party members," he said, were purveyors of "false vigilance." Such avid "bawlers" and "signalers" (*signalizatory*) tried to ferret out information about associational ties: "Instead of investigating enemies

---

27 TsAOPIM, f. 432, o. 1, d. 193, ll. 1–16.
28 Khlevniuk, "Party and NKVD," p. 21.

according to what they did," Efanov noted, "they looked at who met and greeted whom." They further "tried to distinguish and promote themselves at the expense of those who were excluded, and aimed to protect themselves from potential accusations by applying indiscriminate repression against others." Many members, however, had benefited from the exclusions of others; after all, posts had to be filled. And who among them had not tried to distance himself from someone in political trouble by writing a preemptive *zaiavlenie?* Should party members still find the definition of false vigilance confusing, Efanov clarified the lesson by naming names, putting it in terms that everyone could understand. He called one party member, Khromogin, to account, sarcastically anointing him a "vigilant hero because he allegedly unmasked this and that." "He is still unmasking much," Efanov continued with a sneer. "He drops by the shops and notes who works with whom and who meets with whom." Party members, he instructed, were to stop writing *zaiavleniia* and launching investigations based on tenuous associational ties. Zealous displays of loyalty and preemptive denunciations, two of the most common strategies for self-protection, would no longer be tolerated. Efanov concluded by encouraging party members to identify and expel those who belonged to this new category of "bawlers, signalers, and careerists."[29]

During the ensuing discussion, party members used the resolution as a weapon with which to attack comrades for their appalling behavior over the past year. Serebriakov, head of the agitation sector (*agitpunkt*), spoke out angrily against Starichkov, the former head of the party committee. "In 1937, my brother was arrested," he began. "He is ten years older than me. I had not even seen him since 1917.

[29] TsAOPIM, f. 432, o. 1, d. 193, ll. 1–16.

I knew about the arrest through my father, and of course, I went to the party committee and informed Starichkov that my brother had been arrested, but I told him I did not know why. Starichkov said to me, 'You are not such a child that you should not know why he was arrested. It is clear. He is an enemy of the people.' In August 1937, I received a copy of the court decision exonerating my brother. As a result of all this, I went to the party committee many times, and I even entered a sanitarium for nervous illness." Serebriakov, like many others, had been literally sickened by fear. His statement opened the floodgates to a river of recrimination. Every comrade seemed to bear some terrible grudge against another, the sum total of which implicated everyone in a messy collective crime. Kruk, a member of the factory administration, accused Starichkov of having falsified the protocols of party meetings that were sent to the district committee, and in his own case of allowing district officials to see that "Batsheev accused me of being an enemy of the people." Kulimov, an inspector, attacked him in turn: "Kruk wants to shift all the blame onto one person, but this is wrong." Kruk, incensed, stood up and started for the door. "Don't walk out, Comrade Kruk," Kulimov yelled after him. "You cannot say that you were pure. In fact, Iasvoin [the former Dinamo director who was subsequently arrested] brought you with him when he came to the factory." Turning back to the audience, Kulimov declared, "This fact is indisputable: we need to consider that Kruk's speeches are aimed at freeing himself from blame and dumping it onto others. He is supposedly innocent, a little sheep felled by a blow from the former party committee secretary, Comrade Starichkov." No sooner had Kruk left the meeting than Khromogin, an organizer in the foundry whom Efanov had earlier singled out as a "bawler," rose to defend himself. He noted with evident agitation, "Not long ago I showed up for work, and they threw at me this accusation of 'bawler,' which I do not deserve. I am raising this question here at the meeting in order to determine whether I am a 'bawler' or not. I have worked in this factory for fifteen years. . . . I reject this accusation thrown at me that I am a bawler. I reject Efanov's accusation."[30]

But if Efanov considered Khromogin a bawler, other party members now hurled the same epithet at Efanov himself. Khailov, who had been expelled from the Party in May 1937 and then reinstated, came to the secretary's defense. He had other bawlers in mind, including Bakhmutskii, one of the more zealous denouncers, who had figured prominently in his expulsion. "There were bawlers in the party committee," Khailov insisted, "who did not help to clarify things. It was not a healthy situation, but rather one of intimidation. In my opinion, Efanov is being called a bawler incorrectly. In my opinion, Bakhmutskii is the main bawler." Bakhmutskii had evidently boasted about his close connection to the NKVD, and Khailov now complained, "He made a statement that that enemy of the people Tolchinskii called me an idiot under interrogation. He did this in order to demonstrate that he knew about the business with Tolchinskii and to imply that I could be arrested, too." Razin, an employee in the department of technical control, had little interest in the venomous relations between Khailov and Bakhmutskii. Instead he shifted the focus back to Khromogin, accusing him of paradigmatic "bawling" behavior: Khromogin, he reminded his listeners, had attacked others for failing to unmask enemies even though he himself had worked closely with, and likewise failed to expose, those same enemies. Another party member, annoyed that the discussion had strayed from Bakhmutskii, called out,

30 TsAOPIM, f. 432, o. 1, d. 194, ll. 16–21.

"Bakhmutskii wanted to show himself in the role of an unmasker."[31] The meeting, a litany of old wounds, festering resentments, and fresh claims, did not mark an end to the zealous pursuit of unmasking in the factory. It did, however, stir up new roiling currents of accusation and counteraccusation as party members reviewed the ugly history of the previous year.

Moreover, in contravention of the Central Committee's resolution, Dinamo's party organization continued to expel members on the basis of their associational ties. A mere five days after the meeting, hundreds of party members gathered again to review cases of expulsion. Bystritskii, an engineer, was excluded for having ties to two party members who had been arrested earlier, after another member informed the party committee of the arrest of Bystritskii's brother in Leningrad. Bystritskii himself was arrested shortly thereafter. The committee also expelled Mironov, a foreman in the hard insulation shop and organizer in the electrical shop, for his associational ties.[32] Such ties, along with *zaiavleniia*, continued to provide the main evidence for expulsions.

The Central Committee's resolution had little more effect on relations among comrades and coworkers in other factories. Party organizations in Trekhgornaia Manufaktura, Krasnyi Proletarii, and Likerno-Vodochnyi distillery all continued to expel members through the summer of 1938. By now, many of these behaviors and practices had become institutionalized, and there was no real pressure applied from above to change them. When a representative from the district committee, Evteev, attended a party meeting in Likerno-Vodochnyi, he did not encourage the sorts of

31 *Ibid.*
32 TsAOPIM, f. 432, o. 1, d. 194, ll. 22–30. On Bystritskii's arrest, see f. 432, o. 1, d. 188, l. 11.

recriminations prompted by the Central Committee's resolution; to the contrary, he made every effort to maintain the established atmosphere of fear and intimidation. Taking his cue from the resolution, Geche, a party member, complained that his comrades habitually shunned him for his Latvian origins and his ties to a coworker who had been arrested. "I consider the behavior of other Communists toward me to be wrong," he said. "I am a member of the party organization, and they will not sit with me because I worked with Gul'bis. I went to the club, and everyone sitting around me got up and left." He continued, "I go to the courtyard. They ask me, 'You're still alive?'" Geche concluded, "I say, if there is some suspicion about me, take me away. If I am a Latvian Nazi, take me away. If something is wrong, tell me. But people here just try to get farther away from me." Another party member, Ivanova, confirmed his account: "Everyone has begun to avoid Geche. We should check things out, but we need to check carefully, not like this. They have even stopped saying hello to him." She also protested her own treatment: "There is not a single meeting when I am not reminded that I was friendly with the enemy Kogan." In spite of the Central Committee's resolution, which demanded an end to shunning and guilt by association, Evteev sharply reprimanded both Geche and Ivanova. "Geche spoke here and said no one would greet him. This is not the point," he said. "The point is that party members who worked with Gul'bis should tear out whatever roots may remain of his enemy activities." He then admonished Ivanova, "You speak in the pose of the offended, Comrade Ivanova. You received a reprimand. Was this correct? In my opinion, it was correct." Turning to the audience, Evteev asked, "Can she be offended? No." He also chastised Ivanova for defending Geche. Noting that both of their statements had been "unclear," he ominously suggested that their words should be examined more closely: "It seems to me that our entire party organization needs to study such speeches and raise party vigilance."[33] Evteev's message was clear: members were not to defend one another against even the most specious of attacks, nor were they to complain about the insidious rumors that were destroying relations among comrades. If they did, there would be consequences: the party organization would "study" their words. Evteev, a representative of a higher party organization, thus intimidated the protesters into silence.

"UNMASKING" THE "SLANDERERS"

In Dinamo, the factory newspaper, *Kirovets*, which had previously goaded the shop organizations to unmask spies and wreckers, now pushed them to identify "bawlers." Just as Efanov had adopted the language of the Central Committee's resolution in his speech to Dinamo's Communists, so did the editor of the factory newspaper copy Efanov's speech, recycling its phrases for dissemination to the factory's employees. Using the formulation that "mistakes" made in excluding "honest Communists" had hurt the struggle against the "Trotskyist-Bukharinist Fascists and their hirelings," *Kirovets*, too, attempted the tricky political balancing act of defending the earlier repression while condemning the expulsion of "innocents." Many of the accusations against party members, one article conceded, had proved to be little more than a "house of cards built on sand."[34] Another charged that "bawlers, wanting to appear supervigilant, cried out at every opportunity about the dominance of enemies and wrote slanderous *zaiavleniia*, pouncing and casting aspersions

33 TsAOPIM, f. 428, o. 1, d. 1, ll. 12 ob, 76, 57, 101, 101ob.
34 "Protiv Fal'shivoi Bditel'nosti," *Kirovets*, January 19, 1938, p. 1.

on honest Communists." *Kirovets* noted that the party organization had failed to check these "lying *zaiavleniia.*" The paper offered no critique of its own role in publicizing accusations and targeting victims, though it now prodded the party organizations to rectify past mistakes by identifying those responsible for them.[35]

Kirovets published accounts of three cases of "mistaken" expulsion to illustrate the Party's change in course. The editor's aim here, however, was not simply to right past wrongs; rather, the examples were carefully selected to redraw the line between the innocent and the guilty, as well as to set limits for any discussion of the repressions. After all, not all expulsions were mistakes, and party members needed to learn how to distinguish a true enemy from a wronged comrade. The protagonist in the first case was Denisov, former head of the crane shop, who had been expelled for having a tie to an enemy. His expulsion was based on information in a *zaiavlenie* written by a fellow party member, who had heard it from some woman – who in turn claimed to have been told by Denisov's mother-in-law – that Denisov frequently spoke with an "unmasked enemy of the people." The injustice was subsequently compounded when Kovalevskii, a party organizer, fired Denisov from his job. Kovalevskii, the newspaper reported, had "racked his brains for a long time trying to figure out how to get rid of Denisov." First he urged everyone in the shop to recall any infraction he might have committed, and then he fired him "for disrupting labor discipline." Unconvinced by this charge, the workers in the crane shop did not support the dismissal of their boss. *Kirovets*, which had earlier fanned the fires of expulsion, now pushed for Denisov's reinstatement.

35 "Po Bol'shevistski Ispravit' Dopushennye Oshibki," *Kirovets*, February 5, 1938, p. 1.

Of particular note, according to the paper, was that the propagandist who discussed the Central Committee's resolution with the workers in Denisov's former shop had failed to mention Denisov's case. "The silence of this agitator seems strange," the editor pointedly remarked. What was more, Kovalevskii, who had fired Denisov, still had not spoken with him or taken responsibility for his actions.[36] The paper stressed the lack of evidence for the allegations, the spurious reasons for dismissal, and the workers' support of their former boss. According to *Kirovets*, Denisov was a good example of a "mistake."

In its coverage of such "mistakes," *Kirovets* focused mainly on comrades who had been expelled for having questionable associational ties, for failing to denounce others, or for not unmasking "enemies" who were later arrested. The second case it treated in detail was that of Iosilevskii, a worker in the fourth instrument shop. Explaining that Iosilevskii had been excluded for "sympathizing in spirit with an enemy of the people," the writer of the article tartly asked, "How did this 'unmasker' know the spirit of Iosilevskii? We do not know." And finally, the paper devoted several articles to the case of A. S. Fomin, former head of the fourth instrument shop, expelled in March 1937 for having ties to coworkers who were arrested as Trotskyists (see chapter 2). Fomin was charged with not helping his party organization to unmask his "enemy" coworkers and with having failed to write *zaiavleniia* about them.[37] These charges, which could be leveled against any party member who worked with someone who was later arrested, had set off the flurry of preemptive *zaiavleniia* that had ultimately proved so damaging.

36 "Za Chto Sniat s Raboty Denisov," *Kirovets*, February 1, 1938, p. 2.
37 TsAOPIM, f. 432, o. 1, d. 179, ll. 75–79.

Kirovets now revealed some new information about Fomin. After Dinamo's party committee excluded him, the district committee received another denunciation, claiming that Fomin had deserted from the Red Army during the Civil War, an accusation that was later shown to be false. The Moscow party committee eventually overturned the lower decisions and chided the district and party committees for their failure to check the facts. When *Kirovets* urged its readers to "study the Fomin case," it was essentially providing Dinamo's party organization with general guidelines for reversing expulsions. Taken together, the three cases described – Denisov, Iosilevskii, and Fomin – highlighted the "mistaken" party practices most anathematized by the Central Committee's resolution: exclusion on the basis of associational ties, the prosecution of unsubstantiated allegations, and the failure to verify charges. These were the very same practices that had led to the destruction of the party organizations from within. "Slander," the *Kirovets* editor asserted, echoing the rhetoric of the resolution, "is the favorite method of enemies of the people."[38]

Kirovets now called for the party committee to identify and punish those responsible, noting, "The party committee has still not considered who was helped by these exclusions or who slandered this or that Communist, and it has not held the slanderers accountable."[39] Just as the paper had publicized cases of incorrect expulsion, it also named slanderers who should be brought to justice. Among these

38 In *Kirovets*, "Protiv Bezdushnogo Biurokraticheskogo Otnosheniia k Chlenam Partii," January 18, 1938, p. 3; "Protiv Fal'shivoi Bditel'nosti," January 19, 1938, p. 1; "Po Bol'shevistski Ispravit' Dopushennye Oshibki," February 5, 1938, p. 1; "Neponiatno Molchanie Agitatorov Kranovo-Pod"emnogo," February 4, 1938, p. 2.
39 "Po Bol'shevistski Ispravit' Dopushennye Oshibki." *Kirovets*, February 5, 1938, p. 1.

was one Rodionov, a worker and candidate for party membership, who had written a *zaiavlenie* against Zinoviev, a young Komsomol organizer. Rodionov claimed that Zinoviev's father was a kulak and owned seven horses and a two-story house. The allegation proved to be untrue: the man was in fact a railroad worker. *Kirovets* then disclosed that Rodionov was guilty not only of slander but of financial speculation as well. His wife bought milk from a neighbor who had a cow and resold it at a profit to workers at the factory. The paper directed the party organization in Rodionov's shop to "unmask this careerist."[40] Yet Rodionov, a worker in a machine shop, could hardly be considered an egregious example, even among Dinamo employees, of the slanderers and careerists who had benefited from the repression. If anything, his story was more typical of a victim's. After falsely denouncing another party member, he was exposed as being guilty of petty infractions for which he was then himself denounced in turn. Perpetrator and victim, he was accused of the grand crime of "speculation" for his wife's sale of milk from a single cow.

Throughout the late winter and spring of 1938, the pages of *Kirovets* were filled with the names of alleged slanderers and "self-overprotectors" (*samo perestrakhovshchiki*) who tried to shield themselves by denouncing others. Sh. G. Terushkin, an older party member, was publicly criticized for writing "packets of slanderous *zaiavleniia*" and "discrediting honest Communists." One article openly acknowledged that the strategies of self-protection adopted by party members had led to the self-devouring processes of the previous year.[41] The paper urged the party organizations to punish the

40 "Kleveta," *Kirovets*, February 9, 1938, p. 2.
41 "Umet' Razlichat' Druga ot Vraga," *Kirovets*, February 17, 1938, p. 2.

slanderers and to continue unmasking enemies, but its exhortations had little effect beyond promoting additional quarrels, accusations, and personal tragedies.

ORGANIZATIONAL PARALYSIS

Notwithstanding the mandate from the Central Committee, the party organizations found it difficult to dispel the fear that now governed relations among their members. Gripped by mistrust, party members were incapable of carrying out even the most basic of organizational tasks. In April 1938, party organizations throughout the country held elections for their local committees. In Dinamo, more than six hundred party members attended the accounting and election meeting. In his summary report, Efanov praised the great purging work that the party organizations had done over the past year. But the atmosphere was so poisonous that the audience had trouble selecting and approving new candidates: no one, it seemed, was pure enough to stand for election. Shilov, a member of the department of technical control, attacked Serebriakov, head of the agitation sector and a nominee. "What about party member Serebriakov?" he asked. "He has made a lot of mistakes. What were they? I can enumerate them." And he proceeded to give a full accounting of Serebriakov's various mistaken formulations, his ties to enemies, and his failure to denounce those enemies. "I think our party committee needs to check out people a lot more carefully," Shilov declared. Not only did he consider Serebriakov a poor candidate, but he even suggested that he deserved to be expelled: "I feel strongly that he should not be allowed to keep his party card. I am surprised that people such as Serebriakov and Razumovksii [head of the party organization in the mechanical blank preparation shop] have the confidence of the party committee." The audience applauded this last remark. The candidates tried to defend themselves using the by now familiar strategies of blame shifting, aggressive accusation, and naming names. Razumovskii, who evidently had a habit of referring to himself in the third person, explained that he had written a recommendation for a party member who was later arrested only because the party committee urged him to do so. About his exposure by a national newspaper for his failure to "signal," he said, "they want to pour all the guilt on Razumovskii. This is wrong." He asked the audience how he could be expected to identify as an enemy someone who was supported and even praised by the Party. Angrily, he responded to one critic, "Now they are talking about the drunkenness of Comrade Razumovskii. With whom did I drink, Comrade Chalov? If I criticized you, then you may cover yourself, but it does not follow that you may tell an outright lie about me. I suggest that this business be noted and investigated." The cycle of blame thus continued: attacked for having an enemy tie and for excessive drinking, Razumovskii immediately called for an investigation of his critics. Golovanov, an organizer in the warehouse, urged that Martynov, an older foreman, be removed from the list of candidates because he had once said something disparaging about the state bonds that party organizers pressured workers to buy. Golovanov also complained that the party committee had ignored his own denunciations of certain "dubious people" who had relatives abroad or were "inclined to Trotskyism." Ionov, a member of the factory guards, offered a groveling apology: "I made a big political mistake," he announced. "I was overconfident about Zhukov [Dinamo's former director], a party member since 1918. I thought he was more developed than I was." Someone in the audience yelled out, "You were related to him! Yes, he was your relative, your brother-in-law!"

Evsineikin, an organizer in the welding shop, broke in and addressed Ionov directly: "Why are you talking about this enemy of the people whom you regarded as being more literate than you? You lived in the same apartment with him. Rozengol'ts was arrested a long while ago and shot, but at the time, you said nothing about it. And now, when they have begun to unravel the case without you, you talk about this. Now is not the time to confess your innermost feelings. We must root out enemies of the people." Krysin, a member of the union factory committee, tattled on Kovalevskii, the party organizer responsible for firing Denisov. He reported that Kovalevskii had interrupted two lessons for workers on socialist labor. "This is of such political importance," Krysin announced indignantly, "that the party committee needs to give it particular attention." He demanded that the committee stop treating Kovalevskii "with liberalism."[42]

The meeting, a long parade of speakers offering up defensive apologies, petty allegations, and bombastic soliloquies, revealed that Dinamo's party membership had lost any purpose beyond mutual denunciation. Organizational structures had collapsed. The comrades could not select a list of candidates for election to the party committee because they were unable to stop squabbling, making accusations, and demanding new investigations. Efanov seemed powerless to steer them in the new direction mapped out by the Central Committee's resolution. New phrases simply augmented old practices. The meeting ended with a sharp rebuke from Timofeev, a representative from the Moscow party committee. "Comrades," he said impatiently, "of course wreckers did a lot of damage, but you cannot be occupied only with this all the time." Yet Timofeev himself could not resist feeding the insatiable obsession with enemies by relating several recent examples of wrecking in maternity

42 TsAOPIM, f. 432, o. 1, d. 188, ll. 57–60, 67, 71–72, 81–86.

clinics and bread factories in Moscow. Enemies, he said, had infected babies with influenza and disrupted the delivery of bread to the shops. "Who did this?" he asked. "Wreckers." Then he chided the audience, asserting, "Your main mistake was that eighteen enemies of the people were arrested by the NKVD before they were unmasked by you." He encouraged the rank and file to demand further investigations: "You need to ask *why* the people who worked with these enemies of the people failed to unmask them."[43] Timofeev thus sent a mixed message: party members should stop focusing exclusively on enemies but must keep searching out *new* enemies among those who failed to unmask others.

SHUDDERING TO A HALT

Throughout the summer of 1938, the national and factory newspapers continued to call for the unmasking of slanderers.[44] Calls to action proclaiming "Slanderers Remain Unpunished!" appeared in articles urging the party organizations to identify and investigate those responsible for the expulsions of innocent people. The newspapers even conceded that their own editors had failed in these tasks, unmasking too few such enemies in the press. Reminding their readers that "every case of incorrect exclusion played into enemy hands," they insisted that officials needed to recheck all documents, including *zaiavleniia*, and punish those who had made baseless accusations.[45] Yet despite the papers' goading, the local party organizations did little to pursue the matter, and for good reason: if

---

43 TsAOPIM, f. 432, o. 1, d. 189, ll. 40–41, 44. See also "Dnevnik Otchetno-Vybornogo Partiinogo Sobraniia," *Kirovets*, April 11 and 13, 1938, p. 2.

44 "Vypolnenie Reshenii Ianvarskogo Plenuma TsK," *Kirovets*, September 1, 1938, p. 2.

45 "Po Bol'shevistski Vypolnit' Postanovlenie Ianvarskogo Plenuma TsK VKP (b)," *Kirovets*, August 8, 1938, p. 2, reprinted from *Pravda*, August 7, 1938.

they were to prosecute every member who had slandered another, most of the remaining cadres would join their former comrades in the prisons and graves to which their allegations had consigned them. Party members who had survived 1937 were naturally reluctant to remand themselves to prison. Justice was a dangerous business, and where would it end? In all likelihood, a thorough exclusion of slanderers would have destroyed the Party altogether.

The officials who attended district, city, and provincial conferences in Moscow in the summer of 1938 made their usual speeches about "rooting out Japanese-German Trotskyist Bukharinite agents of fascism until the end."[46] Yet their fiery rhetoric notwithstanding, the hunt for enemies was losing momentum. From an organizational standpoint, the repressions had already crippled the Party's ability to organize within the factories. The party organizations in the shops were in a state of semi-collapse. In Dinamo, members arrived late to meetings and left early, without asking permission. Khorikov, the director, cancelled several political sessions. Organizers stopped doing their work.[47] In 1937, party leaders had ordered local officials to "study" their members' biographies; enemies were creeping into the ranks, they maintained, because the officials did not know their own cadres. Yet the ensuing repressions increased, rather than decreased, the level of anonymity within the Party. District and provincial committees were greatly compromised by the effects of the purges. So many people had been arrested, excluded, promoted, or transferred that organizational links were seriously weakened.

46 "Iz Resheniia Obshchezavodskogo Partiinogo Sobraniia," *Kirovets*, July 20, 1938, p. 2.
47 "Nepravil'naia Otsenka," *Kirovets*, March 24, 1938, p. 2; "Razvernut' Bol'shevistkuiu Samokritiku na Otchetno-Vybornom Sobranii," *Kirovets*, April, 7, 1938, p. 1.

One party member noted, "Before, I always knew what was going on in the district committee, but now things have gotten worse. Now they call us together very rarely. When the district committee in Moscow was broken up [through arrests], we thought our ties would be strengthened, but the opposite occurred."[48] Even as the threat of war loomed ever larger, the repressions had disrupted production, destroyed the authority of managers and shop heads, and paralyzed the Party's ability to mobilize workers. The significance of these developments was not lost on the country's leaders, who grew more and more worried about defense, production, and labor turnover.

In June 1938, two Dinamo engineers published an article that would have been unthinkable just a year earlier. Abandoning the relentless concern with sabotage and wreckers that had prevailed in every industrial enterprise since the Kemerovo trial in 1936, the engineers focused instead on the "careless attitude" of workers and technical personnel, and its attendant costs. They noted that the factory had logged 6,334 hours of stoppage in 1937 due to breakage and accidents. In part this was the fault of shop heads who ran machines that were in need of repair, thereby exacerbating the damage, but the greater share of the blame, the article suggested, belonged to the workers, who lacked not only the necessary technical skills but also a knowledge of the "basic rules and instructions" for operating machinery. Coining what would soon become the signature phrase of a new state campaign, the authors bemoaned the "absence of production discipline in the shops."[49]

By early fall, the factory newspapers had finally stopped calling for party committees to punish slanderers or unmask enemies of

48 TsAOPIM, f. 432, o. 1, d. 188, l. 51.
49 "Obiavit' Besposhchadnuiu Bor'bu s Avariiami Oborudovaniia," *Kirovets*, June 20, 1938, p. 1.

any sort. In October, the NKVD issued an order specifying that wives of enemies were henceforth to be arrested only if they were themselves suspected of counterrevolutionary activity.[50] In November, party leaders drew up a list of slogans and disseminated it to the local organizations for use in the anniversary celebration of the revolution. The only slogan referring directly to enemies – "Root Out Enemies of the People, Trotskyist Bukharinite and Bourgeois Nationalist Spies and Wreckers, Hirelings of Foreign Espionage. Death to Traitors of the Motherland" – occupied thirty-seventh place on the list.[51] Hunting enemies was no longer the Party's main priority. Shortly after the anniversary celebration, on November 17, 1938, Stalin halted the mass and national operations and transferred responsibility for sentencing from the infamous extrajudicial "*troiki*" back to the courts. Two days later, Ezhov resigned as head of the NKVD and admitted that he had failed to identify masked enemies among his own leading officials. The same process of self-devouring that had destroyed the local party organizations now consumed the top levels of the NKVD. L. P. Beria replaced Ezhov as head of the agency and then personally arrested him five months later, in April 1939. Charged with spying for both Poland and England, Ezhov was shot in 1940.[52]

Throughout the fall of 1938, Dinamo continued to struggle with serious production problems. In a meeting with party members, Khorikov, the director, acknowledged that there had been "a lot

---

50 Kuhr, "Children of 'Enemies of the People,'" p. 213; Alexopoulos, "Stalin and the Politics of Kinship," p. 109.

51 "Lozungi TsK VKP (b)," *Kirovets*, November 4, 1938, p. 1. The slogans were published in the national press as well.

52 J. Arch Getty and Oleg V. Naumov, *The Road to Terror: Stalin and the Self-Destruction of the Bolsheviks, 1932–1939* (New Haven, Conn.: Yale University Press, 1999), pp. 530–40, 555.

of spontaneous turnover [*samotek*] and unrest." The factory had not received many supplies and materials necessary to its functioning, including fuel. Khorikov did not, however, try to pin the blame for these difficulties on wreckers or other enemies. During the debate that followed his speech, party members rudely vilified both him and one another for the production problems, but they, too, shied away from making political accusations. Instead, the shop heads blamed Khorikov, and Khorikov blamed the shop heads in turn. One party member declared, "The [stamping] shop is such a mess. This is hell, not a shop." Still, with the exception of a certain insolent tone toward authority, a holdover from the earlier democracy campaign, the discussion was much more reminiscent of those held in 1935 than in the years since. Labor discipline, workers' absences, and technical and administrative issues had supplanted masked enemies as the main business of the day.[53] In December 1938, the state passed new legislation aimed at reducing absenteeism, lateness, and idleness in the workplace.[54] Its focus had shifted from "fifth columnists" to defense production and errant workers.

THE OFFICIAL VIEW

By the spring of 1939, the main wave of mass repression was over. Yet the political culture took far longer to change, as fear and

---

53 TsAOPIM, f. 432, o. 1, d. 203, ll. 3–4, 51–54, 56.
54 Decree of SNK SSSR, December 20, 1938, "O Vvedenii Trudovykh Knizhek," *Izvestiia*, December 21, 1938, p. 1; Decree of SNK SSSR, TsK VKP (b), VTsSPS, December 28, 1938, "O Meropriiatiiakh po Uporiadocheniiu Trudovoi Distsipliny, Ulushcheniiu Praktiki Gosudarstvennogo Sotsial'nogo Strakhovaniia i Bor'be s Zloupotrebleniiami v Etom Dele," *Pravda*, December 29, 1938, p. 1. On legislation, see Donald Filtzer, *Soviet Workers and Stalinist Industrialization: The Formation of Modern Soviet Production Relations, 1928–1941* (London: Pluto Press, 1986), pp. 310–11.

mistrust continued to characterize relations among those both within and outside the Party. Soviet citizens carefully guarded their public speech, agonized over slips, and were afraid to speak honestly about politics even with their closest friends. People's inner urge to be candid with others was at war with their ever-present anxiety about informers. This wariness not only deformed the people who survived the terror, but shaped subsequent generations as well. Not until M. S. Gorbachev came to power in 1985 did fears of free speech, informers, and punishment begin to dissipate.

In March 1939, delegates to the Eighteenth Party Congress convened in Moscow. A. A. Zhdanov, secretary of the Central Committee and head of the Leningrad city and regional party organizations, gave a keynote speech ostensibly enumerating organizational revisions to the Party's charter. In fact, several of these represented significant alterations in the overall orientation of the Party itself, which was now occupied with trying to ready the country for war. First, Zhdanov noted that it was no longer necessary to favor workers for party membership, or to use social origins as a factor at all in considering new members. Profound changes in the class composition of the Soviet Union in the 1930s, including the elimination of such "exploiting elements" as kulaks, capitalists, and merchants, had dissolved class boundaries among workers, peasants, and the intelligentsia. Zhdanov now recommended that a single requirement be imposed on all candidates for membership: the provision of recommendations from three current party members who had known the nominee for at least three years. (The time frame would later be reduced to only one year, because the upheaval and loss of cadres had made it so difficult for candidates to meet the three-year standard when procuring recommendations.) The Party was desperate for new cadres to replace those who had either been executed or disappeared into the camps. If the terror and purge had constituted a fierce winnowing process that eliminated many party members, the new rules considerably loosened the criteria for membership.

Zhdanov also provided a list of new "rights" for all party members, including the rights to criticize any party official, to elect and be elected to party organizations, to participate in one's own disciplinary case, and to address a *zaiavlenie* to any party organization up to the Central Committee. These were presented, collectively, as a means of undermining bureaucracy and protecting party members against local officials, but their introduction was also a tacit acknowledgment of both the damage suffered by the local organizations and the prevailing practice of pushing appeals beyond the local level. Zhdanov called for the abolition of "mass purges," or group expulsions based on shared characteristics, noting that such actions had entailed "many mistakes" and "numerous unsubstantiated exclusions"; in particular, he said, "enemy elements" had exploited them to "slaughter honest officials." Yet Zhdanov made it clear that his use of the term "mass purges" referred not to the exclusion and arrest of those party members who were deemed "enemies" in 1937, but rather to earlier expulsions for "passivity."[55]

Zhdanov now reiterated the message of the Central Committee's January 1938 plenum: the purge had been fundamentally correct because it strengthened the Party's unity. His only criticism of the repressions pertained to the excesses provoked by the slanderers, who had seized on the charge of having a "tie to an enemy of the people" as an excuse "to exterminate honest Communists." He noted the "peculiar conveyor" by which anyone connected to an excluded

---

55 *XVIII S"ezd vsesoiuznoi kommunisticheskoi partii (b), 10–21 Marta 1939. Stenograficheskii otchet* (Moscow: Gosudarstvennoe Izdatel'stvo Politicheskoi Literatury, 1939), pp. 672, 511–19.

person was likewise excluded or fired from work. Party members, he explained, were to be judged not "biologically," according to their relatives, but on their own merits. "Careerist elements" and "masked enemies" had used repression to destroy the Party and sow suspicion within its ranks. Some people had written "literally hundreds" of unsubstantiated *zaiavleniia*, and even now, "slander under the flag of 'vigilance'" remained the preferred method of enemies.[56] Zhdanov, however, went no further than the Central Committee's resolution of the previous year had gone in criticizing the repressions within the Party. Slanderers would be punished; reinstatement, if warranted, would rectify any mistakes. Organizational changes and new enrollment rules would reverse the present shortage of cadres. The Party had freed itself from spies, enemies, and wreckers, clearing the path for the promotion of new, younger cadres into leadership positions.[57] It was time to look to the future.

THE LIMITS OF DISCUSSION

Within the party organizations in the factories, bawlers and slanderers were the caboose on the terror train, the last group to be expelled and arrested. The NKVD arrested a number of highly placed party officials to serve as examples to others. These aggressive purgers were interrogated and forced to confess to being masked enemies who had aimed to destroy their local and regional party organizations through slander. At the Eighteenth Party Congress, Zhdanov read aloud from one such confession by a provincial party

56 *Ibid.*, pp. 520–23.
57 *Ibid.*, p. 529.

secretary: "During a period of five to six days, I dispersed the provincial committee's entire staff: I removed almost all of the members of the leading departments, got rid of twelve to fifteen instructors, and replaced even the technical employees. All of this was done under the banner of contending with enemies and ridding the provincial committee of those who were lacking in vigilance. After cleaning house in the provincial committee under this banner, I then attempted to destroy the city and district committees. In a short time, I removed fifteen secretaries from work, along with a series of officials about whom I had no compromising material. I created the appearance of a struggle against enemies, embittering those people, who did not deserve to be removed, against the ranks of the Party. Moreover, I also dismissed a number of participants in our counterrevolutionary organization, transferring them to lower positions and thus saving them from exposure."[58]

This provincial secretary, like so many of his peers, was guilty of sending honest Communists to prison and execution, but despite Zhdanov's claims, he was not, in all likelihood, a masked enemy bent on destroying the Party. Rather, he probably acted out of a mixture of zeal and fear, at once a loyal servant and an independent agent of the terror. Confessions such as his, extracted by NKVD interrogators and shaped by them in accordance with the Central Committee's attack on slanderers, provided party leaders with convenient scapegoats. A spurious motivation grafted onto an accurate description of repressive actions produced a "masked slanderer," the perfect perpetrator of so-called excesses. In essence, local "slanderers," of whom there were many, took the blame for

58 *Ibid.*, p. 521.

fulfilling the Party's earlier instructions to root out enemies. Like Ezhov, the disgraced and by now doomed former head of the NKVD, they became victims of the very process they had once directed.

How were party members to distinguish between the proper repression of the guilty and the "mistaken" repression of the innocent, between vigilance and slander? Party leaders never answered this question, and party members were not encouraged to probe too deeply into the past. Everyone understood that arrest and execution were definitive proof of guilt, and that reinstatement provided a reliable imprimatur of innocence. Thus, working backward, a "slanderer" was someone who wrote a *zaiavlenie* about a fellow party member who was excluded as a result but then reinstated, while a "vigilant" member was one who provided information about a person whose consequent expulsion was followed by an arrest. Similarly, the "overprotector" refused to rehire or recommend an expelled member who was subsequently reinstated, whereas an "enemy" hired or recommended one who was later arrested. Actions undertaken in the present could be assessed only in relation to some future event, as yet unknown and unknowable. Not surprisingly, party members found it difficult to orient themselves.

In early 1939, in advance of the congress, summaries of the main points of Zhdanov's speech were distributed to the local party organizations for discussion. In Dinamo, party members cautiously explored the meaning of what they had experienced and what they had done over the past two years. Ovchinnikov, a thirty-six-year-old party member who had joined the Party as a teenager in 1919, in the middle of the Civil War, tried to make some sense of the terror's upheaval. "It was hard for us to struggle with all of the many kinds of slanderers who were among us," he began. He cited as an example A. M. Besprozvannyi, a partisan commander in the

Civil War, mechanic, and former party committee secretary, who had been one of Dinamo's most ardent purgers until he was arrested.[59] Ovchinnikov reminded his comrades of a comment he had once made: "Remember the enemy of the people Besprozvannyi, who said, 'You old workers of the Dinamo plant, stop your idle chattering. This is not your business! You have to listen to what people say to you. Were enemies beating us, did they beat us? Time will show who is right.'" In relating this incident, Ovchinnikov unwittingly provided a rare glimpse into the reactions of those on the shop floor, implying that at least some of the older workers had questioned the Party's justifications for the repressions and spoken critically of them among themselves. Besprozvannyi had warned them to be quiet and mind their own business, but later this defender of the terror would himself be deemed an "enemy of the people." Ovchinnikov now wondered if perhaps the older workers had not been right to doubt the wisdom of the repressions. He continued, "I would like to say that the decision to liquidate the purge is timely. I think it is time. It is not useful for us; in fact, it is harmful. We gave a lot of energy to this. In short, at times we understood nothing, and enemies of the people used this tribune for their activities." Ovchinnikov then came to a remarkable conclusion about the forces behind the terror: "Who needed this?" he asked his comrades. And he answered plainly, "*Enemies* needed this. For me, a Communist, such things are not necessary. Our enemies used the purge as a tribune."[60]

With this brave speech, Ovchinnikov became the first person ever to speak out publicly against the purge in a Dinamo party meeting.

---

59 A. I. Efanov, *Istoriia zavoda 'Dinamo'* (Moscow: Izdatel'stvo VTsSPS Profizdat, 1964), vol. 2, p. 174, provides a brief biography of Besprozvannyi, who was later rehabilitated.
60 TsAOPIM, f. 432, o. 1, d. 203, ll. 145–47.

Emboldened by the idea that "slanderers" had been responsible for the repression of innocent people, he went considerably further than Zhdanov would go in his subsequent address to the party congress. In his homespun analysis, Ovchinnikov stated simply and clearly that the purge was "not necessary." Enemies had used it to hurt the Party and destroy innocent Communists. Nothing good had come of it. Here he stopped, one small step short of suggesting that the true enemies of the Party and its ideals were those who had launched and fueled the terror. This was most decidedly not Zhdanov's message. Another party member quickly spoke up to correct Ovchinnikov's "incorrect view of the purge": "He said it was useless. This is wrong. It is the best means of struggling against enemies."[61] In the ensuing debate, party members complained about their personal experiences with slander, but no one addressed the more troubling points Ovchinnikov had raised. Zhdanov had set the limits of discussion, and party members patrolled them vigilantly to ensure that no one, whether through ignorance, independent thought, or verbal clumsiness, strayed beyond them. Not until after Stalin's death and Khrushchev's revelations would the Party revisit the issue of the repressions, open the camps, give amnesty to the surviving political inmates, and rehabilitate the reputations of some of the "enemies" of the 1930s.

CONCLUSION

If the Party made only a modest effort in 1938 and 1939 to reinstate the innocent, it never undertook a full reckoning of the guilty. The bawlers or slanderers were among the last group of party members to

61 TsAOPIM, f. 432, o. 1, d. 203, l. 155.

be sent to the camps, along with the NKVD interrogators, or "bone breakers" (*kokol'shchiki*), who had extracted so many confessions.[62] It may seem a mocking sort of justice that the most aggressive purgers and torturers should have followed their victims to prison and to execution. Yet many of the victims, while innocent of the charges leveled against them, had nevertheless also written *zaiavleniia* against others. If the party meetings showed anything, it was that a firm line between innocent victim and bawling perpetrator was difficult to draw. The questions raised by Ovchinnikov were never discussed openly. Why had party members, in his word, put so much "energy" into destroying their own comrades and organizations? And who, in the end, should bear responsibility for that destruction?

In 1939, party leaders offered very narrowly construed answers to these questions. While they obliquely recognized and identified the strategies of self-protection that had consumed the party organizations, they did not consider the process of self-devouring as part of a larger organizational dynamic involving *all* party members. Rather, they faulted the "bawling careerists," an invented category that included only a relative few of the most aggressive denouncers. Just as party leaders had once blamed local party activists for excessive zeal in collectivization, so did they now hold "bawlers" responsible for "excesses" in repression. The Central Committee's 1938 resolution and Zhdanov's keynote at the Eighteenth Party Congress in 1939 both employed this fictive new category of "enemy" as a straw man to disrupt what had become a self-replicating process. The campaign against "bawlers" aimed to discourage party members from denouncing one another, and though many had trouble giving up such conditioned strategies and behaviors, the effort was at least

62 Khlevniuk, "Party and NKVD," p. 30.

partially successful. By the fall of 1938, the local party organizations had stopped hunting for enemies within their ranks.

In this sense, control over the repressions finally rested with Stalin and other central party leaders. They launched the terror, and they brought it to a close. Yet neither its beginning nor its end can be isolated from larger events and social responses. The decision to broaden repression in the fall of 1936 by involving the rank and file of every organization and institution was provoked by the initial lack of interest, on the local level, in hunting for enemies. It was precisely this decision that imparted a mass, uncontrolled element to the terror and transformed the political culture of the nation. The resulting denunciations, fear, mistrust, breakdown of solidarity, and eventual erosion of the Party and other mass organizations at last forced the leadership to call a halt. Party leaders were not unaware of the toll the terror had taken; in fact, the Central Committee's resolution can be read as a reaction to the havoc and ruin that the terror wreaked at the local level. By 1938, the party organizations had been severely crippled. Busy destroying themselves, they were unable to enroll new members, reinstate those who had been expelled, or elect candidates to office. Party members and officials could not hold even a simple meeting without denouncing one another, nor could organizers do any mass organizing among workers. But at the very moment when Zhdanov was delivering his speech to the Eighteenth Party Congress, in March 1939, the Nazis were occupying Czechoslovakia. Party leaders moved to reassert control over a process run amok, to unfreeze enrollment, redraw clear lines of authority, and loosen the paralyzing grip of fear on those who remained in the local organizations. Yet who among the surviving party members had not written a preemptive *zaiavlenie*, shunned a comrade, or parried one accusation with another? The terror had reached far beyond former oppositionists, beyond any targeted social or national group. It was a profoundly violent process whereby the country began to resemble a body in the throes of some terrible autoimmune disease, attacking and destroying its own organs, nervous system, flesh, and blood. Sentencing one more group of scapegoats to execution or the camps could not undo the deep damage inflicted on organizations, institutions, and most importantly, simple human relationships.

CONCLUSION: A HISTORY WITHOUT HEROES

N. S. Khrushchev stood at the rostrum at the Twentieth Party Congress, in 1956. He spoke at length about Stalin's crimes and the terror he had perpetrated against the Soviet people. Suddenly, a voice called out from the vast hall, "And what did you do, Comrade Khrushchev, when all of this happened?" Khrushchev stopped speaking and looked out over the seated delegates. "Who said that?" he demanded. The delegates froze. No one said a word. Khrushchev paused for a long moment as he surveyed the silent crowd. "That's what I did," he said. "Exactly what you are doing now."

– Soviet-era anecdote

PARTY MEMBERS, WORKERS, SHOP HEADS, ENGINEERS, managers, and others in the factories became both agents and victims of a political culture bent on identifying and destroying enemies. No one in the factories was able to escape this culture. After each of the Moscow trials, workers attended mass demonstrations, factory-wide meetings, and small group discussions in the barracks and the shops. Radio loudspeakers in the factories blared news of the trials. Workers across the country took mass, public pledges to examine every industrial bottleneck and accident for signs of wrecking. The factory newspapers functioned as small motors of terror, informing workers and party activists of accusations and spurring them to investigate specific shops and individuals. The leaders of the factories were regularly humiliated in the press. Each day brought new, shocking headlines that set employees abuzz. At the same time, NKVD arrests affected the leadership of the factories at every level. Every director, organizer, instructor, shop and department head, engineer, and foreman, whether party member or not, had associational ties to others above and below. Arrests rippled outward to envelop the victims' associates, friends, and relatives, at work and at home.

People responded both individually and collectively to the propaganda, the mania for spies and saboteurs, and the arrests occurring everywhere around them. Engineers denounced one another for technical and industrial mishaps, party members reported long-standing political suspicions about their comrades, and workers complained about the arrogance of their bosses. The great campaign against terrorists and spies encouraged ordinary people to abandon whatever scruples they felt about reporting mere suspicions. Many trusted the NKVD to investigate the charges and bring justice to bear on the accused. Employees who worked side by side wrote reciprocal denunciations and then continued to work together, each unaware of the other's betrayal. Such denunciations, or *zaiavleniia*, often resulted in investigations and arrests. Party members were arrested and then expelled from the Party, or expelled and then arrested; the exact sequence was unimportant. Arrest and expulsion propelled each other, leading to investigations that widened the circle of culpability by drawing in mentors, coworkers, and family members. The party committees and shop organizations were soon occupied almost entirely with "unmasking" the alleged enemies in their ranks. Tumultuous factory-wide party meetings, attended by upward of five hundred members, supplemented smaller, regular meetings of elected shop and factory representatives as part of the campaign for party democracy. The factory newspapers reported on the proceedings in detailed articles available to all factory employees.

In meetings of the shop and party committees and the general membership, party members displayed a limited range of behavior. No one, for example, spoke out publicly against the mounting arrests or questioned the logic of guilt by association. Voices of reason were drowned out by the clamor to attack, counterattack, denounce, and convict. Comrades and coworkers eagerly involved the NKVD, drawing attention to specific people through accusatory speeches and *zaiavleniia*. If presented with a choice of possible punishments when considering a disciplinary case, members frequently voted for the most severe penalty available. Larger meetings proved more punitive than smaller ones, with the loudest, harshest speakers prevailing.

Was people's behavior governed by a genuine belief in a terrorist threat to the state? Or were their actions shaped by the opposite – namely, fear of the state and its terror? Did the majority view themselves as secure citizens or vulnerable targets? Tracing behavior in party meetings over time, we can detect a shift from belief to fear. This shift was not uniform; it did not affect all individuals in the same way or at the same time. During the first Moscow show trial, in August 1936, few party members, workers, or factory employees could foresee that the state's prosecution of prominent former oppositionists would soon be transformed into widespread arrests. Public declarations and private comments indicated that most people perceived that a great gulf existed between themselves and the famous revolutionaries on trial.[1] Many believed the state's warnings

1 On popular responses to the trial, see Wendy Z. Goldman, "Terror in the Factories," in Donald Filtzer, Wendy Z. Goldman, Gijs Kessler, and Simon Pirani,

about an internal terrorist threat and considered it their patriotic duty to report suspicions about coworkers and comrades. In Dinamo and other factories, the first trial inspired a flurry of *zaiavleniia*. Yet as people's experiences with denunciations, expulsions, and arrests grew, so did their awareness of personal vulnerability. They found it increasingly difficult to sustain the belief that all of those arrested were truly guilty, and that the state was targeting only terrorists, spies, and saboteurs.

Party members were compelled to provide *zaiavleniia* about any contact they had with alleged enemies. Following the arrest of a relative or friend, many agonized over whether to conceal such contact or provide a full report. Either choice carried potentially grave consequences: concealment, on the one hand, could, if discovered, lead to expulsion and arrest, while full disclosure, on the other hand, could result in a dangerous investigation and interrogation. As party members wrestled with this dilemma, they began to question their assumptions about the NKVD and the state. Doubt undermined belief. Gradually, people began to understand that anyone was susceptible to attack. Their experiences in meetings, either as victims or as prosecutors, fostered a keen awareness of the meaning of political vulnerability. They understood that even a comrade such as Aleksandr Somov, head of the party committee in Serp i Molot, possessed of an impeccable proletarian background and political record, could suffer a rapid reversal of fortune. Once people grasped this simple lesson, which was reinforced by each new arrest, their behavior revealed that fear was supplanting faith. They became guarded, cautious, and wary of others. Often their own hidden

eds., *A Dream Deferred: New Studies in Russian and Soviet Labour History* (Bern: Peter Lang, 2008), pp. 193–218.

biographical or political liabilities made them more, not less, aggressive in denouncing and accusing others. Anxious to conceal weaknesses, each individual acted out of a uniquely personal mixture of belief and fear. Mariia Zhidkova, for example, denounced Esfir Krivitskaia as an emotional reaction to the arrest of her own brother. Believing that arrest to be a "mistake," Zhidkova was appalled by Krivitskaia's seemingly lighthearted response to the fate of those around her, and promptly denounced her to the NKVD.

At meetings, everyone publicly upheld the line that the Party was expelling dangerous enemies. All sought to demonstrate their loyalty through their public presentations of self, often by unmasking potential enemies or participating in attacks by the group. In fact, party members who did not participate actively in attacking or unmasking others got into trouble for "overlooking" or "protecting" enemies. The fiercer such public displays of fealty became, the more people were victimized by them. The purge soon fed itself, as every arrest provoked fresh investigations of associational ties, additional accusations, and new victims. Within the group, this dynamic created an inescapable contradiction: the greater the number of victims and the more spurious the attacks, the harder it became to maintain faith that all of the victims were truly enemies. Party members and others in the factories were thus drawn into and caught up in a collective process that inexorably created cynics, doubters, and liars. In the end, everyone seemed to be guilty of something: having a Trotskyist friend, an imprisoned mentor, an immigrant spouse, or a relative living abroad; casting an ill-advised vote in a long-ago meeting; telling a biographical lie or omitting some damning detail during a membership review. The very process of ferreting out lies turned loyal party members into liars. It corroded and destroyed the party organizations, as well as the larger factory collective, from within.

Every meeting provided lessons that reinforced certain behaviors and criminalized others. Party members quickly absorbed these lessons, then taught them to others. Over time, increasingly minor transgressions had ever-greater consequences. Silence in meetings, for example, became a sign of enemy support. The failure to foresee an NKVD arrest and write a timely denunciation was punished by investigation and expulsion. Refusal to renounce a spouse, child, or parent who was arrested could lead to expulsion, job loss, or even imprisonment. Using stenographic records to follow the participation of specific people through this painful period of party meetings, we see how their attempts at self-protection – in the guise of preemptive and confessional *zaiavleniia*, aggressive countercharges, the naming of names, and efforts to demonstrate "total loyalty" to the Party – broadened the scope of repression. The devilish paradox of the terror was that individual strategies for survival, at their most successful, served only to heighten the risk to coworkers, family, and comrades.

Yet even in the midst of this self-generating, self-consuming process, small acts of kindness and decency occurred. After the Kirov murder, some local and factory party officials tried to protect former Trotskyists, shield them from attack, and defend their contributions to production. They attempted to quash investigations by allowing *zaiavleniia* to "marinate" and ignoring baseless or trivial charges. They counseled party members to remain silent about arrested or excluded relatives. They emphasized the need for evidence in the rush to judgment. As the number of arrests grew, many people secretly aided their relatives in exile or in prison despite the risk of expulsion or worse. Some brave souls such as Varvara Torbeeva, a party member and worker in Dinamo's first instrument shop, refused publicly to renounce spouses or close family members. Others helped orphaned grandchildren or the children of arrested relatives, gathering the remnants of a family and trying to preserve it in some form. Some people kept silent in meetings and abstained from joining in on the group's attacks on others. In rare instances, comrades defended one another and voiced doubts about the accusations being leveled. Many more refrained from telling everything they knew: several of Somov's coworkers, for example, withheld details about Krivitskaia's frequent visits to the open hearth furnace. During meetings, some voted against the majority, favoring more lenient punishments for their comrades' transgressions. Over time, however, party organizations demonized and punished all of these behaviors. As a result, such modest acts of individual decency and solidarity became riskier and less common.

People exhibited a variety of different, often conflicting behaviors in response to what was going on around them. Any one person might make fiery speeches and write *zaiavleniia* against others while secretly assisting so-called "enemy" relatives. A notable exemplar of this was Sheinin, the deputy director of Dinamo, who denounced his friend Tolchinskii, the technical director, even as he himself sent aid to relatives who had been exiled for Trotskyism. The terror created a deep split between public pronouncements and private practices. Both individuals and groups embodied and enacted this quality, which was later to become known as "dual-mindedness." Yet such splitting did not entail only public loyalty and private subversion; one person might also protect some comrades and attack others, both publicly. Among party members at the local level, the line between victims and perpetrators was hopelessly blurred. Everyone participated in the hunt for enemies, and everyone lived in fear of being attacked themselves.

In the end, this is a history without heroes. The record reveals no grand gestures of personal sacrifice, no attempts to organize a collective response to the prevailing political culture. Whatever small acts of resistance people did manage to undertake were accomplished individually, quietly, and in secret. In this sense, there were no examples for others to emulate, no resistance groups to contact, no models to follow. People outwardly supported the repressions, actively participated in them, and had to struggle privately with the consequences.

How does this microhistory of events in the factories affect our larger understanding of the terror? What was the relationship between the larger political culture of enemy-hunting and the NKVD's arrests of individuals and groups? The terror escalated in phases as the state added new groups to its list of security threats, and as associational ties endangered increasing numbers of people. In the factories, it began with the state's attack on former oppositionists after the Kirov murder, broadened into a ubiquitous political culture devoted to the unmasking of wreckers and enemies, and culminated in the mass and national operations against targeted population groups. Denunciations, *zaiavleniia*, investigations, and newspaper accounts were all crucial to this culture of finger-pointing. They also brought damaging information about people's associational ties, previous political records, and social origins to the attention of various authorities. The heads of factory party committees forwarded the information they received to the district and city committees and to the NKVD. As more party committee heads were called to account for neglecting to follow up on *zaiavleniia* against members who were subsequently arrested, fewer were willing to risk their own lives by ignoring unverified accusations. Over time, officials "marinated" less and less of this material, instead automatically forwarding nearly every denunciation to the NKVD as a hedge against the possibility of its subject's arrest. Although NKVD officials did not act on every *zaiavlenie* they received, the information contained therein alerted them to the existence and whereabouts of specific individuals and prompted further investigations. Local NKVD organizations relied on denunciations, informers' reports, police records, watch lists, and other sources of information throughout the 1930s. They needed a good deal of information in order to compile their lists of victims, and unfortunately, many in the Party as well as in the general population were all too willing to provide it.[2]

Party leaders made close connections between political and social policing, and between the attack on former oppositionists and the mass and national operations. They frequently voiced the fear that former oppositionists might unite with former kulaks and members of other disenfranchised populations to tap the social discontent created by industrialization and collectivization. These fears provided a central theme for the Moscow show trials and shaped the charges against their defendants. At the Central Committee plenum of February–March 1937, party leaders repeatedly emphasized the threat posed by a potential alliance of political oppositionists, exiled former kulaks, and other dispossessed groups. Throughout the earlier part of the 1930s, policing practices directed against dispossessed and criminal elements had been distinct from those aimed at political opponents, but by 1937, these two operational trends merged. Leaders of the Party and the NKVD came to view suspect social and national populations as a political threat prone to armed uprising in the event of war.[3]

---

2 David Shearer, *Policing Stalin's Socialism: Repression and Social Order in the Soviet Union, 1924–1953* (New Haven, Conn.: Yale University Press, 2009), p. 196; Sheila Fitzpatrick, "Signals from Below: Soviet Letters of Denunciation of the 1930s," *Journal of Modern History*, vol. 68, no. 4 (December 1996), pp. 859–60. Fitzpatrick notes that often there was no further information regarding the outcome of the denunciations she reviewed, except perhaps a note indicating that the denunciation had been forwarded to another organization such as the NKVD, the procuracy, or the local party organization.

3 Shearer, *Policing Stalin's Socialism*, pp. 300–3.

Attacks on former oppositionists were linked to the mass and national operations not only in the minds of party and NKVD leaders but also through the experiences of ordinary people, both party members and regular citizens. The mass and national operations, concealed from the public, devastated not only the actual members of the affected groups but also their relatives, coworkers, and friends. If we focus on how people *experienced* the terror, the discrete victim categories blur and dissolve. Although people were targeted by category, they lived within families, social structures that might unite in one entity a number of different targets of the state. Taken together, the state's motivations for sponsoring the terror and people's personal experiences of it make it impossible to decouple the political attacks against former oppositionists from the mass campaigns against marginalized social and national groups.[4]

Even the most dedicated of party members were connected, through family ties, to one or more of the state's seemingly discrete categories of victims. The mass culture of enemy-hunting made a potential enemy out of almost everyone. Party members and others attempted to shape their biographies to conform to an impossible standard of purity, but as sources from the factories show, even the "purest" Communists had complex political histories or compromising familial or associational ties. Party members in the factories presented countless confessional *zaiavleniia* concerning

---

4 Paul Hagenloh emphasizes the distinction between the mass and national operations and political terror. He notes, "The mass repression of 1937 and 1938 was no mere expansion of ongoing purges within the Communist Party and the Soviet state; it was an explosion of police repression with roots in the histories of Soviet policing, social engineering, and state violence stretching back to the very beginnings of the Bolshevik regime." *Stalin's Police: Public Order and Mass Repression in the USSR, 1926–1941* (Baltimore: Johns Hopkins University Press, 2009), p. 6.

their relatives and spouses. Some had fathers who were traders, village priests, or prosperous peasants; others had Latvian, Polish, or German connections. Many had relatives with problematic political histories. Pavlov, a garage worker, reported the arrest of a kulak brother-in-law; Krivitskaia's husband kept his kulak brother a secret; Margolina's brother-in-law and brother were arrested for Trotskyism and associational ties to Trotskyists; Sharova's husband, a railway worker, was charged with wrecking after a switching accident, as was Iarkin's cousin after the death of some cattle on the state farm where he worked; Shtrul was a Latvian with two Trotskyist brothers; Malyshev thought his father might have been a rightist; and Pereversev's aunt and uncle had been members of an anarchist organization in the 1920s. The turbulent social and political history of the Soviet Union left its stamp on every family. By 1938, the local party organizations could scarcely find a single member "pure" (*chistyi*) enough to stand for election to the district committees.

Some historians have argued that the terror's reach in the factories did not extend to "ordinary" workers but was instead limited only to "elites," party officials and industrial leaders.[5] While it is true that shop heads and managers were much more apt to be arrested than workers, it would be a mistake to conclude from this that workers were unaffected by the terror. Outside of the major cities, many of the victims rounded up to reach target figures for arrests in the *national* operations were former kulaks who worked in factories. (The plants in Moscow and other leading cities had already been purged, in the early 1930s, of this group and others lacking passports.) In small industrial enterprises in rural areas, coworkers would have

5 See, for example, Robert Thurston, *Life and Terror in Stalin's Russia, 1934–1941* (New Haven, Conn.: Yale University Press, 1996).

been aware of the arrests and frightened by them, but would have had no way of knowing that these victims were being imprisoned because they were former kulaks, now targeted by regional NKVD officials to fill their arrest quota for foreign spies. In essence, workers saw fellow workers disappear from their accustomed places in the factories, and understood that workers, too, were being seized.

Moreover, even in Moscow, ordinary working-class families were vulnerable to the terror. In the 1930s, the majority of party members in the factories (over 90 percent of those in Dinamo, for example) came from working-class or peasant origins. Furthermore, most of the managers, engineers, and shop heads themselves had scant education and had only recently been promoted out of jobs in production. Their parents and grandparents were workers or peasants, and their spouses generally came from backgrounds similar to their own. G. N. Fridman, for instance, was born into a working-class family and began working in Dinamo in production. Fascinated by the electric locomotives, he spent his every spare minute tinkering with their motors. After the Party provided him with some training in electrical engineering, he was promoted from ordinary worker to head of the experimental station of mobile prototypes. In 1937, he was excluded from the Party at the age of twenty-six as a "supporter of enemies of the people."[6] Fridman, like many bright and enterprising technical and managerial personnel, was representative less of a supposed "elite" than of the rapid upward mobility made possible by socialism. When these newly elevated professionals were arrested, they left behind ordinary families to bear the shame and suffer the consequences. Working-class and peasant wives and mothers stood

6 Tsentral'nyi Arkhiv Obshchestvenno-Politicheskoi Istorii Moskvy (TsAOPIM), f. 432, o. 1, d. 179, ll. 127–28. A. I. Efanov, *Istoriia zavoda 'Dinamo'* (Moscow: Izdatel'stvo VTsSPS Profizdat, 1964), vol. 2, pp. 170, 241.

in lines outside the prisons, sacrificed their own meager stores of food to make up parcels for relatives in the Gulag, lost access to housing for themselves and their children, and were fired from their jobs. The repressions affected not only the individual members of discrete victim groups but their entire families. Torbeeva, for instance, was kept in the dark about the fate of her husband, Torbeev, who had been arrested for Trotskyism. Torbeev is counted among the victims of repression against "Trotskyists," but what about his wife? She, too, was a victim, but to what group does she belong? Our microhistory of the factories suggests that to conceptualize the terror by looking only at categories of arrest is vastly to underestimate its effects on families and thus on Soviet society at large.

Just as a single family might include members of various victim groups, an individual, too, often had multiple identities. The victims themselves confound our attempts to understand the terror solely through the discrete categories laid down by the state. Krivitskaia, for example, was at one and the same time a party member, a Polish emigrant, a worker, the wife of a party member expelled for concealing a kulak brother, and the alleged lover of the head of Serp i Molot's party committee. Our story focuses on party members in five factories, yet its various chapters convey some sense of the dense web of familial and associational ties running between these people and their friends and acquaintances, spouses and former spouses, near and distant relations, colleagues, bosses, and rivals, connecting them to various victim categories as well as to "ordinary" Soviet citizens. Party members were neither more isolated from victimized groups nor more likely than others to be associated with them. In this sense, at least, the rank and file were much like everyone else, tied through family, comrades, and coworkers to refugees from the east and west, to so-called "kulaks" and other disenfranchised elements, and to former oppositionists. There was no hard line between victims and survivors, between party members and ordinary people, between those who were targeted and those who were not. The terror cut a wide swath across Soviet society, leaving almost no one untouched or uninvolved.

By 1938, the factories were in a state of feverish disorganization. Foremen, technical personnel, shop and department heads, engineers, and directors had fallen victim to expulsion, arrest, and execution. The Soviet Union was preparing for war, yet the industrial leadership had been seriously compromised. The factory newspapers publicly derided all authority, and leaders at every level were terrified to make decisions. The party organizations, the main organizers within the factories, were destroying themselves from within. Preoccupied with hunting enemies within their own ranks, they were paralyzed by inaction when it came to their organizational duties, and had been neither enrolling new members nor processing the accruing appeals for reinstatement. No one wanted to write a recommendation for, or move to overturn the expulsion of, an individual who might still be arrested. And no one knew who might be arrested next. Party members had grown weary of the endless purging. The campaign to identify and expel bawlers found few enthusiasts – and understandably so, given that almost everyone who remained in the Party at this point was a bawler. Members had gone after others aggressively in order to protect themselves, a shared behavior for which they were now unwilling to expel their comrades or be expelled in turn. Every accusation of bawling could easily be met with a counteraccusation. The factory newspapers tried to stir up interest in this last group of enemies, but their efforts soon sputtered to a halt. Party members tacitly recognized that everyone was potentially guilty of something. The emphasis on wrecking was replaced by a new campaign to reimpose labor discipline and mobilize the factories to prepare for war.

Many historians contend that Stalin, and Stalin alone, was responsible for the repressions because he wielded the power to start and to stop them. Everyone else, including the small coterie of leaders surrounding him, was helpless before his will to power.[7] According to this view, Stalin gutted the Central Committee that had been elected in 1934 and turned the Politburo into a group of servile lackeys. Commissars, regional party leaders, and military officers all trembled before him. Party leaders offered support for this interpretation, later blaming Stalin, the NKVD, and the political culture for the horrors of these years. None took responsibility publicly for playing a part. L. M. Kaganovich, a strong supporter of Stalin, put it all down to the "general mood." "It was impossible to go against public opinion at that time," he explained. "The situation was such in the country and in the Central Committee, the mood of the masses was such, that there was no thought of acting in any other way." N. S. Khrushchev, who presided over the terror as head of the Moscow party committee, pointed a finger at the NKVD. "What kind of control was there here," he asked, "when the party organs themselves had fallen under the control of those whom

7 Historians across the political spectrum have advanced this perspective, including Vadim Rogovin, a Trotskyist, and Roy Medvedev, a Communist, as well as Robert Conquest and Richard Pipes, both staunch anti-Communists. Oleg Khlevniuk writes, "The NKVD orders guiding the mass operations in 1937–38 show that the Great Terror was a centrally organized punitive action, planned in Moscow, against a potential fifth column perceived as capable of stabbing the country in the back in the case of war. Substantial evidence shows that the author of these purges was Stalin and that he initiated the operations." See Oleg V. Khlevniuk, *The History of the Gulag: From Collectivization to the Great Terror* (New Haven, Conn.: Yale University Press, 2004), p. 148.

they were supposed to be controlling?"[8] And NKVD leaders, too, deemed others at fault. S. Redens, the NKVD chief of Kazakstan, in a private conversation with his deputy, M. Shreider, decried the torture of prisoners they both oversaw in the prisons. He noted that Dzerzhinskii, former head of the Cheka, "would have the lot of us shot for the way we're working now."[9] Thus even the most potent perpetrators cast themselves as victims of individuals or forces they had been powerless to resist.

For all that perpetrators and participants tried to act the part of victims in an effort to escape responsibility, people at all levels were ensnared in a process that was both beyond their control and of their own making. They had few choices and little room to maneuver. In the factories, people denounced comrades out of a sense of patriotic or political duty, fear, self-interest, or self-preservation. The sources document the rabid accusations at meetings, the instigation of the factory newspapers, the votes to impose harsh punishments, the calls for further investigation, the cruelty of comrades toward one another. We have seen how people's behavior was shaped by specific group dynamics, and how individual strategies intended to ensure survival succeeded only in widening the terror's reach.

The party meetings of 1937 and 1938 are long over. Only ghosts now roam the shuttered shops and halls where hundreds of people

---

8 F. I. Chuev, *Tak govoril Kaganovich. Ispoved' stalinskogo apostal* (Moscow: Rossi-iskoe Tovarishchestvo 'Otechestvo', 1992), pp. 89, 105, and *Voprosy Istorii*, no. 5 (1990), p. 64, both quoted in Vadim Zakharovich Rogovin, *Stalin's Terror of 1937–1938: Political Genocide in the USSR* (Oak Park, Mich.: Mehring Books, 2009), pp. 148, 159.

9 M. P. Shreider, *NKVD iznutri: zapiski chekista* (Moscow: Vozvrashchenie, 1995), p. 42, as quoted by Orlando Figes, *The Whisperers: Private Life in Stalin's Russia* (New York: Metropolitan Books, 2007), pp. 284–85.

once gathered to judge their comrades. Party members put central directives into action and thereby created a process driven by its own self-generating dynamic, which devoured victims and perpetrators indiscriminately. The Soviet Union in the late 1930s was a society threatened by external enemies. Fascism was ascendant in Germany, Austria, Italy, Hungary, and Spain, and Hitler's armies were moving east. The assassination of Kirov, social discontent, and the fear of war were sufficient to convince party leaders and the majority of Soviet citizens that strong governmental action was necessary. Yet the abrogation of civil liberties and judicial rights was merely the first step of many taken to vanquish the threat posed by alleged terrorists. Soon the entire population was embroiled in the hunt for enemies, and state actions against terrorism had cohered into a full-blown terror. The "Great Terror" was not solely a set of directives and operational orders launched from above. It was also embedded in the fabric of a fierce political culture that influenced the entire population. People reacted to and actively shaped a process that was simultaneously of their collective making and beyond their individual control. What is most instructive and frightening about these years is how easily ideological righteousness, belief, fear, and self-interest combined to create a citizenry capable of destroying its own. And therein lies the most difficult and important lesson of all.

INDEX

totalitarianism, 4, 5
Tregubov, 119, 135
Trekhgornaia Manufaktura, 3, 23, 24, 140,
    156, 161, 167, 170, 171, 179, 182, 252,
    273
Trotsky, L. D., 28, 37, 38, 39, 41, 43, 51, 53,
    59, 102, 109
Trotskyism and Trotskyists, 5, 24, 27,
    33–40, 44, 58, 60, 64, 67, 73–78, 85,
    86, 91–98, 101, 102, 105, 107–111,
    115–119, 121, 124, 137, 153, 155,
    157–161, 168–170, 175–178, 179, 180,
    183, 184, 185–188, 190–193, 216, 225,
    226, 228, 253, 275, 277, 281, 284, 286,
    303, 304, 308, 310
Tukhachevskii, M. N., 79

Union of Electrical Machine-Building
    Workers, 88
Union of Ferrous Metallurgical Workers,
    53, 204
unions, 2, 4, 21, 26, 65, 79, 125, 127, 138,
    252, 255, 257
upward mobility, 11, 90, 146, 149, 152,
    309

Viktorov, V., 104, 119, 135
Voroshilov, K. E., 102, 178
VTsSPS, 25, 106
Vyshinskii, A. Ia., 38, 40, 41, 55, 74, 92, 94,
    99, 112, 136, 217, 226, 248, 266

women, 56, 147, 156

workers, 10, 22, 26, 28, 34, 41, 53–57, 66,
    68, 69, 75, 79, 83, 89, 91, 99, 147, 149,
    161, 205, 218, 255, 266, 279, 285, 288,
    293, 298, 299, 308–309
and wrecking, 45, 47–54
wreckers and wrecking, 15, 21, 25, 27, 28,
    43–55, 58–60, 62, 64, 70, 75, 76, 78,
    79, 81–87, 92–94, 97–101, 111–114,
    117, 118, 126–129, 131–133, 136, 137,
    163, 171, 174, 178, 196, 203, 205, 213,
    251, 275, 282, 285, 287, 290, 298, 305,
    311

zaiavleniia, 29–31, 42, 52, 72, 80, 91–100,
    108, 112–114, 121–126, 129, 130, 133,
    136, 138, 144–146, 156, 163, 165, 170,
    172, 175, 176, 182, 183, 188–190, 192,
    194–196, 202, 203, 207, 208, 209,
    216–219, 224–234, 238, 241, 245, 252,
    256, 262, 263, 269, 273, 275–279, 283,
    289, 292, 295, 296, 300, 301, 304–305,
    307
Zhdanov, A. A., 64, 65, 133, 166, 288–292,
    294, 296
Zhidkov, D., 207–210, 214, 218, 225, 226
Zhidkova, M. F., 201, 202–212, 214–219,
    224, 225, 226, 229–235, 238, 239, 242,
    244, 246–249, 257, 302
Zhukov, M. E., 83, 84, 86, 88, 105,
    113–116, 123, 128, 130, 135, 137, 281
Zil'berman, 119, 135
Zinoviev. G. E., 28, 32, 33, 38, 43
Zinovievites, 32–39, 77, 78, 107